Independent Politics

Independent Politics:

The Green Party Strategy Debate

Edited by Howie Hawkins

Haymarket Books
Chicago, Illinois

For additional source information, please see page 324.

First published in 2006 by Haymarket Books
P.O. Box 180165
Chicago, IL 60618
773-583-7884
www.haymarketbooks.org

This book has been published with the generous
support of the Wallace Global Fund

Cover design by Josh On

Library of Congress Cataloging in Publication Data
Independent politics : the Green Party strategy debate / edited by
Howie Hawkins.
p. cm.
ISBN-13: 978-1-931859-30-1 (pbk.)
ISBN-10: 1-931859-30-2 (pbk.)
1. Greens/Green Party USA. 2. Presidents--United States--Election-
-2004. 3. United States--Politics and government--2001- I.
Hawkins, Howard.
JK2391.G74I53 2006
324.273'8--dc22
                                    2006010223

Printed in Canada

1 3 5 7 9 10 8 6 4 2

Contents

Dedicated to the memory of
Walt Contreras Sheasby

Ten Key Values of the Green Party

There is no definitive list of the ten key values. They were first adopted as a discussion paper in 1984 and have been modified several times. Many state and local parties have adopted their own versions. Perhaps the most widely used version is the one ratified at the Green Party Convention in Denver, Colorado, June 2000, which is reprinted below.

1. GRASSROOTS DEMOCRACY
Every human being deserves a say in the decisions that affect their lives and not be subject to the will of another. Therefore, we will work to increase public participation at every level of government and to ensure that our public representatives are fully accountable to the people who elect them. We will also work to create new types of political organizations that expand the process of participatory democracy by directly including citizens in the decision-making process.

2. SOCIAL JUSTICE AND EQUAL OPPORTUNITY
All persons should have the rights and opportunity to benefit equally from the resources afforded us by society and the environment. We must consciously confront in ourselves, our organizations, and society at large, barriers such as racism and class oppression, sexism and homophobia, ageism and disability, which act to deny fair treatment and equal justice under the law.

3. ECOLOGICAL WISDOM
Human societies must operate with the understanding that we are part of nature, not separate from nature. We must maintain an ecological balance and live within the ecological and resource limits of

our communities and our planet. We support a sustainable society that utilizes resources in such a way that future generations will benefit and not suffer from the practices of our generation. To this end we must practice agriculture that replenishes the soil, move to an energy efficient economy, and live in ways that respect the integrity of natural systems.

4. NONVIOLENCE

It is essential that we develop effective alternatives to society's current patterns of violence. We will work to demilitarize and eliminate weapons of mass destruction, without being naive about the intentions of other governments. We recognize the need for self-defense and the defense of others who are in helpless situations. We promote non-violent methods to oppose practices and policies with which we disagree, and will guide our actions toward lasting personal, community, and global peace.

5. DECENTRALIZATION

Centralization of wealth and power contributes to social and economic injustice, environmental destruction, and militarization. Therefore, we support a restructuring of social, political, and economic institutions away from a system that is controlled by and mostly benefits the powerful few, to a democratic, less bureaucratic system. Decision-making should, as much as possible, remain at the individual and local level, while assuring that civil rights are protected for all citizens.

6. COMMUNITY-BASED ECONOMICS AND ECONOMIC JUSTICE

We recognize it is essential to create a vibrant and sustainable economic system, one that can create jobs and provide a decent standard of living for all people while maintaining a healthy ecological balance. A successful economic system will offer meaningful work with dignity, while paying a "living wage" which reflects the real value of a person's work.

Local communities must look to economic development that assures protection of the environment and workers' rights; broad citizen participation in planning; and enhancement of our "quality of life." We support independently owned and operated companies which are socially responsible, as well as co-operatives and public enterprises that distribute resources and control to more people through democratic participation.

7. FEMINISM AND GENDER EQUITY

We have inherited a social system based on male domination of politics and economics. We call for the replacement of the cultural ethics of domination and control with more cooperative ways of interacting that respect differences of opinion and gender. Human values such as equity between the sexes, interpersonal responsibility, and honesty must be developed with moral conscience. We should remember that the process that determines our decisions and actions is just as important as achieving the outcome we want.

8. RESPECT FOR DIVERSITY

We believe it is important to value cultural, ethnic, racial, sexual, religious, and spiritual diversity, and to promote the development of respectful relationships across these lines.

We believe that the many diverse elements of society should be reflected in our organizations and decision-making bodies, and we support the leadership of people who have been traditionally closed out of leadership roles. We acknowledge and encourage respect for other life forms than our own and the preservation of biodiversity.

9. PERSONAL AND GLOBAL RESPONSIBILITY

We encourage individuals to act to improve their personal well-being and, at the same time, to enhance ecological balance and social harmony. We seek to join with people and organizations around the world to foster peace, economic justice, and the health of the planet.

10. FUTURE FOCUS AND SUSTAINABILITY

Our actions and policies should be motivated by long-term goals. We seek to protect valuable natural resources, safely disposing of or "unmaking" all waste we create, while developing a sustainable economics that does not depend on continual expansion for survival. We must counterbalance the drive for short-term profits by assuring that economic development, new technologies, and fiscal policies are responsible to future generations who will inherit the results of our actions.

The Green Party's Missed Opportunity in 2004—and the Opportunity Still at Hand

Howie Hawkins

> *Cowardice asks the question: is it safe?*
> *Expediency asks the question: is it politic?*
> *Vanity asks the question: is it popular?*
> *But Conscience asks the question: is it right?*
> *And there comes a time when one must take a position*
> *that is neither safe, nor politic, nor popular—*
> *but he must take it simply because*
> *Conscience tells him it is right.*
> —Martin Luther King Jr.[1]

Since the very inception of the Green Party movement in the United States in 1984, questions of political independence and organizational democracy have been at the center of often divisive debates. Without resolving those debates, the Greens were able to muddle through and grow around a loose unity in action despite being divided at times into rival national organizations. But in 2004, these unresolved differences rendered the Greens divided in action and, as a result, marginalized in a presidential campaign that was dominated by the militaristic bipartisan consensus of the two big corporate parties.

This book brings together the principal documents and commentaries in the debate over Green Party strategy for the 2004 presidential election within the Green Party and in the broader progressive community. I hope it will help Greens understand and resolve these issues so they can move forward in the future as an independent political party with greater unity in purpose and action based on more democratic structures and processes.

I put it together because I believe the ability of the Green Party to transform our society depends on its political independence and on its adoption of a more democratic structure based on a one-Green, one-vote system of representation in the Green National Committee and conventions. I have tried to fairly present both sides of the debate by letting each side present its position in its own words. In the interest of full disclosure, I should add that I am a founding member of Greens for Democracy and Independence and supported Ralph Nader's presidential bid in 2004.

I am opposed to any split of the Green Party over these issues. At least until elections in the United States are held under a system of proportional representation, we need one united people's party standing in opposition to the corporate-sponsored two-party dictatorship. I want to see these issues worked out among the Greens over time by discussion and democratic decisions. It was in this vein that Peter Miguel Camejo introduced and Ralph Nader supported the "Green Party Unity" proposal to the Green National Convention. That proposal acknowledged the divided opinion among the Greens on presidential strategy for 2004, recommended a dual endorsement of Ralph Nader and David Cobb, and allowed each state Green Party to make its own decision on whether to put Nader or Cobb on its state ballot line in 2004. As Camejo stated in the proposal, "We will move forward to build the party together, accepting that we have differences and that these differences are normal in a democratic organization."[2] That is the spirit in which this collection is offered.

Corporate Rule through the Two-Party System

Since the Civil War, the moneyed class in the United States has organized its wealth into large corporations and controlled the government through its sponsorship of the two-party system. The corporate rulers finance two parties—the Demcocrats and the Republicans—to represent them. That way the corporate ruling class always has its people in power on both sides of the aisle in the legislatures and in the executive branch.

By financing two parties, the corporate powers give the illusion of democracy in a choice between two alternatives. But there is no alternative to the economic and foreign policies that are of primary concern to their wealthy sponsors. On economic and foreign policy matters, a pro-corporate "bipartisan consensus" prevails in both corporate-sponsored parties.

The two corporate parties always have some differences on social issues, such as civil rights in the 1950s and 1960s, and the controversies over gun control, gay marriage, and school prayer of recent elections. These issues are certainly important and progressives can always use them to determine that one of the corporate-sponsored candidates is the lesser evil compared to the other. The problem is that with election contests between the two big parties focused on social issues, the bipartisan consensus on economic and foreign policy goes uncontested. Between elections, both corporate parties work together to execute the economic and foreign policies favored by their corporate sponsors.

Only an independent political insurgency can break us out of this box to challenge pro-corporate economic and foreign policies as well as reactionary social policies. But third parties face formidable obstacles. Ballot access barriers and disparity in campaign funds put every third-party campaign at a disadvantage from the start. The biggest barrier is the single-member-district, winner-take-all election system. That system strongly encourages people to vote strategically for the lesser evil between the two corporate parties instead of for the third party they really prefer. The result has been nearly 150 years of corporate rule through the two-party system, a far more sophisticated system of elite rule than the transparently tyrannical one-party systems many countries have had.

In 2000, the Green Party, with Ralph Nader heading the ticket, mounted the strongest challenge to this two-corporate-party system in three-quarters of a century, winning the largest vote for an independent progressive presidential ticket since the Debsian Socialists of 1904 to 1920 and Robert LaFollette's 1924 Progressive campaign. Since 2000 the Democrats had been constantly attacking Nader and the Greens for "spoiling" Gore's chance to beat Bush. As the 2004 presidential election approached, a question on the minds of everyone who follows politics was, "Would Nader and the Greens run again?"

The Missed Opportunity

As the Greens approached their June 24–27, 2004, convention in Milwaukee, a massive leadership vacuum cried out for an independent presidential crusade against the pro-war, pro-corporate bipartisan consensus of the Democrats and Republicans. The Green Party could have filled that vacuum by uniting behind the independent ticket of Ralph Nader and Peter Miguel Camejo.

Ralph Nader, the iconic progressive who had been prominent on the national stage for forty years, had a résumé with accomplishments and qualifications that dwarfed those of Kerry and Bush. Nader had been instrumental in the passage of more significant legislation than Kerry and Bush combined, perhaps more progressive federal legislation than all the current members of Congress combined, including the National Traffic and Motor Vehicle Safety Act, the Wholesome Meat Act, the Freedom of Information Act, the Clean Water Act, the Clean Air Act, the Community Reinvestment Act, and the acts creating the Occupational Safety and Health Administration (OSHA), the Environmental Protection Agency, the Consumer Product Safety Commission, and the National Cooperative Bank. To help advance the progressive reform agenda, Nader pioneered the concept of citizen action groups with lobbying and litigation capacities. He instigated scores of such groups to deal with consumer rights, energy and environmental issues, union democracy, investigative reporting, corporate crime, women's rights, racial discrimination, poverty, fair trade and corporate welfare, and to monitor the legislatures and government agencies. He had been arguably the most preferred candidate in the 2000 presidential election and might have won the election had it been conducted under a majority preference system instead of the electoral college plurality system.[3]

Camejo had just come off of two runs for California governor—in 2002 and 2003—in which he received by far the most votes any Green gubernatorial candidate had received to date: nearly 400,000 votes, or 5.3 percent, in 2002, and nearly 250,000 votes, or 3 percent, in the 2003 recall election. Exit polls showed that his base of voters was disproportionately Black, Latino, and Asian-Pacific, as well as voters who had previously voted for Greens in lower proportions than other voters. People of color voted for Camejo at twice the rate white people did. Voters who earned less than $15,000 a year voted for Camejo at three times the rate voters making over $75,000 a year did.[4] Nader and Camejo offered policies—from ending the U.S. war in Iraq to creating a national health insurance program to spearheading public works projects to create millions of new jobs—that had broad support among the people. Nader's 2000 campaign had demonstrated his capacity to raise funds and command media attention at the level needed to run a national presidential campaign with a significant impact on U.S. politics.

Since 2000, the Democrats had kept Nader in the national spotlight, keeping his media profile high with their constant whining about Nader's "spoiling" the 2000 election. Nader took most of the heat for the Green Party on this issue. His unbending defense of the Greens' right to run candidates should have earned him the Greens' lasting respect and laid the foundation for another united Nader/Green assault on the corporate-sponsored two-party system. But when delegates at the Green convention chose a "safe states" candidate over Nader, they implicitly affirmed the Democratic hacks' smear campaign against him. For the hacks, this was merely a convenient proxy for Greens or any other independent challenge to the Democrats from their left.

By the time Nader formally declared his candidacy on February 23, 2004, nearly every section of institutionalized progressivism had joined in the Democrats' vitriolic attacks against him. They said his campaign was driven by his ego, as if issues like ending the war and reversing the spread of economic insecurity were irrelevant. They said Nader was throwing away his progressive legacy by increasing Bush's chances for reelection. History may conclude in the end, however, that Nader's insistence on building an independent political alternative to the bipartisan consensus around militarism and corporate domination was a principled and logical extension of his career as a progressive reformer.

When Martin Luther King Jr. came out against the war in Vietnam in 1967, he was also accused of throwing away his legacy. He was the target of withering attacks from the leadership of the Democratic Party, organized liberalism, and the civil rights movement. He suffered a drastic loss of funding from unions, churches, foundations, and wealthy liberals and was completely cut off from former allies in the government by the Johnson administration. King's response was to hold his ground and link his civil rights and antiwar demands. Pushing ahead despite resistance from most of his colleagues in the Southern Christian Leadership Conference and another round of attacks by Democratic liberals, King began organizing the Poor People's Campaign, a radical plan to expand the scope of the civil rights movement into a multiracial, class-based economic justice movement that would channel the discontent expressed in the ghetto riots into a massive nonviolent disruption of the government until it came through with jobs or income for all to end poverty. At the time, King appeared isolated. Within a few years, public opinion had joined him in opposition to the war. Today, his courage in standing against the war and attacking systemic poverty and exploitation are seen as integral to his whole legacy.

Like King, Nader defied the Democratic Party leadership by campaigning independently against a war and a system of economic injustice in which the Democrats were fully complicit. Nader also suffered a loss of liberal allies, funding, and access to government officials for doing so. But as important as his antiwar and pro-justice demands were, Nader's greatest legacy may be his instistence on the right of the people to have alternatives to the two corporate-sponsored parties.

But instead of suporting Nader in 2004 and leading the opposition to the war and corporate domination, the Green Party was divided. Many Greens, probably a strong majority, did want to launch another all-out assault on the corporate-sponsored bipartisan consensus. Others, in an effort to prove they wouldn't "spoil" another election, supported the Democratic ticket as the lesser evil, either directly, or indirectly—with a "safe states" strategy of not competing in the battleground states. In a close vote in the second round of balloting, the Green National Convention chose to run a low-profile campaign with an unknown candidate, David Cobb, whose approach was to support Kerry's attempt to beat Bush.

Unfortunately, by taking this "safe" route, the Green Party handed the Democrats and the media the club with which they were able to cripple the Nader/Camejo campaign. The typical headline around the world read "Greens Reject Nader," with Cobb's nomination mentioned as an afterthought in the text.[5] "By nominating Cobb," a *Los Angeles Times* article noted, "the Greens have a candidate 'with zero name recognition,' said Dean Spiliotes, a fellow at the New Hampshire Institute of Politics. 'It may be a good exercise in building up the party on the local level, but it means the party will drop off the radar. It's a shock, but it is great news for Kerry.'"[6]

Nader consistently accounted for around 5 to 7 percent of prospective votes in the polls in the few months leading up to the Green National Convention in June 2004. After the convention, his poll numbers dropped to 3 to 5 percent during the summer battle for ballot lines and dropped again to 1 to 2 percent after Labor Day.[7] After the initial mention of Cobb's victory over Nader at the Green convention, Cobb was out of the national media for the rest of the campaign. With most of the left and organized liberalism, including the peace movement, supporting Kerry, and with no strong opposition ticket backed by the Green Party, there was no broad challenge to the war, militarism, and corporate rule in 2004.

Questionable Legitimacy of the Green Convention

The legitimacy of Cobb's nomination was a matter of debate even before the result was in at the convention. One source of controversy was the complicated formula used to determine how many delegates each state was entitled to. The formula incorporated the electoral college vote (the traditional corporate-party model dating back to before the Civil War), National Committee delegates (akin to Super Delegates in the corporate-party model and based on a "bounded proportionality" formula that magnified the voting power of small states even more than the electoral college), Voting Strength (Bonus Delegates in the corporate-party model, in this case, the 2000 Nader vote), and Elected Greens (Bonus Delegates in the corporate-party model).[8] The net effect of the representation scheme was to overrepresent states with small Green parties and underrepresent states with big ones. The small parties, many of them not capable on their own of successfully petitioning for a ballot line in the general election, tended to vote overwhelmingly for Cobb. The big parties, notably California and New York, with two-thirds of all the registered Greens in the U.S. between them, voted overwhelmingly for Nader.

Adding to the controversy were the convention rules. The rules were approved by the National Committee beforehand and could not be amended by the convention delegates. The national Green Party bylaws make the National Committee sovereign over the broader National Convention. Many delegates were dismayed at this obvious contradiction of the Green principle of grassroots democracy. The platform could not be amended, only voted up or down by the convention delegates. By contrast, even the Democrats and Republicans have provisions requiring that minority planks with at least 20 percent support in the platform committee be reported to the convention floor for a final debate and vote. The rules for voting on the nomination were also controversial. They required the convention to first vote for no nominee in order to then consider a motion for the endorsement of the Nader/Camejo independent ticket, a complicated process that many delegates felt was biased against a Nader/Camejo endorsement.

Going into the convention, Cobb had received only 12 percent of the cumulative vote of the five states that had Green Party primaries and minority support in most of the other states that held caucuses and conventions. Nader supporters had to vote for stand-in candidates in most states who said they wanted Nader to be endorsed.[9] Yet Cobb had come into Milwaukee with the plurality of delegates pledged to him and came out with a slight majority and the nomination in the end. The problem here was that there was no rule stipulating that delegates had to be elected from states in proportion to the support each candidate had. The Green primary, caucus, and convention votes were, in effect, merely beauty contests. The delegations were chosen separately from the presidential voting in most states. Cobb's campaign was able to recruit pro-Cobb delegates in far greater proportion than the presidential preference voting for Cobb by rank-and-file Greens, especially in the many small state parties with disproportionately big delegations.

A year earlier it had seemed clear the Green Party was intent on running an all-out independent campaign in 2004. Meeting in Washington, D.C., on July 17–20, 2003, the Green National Committee spent most of Friday discussing its 2004 presidential campaign strategy. Ralph Nader sent a message that said he was a possible candidate. Former congresswoman Cynthia McKinney of Georgia sent a message regarding her possible candidacy, saying "nothing can be ruled out." And David Cobb circulated his strategic-states plan among the delegates. Cobb's memo said the Greens should drop out if Kucinich or Sharpton won the Democratic nomination, run all-out if Lieberman won the nomination, or, in the most likely event, follow a *"strategic states" plan* "if a marginally 'moderate' (but still woefully inadequate) candidate wins the Democratic Party nomination.... Most of our resources should be focused on those states where the electoral college votes are not 'in play,'" he wrote. "The Green Party can run a strong campaign in 2004 that grows our party, garners millions of votes, and culminates with George Bush losing the election."[10]

But Cobb's approach did not have much support at the National Committee meeting. While there was no binding vote, a straw poll was taken late Friday in which people were asked to go to three different corners of the room to get a sense of where people stood on the question of strategy. One option was to not run at all. Only a few people went to that corner. A second option was to run a "tactical" campaign, whether it was making a late exit in a close race (suggested by *Green Horizon Quarterly* editor John Rensenbrink and party co-chair Tom Sevigny[11]), adopting Ted Glick's safe-states strategy,[12] or following Cobb's strategic-states strategy. At best, that corner had 25 percent of those in attendance. Conservatively, 75 percent of the Greens went to the corner that stood for an all-out campaign against both corporate parties.

The *Washington Post* headline on July 21, 2003, read, "Greens Want Candidate in 2004; At Party Meeting, Most Rule Out Supporting a Democrat." The reaction from liberal Democrats was to attack. For example, under the headline "Gang Green" on July 23, Michael Tomasky wrote in the liberal *American Prospect Online*: "The Democrats can cure their Ralph Nader problem by attacking him—immediately and ferociously." Tomasky called for a Democrat like Howard Dean "with at least one leg in the liberal soil" to blast Nader and Cynthia McKinney, the other leading candidate among Greens, as anti-Semites for their criticisms of Israeli policies.[13] Democratic leaders like Terry McAuliffe, the chairman of the Democratic National Committee, and Bill Richardson, governor of New Mexico, hit the airwaves decrying another Nader run. More articles from writers identified with the left, like Michael Albert on *Znet* and Tom Hayden on *AlterNet*, hit the e-mail circuits, calling for a safe-states approach by the Green Party.[14] The Anybody-But-Bush movement became fixated on Anybody But Nader.

Cobb Allies with Anybody But Bush (or Nader)

With the Democrats' and progressive media's Anybody-But-Nader blitz providing a tailwind, the Cobb campaign continued to hammer away at Nader, making the political issues at stake personal. The tactic began to work. In December 2002, Peter Camejo had drafted an open letter to Ralph Nader from eight 2002 Green gubernatorial candidates, appealing to him to run again in 2004.[15] But two of these signers, David Bacon of New Mexico and Jill Stein of Massachusetts, changed their mind in late 2003. Bacon appeared at a Kucinich fund-raiser and publicly reregistered as a Democrat.[16] Stein, who was now running for state representative, told Nader in December that his candidacy would turn Democratic voters against Green candidates like her.

Micah Sifry's "Ralph Redux?" carried the torch for the Cobb campaign into *The Nation*. Sifry's article highlighted Cobb's candidacy for the nomination, his strategic-states plan, and his objections to Nader. Despite having witnessed the straw poll at the National Committee meeting, Sifry claimed, incredibly, that those supporting an all-out run were "a distinct minority."

All the Greens Sifry quoted were against a Nader run, including three Green elected officials, Medea Benjamin of Global Exchange, and John McChesney, coeditor of the socialist *Monthly Review*. The quote from John Rensenbrink of Maine summed up how the Cobb campaign's case for a lesser-evil strategy was being linked to a personal attack on Nader:

> People ... are very focused on stopping the right-wing cabal that has taken over the country. Therefore, the focus has to be on defeating Bush. Beyond that, the Green Party needs to project a sense of urgency around saving the country, saving the Constitution, saving the planet. There's a concern that we'll be deflected from that message because of the baggage Ralph Nader has from 2000. I doubt he can get over 1 percent of the vote. He'll have to spend a lot of time dealing with the "spoiler" question, unfairly, but that's where it is. I'd add to that that he doesn't want to be a Green, he runs with his coterie rather than party organizers, he doesn't involve local Green leaders and he doesn't get the racial issue. I fear if Nader runs, he'll drag down every other Green in this country. I love him, but this is sheer practical politics.

Dean Myerson, the recently resigned political director of the Green Party, emphasized the safe-states strategy: "The best strategy to build the party is to not focus on states where we'll do poorly. Why should we hook ourselves to the Democrats' strategy and campaign against them? We should campaign in non-battleground states and safe states."[17]

Myerson put this approach to the Greens directly in his "Statement on Green Strategy 2004 and Call for Dialogue and Action," which was signed by eighteen Greens. Calling the lesser-evil concept "instructive," the signers recognized the Democrats as the lesser of two evils and named defeating Bush as the primary objective for Greens in 2004. They called for debate over which strategy would best achieve that goal: "from not running at all, to running in ways that will focus our campaign energies in certain states, to calls to possibly drop out of the race near election day if it is very close."[18]

Roots of the 2004 Division

Most of the signers of this statement had long been leaders of the American Greens' liberal faction, which has gradually distanced itself from the radicalism of the original Green Party organization in the U.S. The original Green Party organization was called the Committees of Correspondence (1984–1989), then Green Committees of Correspondence (1989–1991), and then Green Party USA (GPUSA, 1991–2001).

After the first national program was adopted in 1990, the liberal tendency's leadership began a split based on a separate Green Party Organizing Committee (1990–1992), which became the Green Politics Network (1992-present), and finally the Association of State Green Parties (ASGP, 1996–2001). They also form the leadership of today's Green Institute, a Green policy think tank.

In 2001, the majority of the Green Party USA joined with the Association of State Green Parties to form today's Green Party of the United States under the terms of an agreement called the Boston Proposal. A small remnant of the old Green Party USA that rejected the Boston Proposal still exists under that name.

The issues the liberals raised in justifying their split contained the seeds of the division of Greens between the Nader/Camejo and Cobb/LaMarche tickets in 2004. The liberals stood for moderating the socialistic nature of the Green Party USA's economic program, for establishing a system of indirect representation by substituting a federation of state parties for the national membership organization, and for being open to cross-endorsing Democrats.[19]

The original impetus for the liberals' split was the anti-capitalist thrust of the first national Green program adopted in 1990. As one of their leaders, Nancy Allen of Maine, put it on the ASGP Coordinating Committee listserv in 2000 during unity talks with GPUSA, "Are you aware that many of the original members of the Green Party Organizing Committee of the Green Committees of Correspondence, which evolved into the ASGP, ... had real problems with the economic vision as a strategy in that document?... and that was one of the reasons that precipitated the split."[20] John Rensenbrink complained that the GPUSA's program "had a knee-jerk anticapitalist and pro-socialist cast to it."[21] Although it was the initial precipitator of the split in the Greens, the economic program was not a factor in the division of 2004. Both Nader and Cobb are nondogmatic and pragmatic reformers when it comes to questions of ownership forms, markets, planning, and regulation.

While the economic program was in the background, the GPUSA/ASGP fight was expressed more in terms of organizational differences. GPUSA was based on individual members, with voting in its National Committee and convention based on delegations proportional to membership in local and state affiliates. It was based on the German Green model of "base democracy," or grassroots democracy, as the American Greens termed it. In this structure, representatives were elected by and accountable to assemblies open to all local members at the base. ASGP argued that the national party should be a federation of state Green parties, with each state party conforming to the statutory requirements of ballot-line parties. These requirements are different for each state and territory, but they generally prescribe party governance by a representative elite in county and state committees selected by petition or primary, not by membership assemblies at the base. ASGP argued for replacing the individual membership model with the representational model used by the two big corporate parties, which was based on abstractions like the electoral college vote, rather than living, breathing members of the party. The electoral college vote was the original corporate party basis for convention delegations, to which Bonus Delegates for voting strength and Super Delegates for

National Committee members and elected officials were later added. In adopting these abstractions to determine state party delegations, the Green Party in the U.S. moved away from its principle of grassroots democracy, where representatives came from membership assemblies and voting strength was proportional to the number of Greens on the ground, not abstractions like the electoral college.[22] It was this abstract structure of representation at the 2004 convention in Milwaukee that enabled the small parties representing a minority of Greens and supporting Cobb to outvote the big parties representing a majority of Greens and supporting Nader.

The other seed of the division in 2004 was the liberal tendency's long-standing openness to selective endorsement of corporate-party candidates. At the first national Green organizing meeting in St. Paul, Minnesota, in August 1984, opinion was divided on whether to organize an independent Green Party, a Green movement that tried to influence both major parties, or a Green Party that took an inside/outside approach, challenging both parties in some races and sometimes endorsing the better of the major-party candidates. Charlene Spretnak, whose book, *Green Politics*, instigated the St. Paul meeting, had suggested that "a bipartisan caucus is probably the shrewdest approach, although Green candidates could run at the local level as Independents."[23] In a follow-up article in *The Nation*, Spretnak suggested that Democratic presidential candidate Gary Hart's 'new ideas' may turn out to be surprisingly Green."[24] One of the Democrats' leading "neoliberals," as they were called at that time, Hart supported military modernization for fast, flexible intervention—that today we associate with Bush's defense secretary, Donald Rumsfeld—as well as the pro-corporate turn toward deregulation, privatization, and regressive tax reforms taken by both corporate parties in the late 1970s. This perspective was quite different from the radicals who were beginning to organize an independent Green Party in the United States because they were attracted by the German Greens' recent electoral victories based on their anti-militarist and anticapitalist program of that period.

When the liberals' Green Party Organizing Committee met in Boston in February 1991, they issued a statement that opened the door to endorsing corporate-party candidates:

The meeting approved a guiding declaration with respect to the question of support for candidates in either of the two major parties: "We strongly recommend that local and state Green parties concentrate their efforts on mounting their own candidacies and forming their own parties. Endorsement of other candidates and participation in caucuses in other parties should be carefully considered, and undertaken only when they advance the cause of Green ideals and the development of the Green movement."[25]

Leading up to the 1996 election, the Green Politics Network sponsored a series of third-party meetings to which they invited the New Party, the Labor Party, the Socialist Party, the Libertarian Party, the Natural Law Party, the Patriot Party (the faction of the Perot movement headed by the old New Alliance Party of Fred Newman and Lenora Fulani), the Independent Progressive Politics Network, California's Peace and Freedom Party, and state Green parties. Organized around the theme of "Transcending Left, Right, and Center: Building the New Mainstream" and with the goal of running a coalition-backed presidential candidate, this motley collection of political tendencies blurred the meaning of independent politics. Rather than defining the term as freedom from the corporate power structure and the parties it sponsors, the conferences suggested that any party that was not Democrat or Republican was "independent," even if the party was not anticorporate, or, like the New Party, sought coalition with the Democrats.

One of the ironies of 2004 is that the liberal tendency harshly criticized Nader for running as a coalition-backed independent and for attending a forum on independent politics sponsored by the Newman/Fulani group. But in 1996 these same liberals had sought to run coalition-backed independent candidates separate from the existing Green Party USA, a coalition into which they invited the opportunistic Newman/Fulani group.[26]

What Is Political Independence?

Another contradiction in the liberal Greens' position in 2004 is that while they gave indirect support to Kerry through the safe-states approach, they criticized Nader for not being a Green. They presented a sectarian notion of political independence as being independent of everyone who is not a Green, blurring the important distinction between corporate-sponsored Democrats and Ralph

Nader who stands with the Greens on the issues. That sectarian conception of political independence is still being articulated by some Greens in the post-election period who maintain the Greens should only nominate Green Party members.

A nonsectarian notion of political independence for the Greens would mean being open to alliances with every progressive independent candidate and party that is opposed to the corporate rulers and the two parties they sponsor. In practice, this notion would mean the Greens do not support Democrats or Republicans in elections. But they would be open to supporting other independent progressive candidates and parties who are independent of corporate sponsorship and share Green platform goals.

It is a question of class. Do the Greens want rule by the corporate elite or rule by the people? This nonsectarian notion of political independence paves the way for productive electoral alliances with other movements that share the Greens' goal of abolishing corporate rule and establishing real democracy, whether it is through a progressive independent like Ralph Nader, or a new insurgent labor-, Black-, or Chicano-based party, or a state-based independent progressive party, such as the Progressive Party of Vermont, the Mountain Party of West Virginia, the United Citizens Party of South Carolina, or the Peace and Freedom Party of California. Openness to these kind of electoral alliances made for the productive Green/Nader alliances in 1996 and 2000 and for the mergers between the Greens and Black-based political formations in Massachusetts (Green-Rainbow Party) and Washington, D.C. (DC Statehood Green Party). The Greens' concept of independent politics should embrace these kinds of alliances among the people against corporate rule. It should not be the Greens against everybody else. It should be the Greens with the people against the corporate ruling class.

Another problematic notion of political independence that is circulating in the postelection period is the idea of an "independent" movement that works inside and outside the Democratic Party. The Greens should acknowledge that there are some genuine progressives in the Democratic Party and work with them on advancing shared policy goals between elections. But the Greens should not support them in elections, because doing so undermines the Greens' very identity as an alternative to corporate rule. Why should voters accept the Greens' argument for independent alternatives if the Greens do not have enough confidence in themselves to run their own candidates?

The Democratic Party as an institution is funded and controlled by its corporate wing. Progressives in the Democratic Party serve to give it a progressive veneer, making it marketable to progressive constituencies, while the policy direction remains firmly in the hands of its corporate-sponsored leadership. The Kucinich campaign demonstrated this function of progressives in the Democratic Party in 2004 when it sought to bring Greens and Nader voters into the Democratic coalition. In the end, however, Kucinich was obliged to campaign for Kerry, who stood against Kucinich's entire platform, from ending the Iraq war and the Patriot Act to instituting national health insurance and fair trade policies.

When a progressive Democrat refuses to buckle to the corporate line, the Democrats isolate him or her. The Democratic Party abandoned Cynthia McKinney when the Democratic Leadership Council allied with Republicans to defeat her in 2002. When she won her seat back in 2004, the Democratic leadership in Congress refused to restore her ten-year seniority, as the Democrats had traditionally done in the past for returning members and as the Republicans also do for their members. The denial of seniority prevented McKinney from resuming her role as thorn in the side of U.S. foreign policy on the House International Relations Committee and its Human Rights Subcommittee.[27]

Without having adopted a principle of political independence, and there being no consensus in the Greens on the very meaning of independent political action, it is not surprising that the Green Party was divided on how to respond to the Anybody-But-Bush tsunami from liberal and left leadership circles. Nor is it surprising that the liberal tendency in the U.S. Greens chose to ally with Anybody But Bush through the safe-states approach.[28]

Pushing Nader Away from the Greens

Cobb had been part of the liberals' leadership network since soon after joining the Greens in 1996, and he carried its safe-states message into the nomination race in 2004. As a December 2003 report on his editorial board meeting with the *San Antonio Express-News* put it, "Cobb's strategy is to concentrate on the forty or so 'safe' states where Bush or a Democrat is likely to win. That way he builds the Green Party without helping Bush.... Cobb said that if his strategy had been in place in 2000, Al Gore would be president today because Nader would not have siphoned off votes from the Democrats in key states."[29]

Cobb would soon find that such open support for the lesser evil through the safe-states strategy was generally unpopular among the Greens. Many Greens realized that if they were not willing to risk "spoiling" elections for the Democrats, there was no point in running Green candidates at all. Cobb particularly irked many Greens by repeating the Democrats' claim that Nader's campaign was responsible for Bush's election. Blaming Nader absolved the Republicans of their suppression of the Black vote in Florida, the Democrats of their refusal to challenge it, and the U.S. Supreme Court of their selection of Bush, where the majority opinion stated that "the individual citizen has no federal constitutional right to vote" in presidential elections.[30] Blaming Nader excused the electoral college system that denied victory to Gore, who won the national popular vote. Blaming Nader perpetuated the corporate media's suppression of their own comprehensive ballot recount finding that Gore actually won the Florida vote.[31] If one accepts that Nader cost Gore two states (New Hampshire and Florida), then one must also acknowlege that Buchanan cost Bush in four states (Oregon, Iowa, Wisconsin, and New Mexico) and that Buchanan cost Gore Florida due to the deceptive butterfly ballot in Palm Beach County. One can cite dozens of conditions necessary for Bush to prevail over Gore. Singling out Nader was more about stopping Nader and the Greens than explaining what really happened in 2000.[32]

Finding "safe states" unpopular with many Greens, Cobb opted to brand his lesser-evil plan less explicitly, calling it the "smart growth strategy." In this version, Cobb said his primary objective was to build the Green Party and his secondary objective was to defeat Bush. He also added that he would campaign in battleground states if Green state parties there wanted him to, although it was doubtful his campaign had the capacity to get on the ballot in many of those states.[33]

Still, it was not Cobb's "smart growth strategy" that won him the nomination. No one has surveyed all the Green convention delegates to see why they voted as they did, but the anecdotal testimony on Green e-mail lists shows that many delegates who wanted an all-out run against the corporate duopoly nevertheless voted for Cobb because they perceived Nader as having abandoned the Green Party when he chose to run independently. That testimony also shows that Cobb supporters emphasized that spin on Nader's decision as they attempted to recruit and win over delegates.

Whatever the pro-Cobb delegates' reasons, it is clear that Cobb and his supporters worked hard to keep Nader from being the Green nominee again in 2004. As Jack Uhrich, finance director of the national Green Party U.S. until December 2003, would write to the Green Party e-mail discussion list in February 2004:

> I was very surprised, when I joined the USGP (United States Green party) staff in October 2001, to find that several members of the USGP leadership were already actively campaigning against Ralph running for President in 2004, and, according to prior leaders I talked to, this had been going on at least since right after the 2000 campaign ended.... In my opinion, it was the actions of several members of the USGP leadership that drove Ralph away from the party, after he held many fundraisers for us, nationally, statewide and locally, and was constantly in the media during and after the 2000 elections, urging people to join the Green Party.[34]

Most of the party's officers in the 2000–2004 period would work to prevent Nader from running again as the Greens' presidential candidate, including David Cobb, the party's legal counsel; Dean Myerson, the political coordinator in the D.C. office; Steve Schmidt, the chair of the Platform Committee; Greg Gerritt, the party secretary; and party co-chairs Marnie Glickman, Ben Manski, Nathalie Paravicini, Anita Rios, and Tom Sevigny. Many Greens were as surprised by Uhrich's comments as he had been by what he witnessed when he joined the staff. The actions against another Nader candidacy by the national officers were conducted without the consent of, or even any discussion with, the party's National Committee of state party representatives.

Annie Goeke, a party cochair until 2002 who served as the party's liaison with Nader after the 2000 election, did try to maintain the partnership that the Greens had with Nader in the 1996–2000 period. The partnership should not have been difficult to maintain given the mutually compatible concerns on both sides: the Greens' desire to be perceived as more than the Ralph Nader party and Nader's wish to remain an independent who was not formally affiliated with any political party. Goeke tried to get the national officers and Nader to agree that the best role for Nader was to remain an independent who supported the Greens. He would support the Greens through fund-raising and in issue-based and election campaigns without becoming involved in internal decision-making. However, Goeke quickly found herself isolated among the national officers in trying to maintain the Green end of this arms-length partnership. After a six-hour meeting between the party's officers and Nader about ten days after the 2000 election, David Cobb told Goeke she was "starstruck." Cobb and other officers began arguing that the Greens had grown beyond Nader and could better appeal to Democratic voters without him.[35]

Nader continued to hold up his end of the partnership, though. Between the 2000 election and the approach of the 2004 campaign, Nader would go to forty-five Green fund-raisers in thirty-one states at his own expense, raising more money than anyone for the Green Party and its state and local affiliates. He praised the Green Party U.S. and its platform in his 2001 book, *Crashing the Party*, as he also did regularly in his public speeches and media interviews.[36] He shared his 2000 campaign volunteer lists with party organizers and the 2000 campaign donor list with the national party.[37] Either he or close staffers attended national Green meetings and met with Greens internationally. Despite this support, most of the national officers of the Green Party wanted to distance Nader from the Greens.

On June 14, 2003, the Green Party of Texas met in Bastrop. There, at the initiative of David Cobb, a decision with national ramifications was made. The party voted to add a new article on the "Presidential Candidate" to its bylaws which would require that in order to be on the Green Party ballot line in Texas, a presidential candidate must be a member of his or her state's Green Party. That, obviously, was directed against Nader, who had long said he would always remain an independent.

Cobb, formerly of Texas but by then a California resident, dominated much of the Texas convention, according to reports by Paul Cardwell, a delegate who was chair of the Green Party of Fannin County, Texas, and Ramsey Sprague, a delegate who was treasurer of the Green Party of Tarrant County, Texas. As Cardwell wrote, "I was inclined to support Cobb until the 2003 Texas state convention in Bastrop. There I changed positions totally. I am chair of the Fannin County (TX) party and was a delegate to that convention. Even though no longer a resident of Texas, Cobb ran the convention with an iron hand, often from the chair, and always giving orders to whomever was presiding."

Sprague reported how Cobb attempted to pack the state executive committee with supporters by proposing a limited-approval voting method by which each delegate had two "yes" votes. Sprague noted that "by allowing 'no' votes in Mr. Cobb's voting method, a well organized clique could determine the outcome of an election by voting 'yes' for their candidate and 'no' for all other candidates." Delegates tried to reject this winner-take-all plurality method of voting proposed by Cobb for the proportional method of preference voting, where delegates would rank their choices in order of preference, which is what the Texas party bylaws actually required. But Sprague reports, "Mr. Cobb either vehemently denied others the opportunity to speak for or against his proposal or berated them as delegates sought more democratic alternatives."[38]

As a former Texas staff member of a proportional representation advocacy group—the Center for Voting and Democracy—Cobb no doubt understood the implications of his voting proposal.

Uhrich reflected the anguish many Greens felt about the Texas bylaw amendment and other maneuvers to separate Nader from the Greens:

> [The Texas bylaw change] is just one of a number of examples where some of our leaders made Ralph feel unnecessarily unwelcome in our party. Some of these actions were innocent enough, though dumb, in my estimation, like not featuring Ralph to do the reply to the State of the Union message. Others were deliberate, like the Texas resolution.... That is part of the reason I find myself so torn about this whole thing. On the one hand, I want to build a party and stay within the democratic guidelines we set to make this decision; on the other, I believe that the one person who has done the most to build that party (and we now see by the polls that he did as good a job as any of us in attracting Black and Latino support—actually doing better than attracting white support), was rejected in a number of ways, sometimes by those who are now complaining that he's not running as a Green. Or is it that he's running at all that angers them? Were they so arrogant to think that, if he didn't run as a Green he wouldn't run at all, and so they felt free to either force him out or try to force him to run

as they wanted? If that is the case, they obviously miscalculated, and now, not only are they stuck, but we are all stuck with this mess."[39]

Nader's Green Path Not Taken

Seeing the Greens divided between independent and lesser-evil strategies in late 2003 and not organized to make a decision until the June 2004 convention, Nader reluctantly concluded that his best option was to declare his candidacy as an independent and then ask the Greens for their endorsement as part of a coalition candidacy should he decide to run.

"I write this with regret," Nader wrote in his December 23, 2003, letter to the Greens withdrawing his name from consideration as the Green presidential nominee, "because of my support for your platform and civic activities, because of our shared political history and because of the numerous efforts I have made, over the years since 1996, to help grassroots Greens build the Party." He noted that

> as part of my exploratory effort, I have met or spoken with Greens from all over the country in extensive conversations, heard from even more through sign-on letters, Kucinich supporters, Greens for Dean, state and local Green groups, newspaper and magazine accounts, including the Green Pages and Green Horizon, etc., all of which illustrate how the reaction to George W. Bush, has fractured—more than galvanized—the Greens as a Party.

Nader concluded that "uncertainty expressed by the Party's leadership regarding the conditions under which the Party may or may not field Presidential and Vice-presidential candidates in 2004 can only be interpreted as a confused retreat."

Nader went on to cite several factors that he felt made a Green run by him impractical. He said the fact that the Greens were waiting until the June 2004 convention before deciding whether to run a candidate and, if so, whether to run safe states or all out, made it difficult for a serious candidate to raise funds and seek ballot access. He also expressed concern that some state Green parties had resolved to deny independents not registered in the Green Party access to their states' ballot line. He closed the letter on an amicable note: "In the event that I should still decide to become a presidential candidate, any collaborative efforts that are possible, especially at the state and local level, would be welcome."[40]

Nader's decision to run as an independent, which some of his non-Green supporters had been pushing him to do since 2002, opened the door for Cobb's anti-Nader campaign and made it problematic for the Greens for Nader network that had been organized in 2003 to build support for a Green-backed Nader run. Most Greens believe that Nader overestimated the influence of the national party leadership on the nomination and convention process. If Nader had gone over the heads of the liberal leadership and appealed directly to the Green base for the nomination in Milwaukee, he probably would have won handily, as even Cobb's supporters concede.[41] States like Texas, that had said they would not put an independent on their state ballot line, probably would have gone along with the national party decision to back Nader and put him on the ballot. Certainly Nader would have risked losing a state ballot line or two running for a Green Party divided on whether to run all-out against both corporate parties. But ballot petitioning for a few additional states would have been much less of a burden than petitioning for all fifty states and Washington, D.C. Had he chosen to seek the Green nomination, it is likely he would have won it and headed up a Green presidential campaign that still had a solid majority of Greens backing him.

In the six months between Nader's decision not to seek the Green nomination and the Green National Convention, Nader was ambiguous with some states about whether he would run on the Green line or an independent line. That hurt him with many Green supporters who were inclined to support his endorsement only if he would appear on their state's Green ballot line. It also lent credibility to Cobb supporters' allegations that Nader had used and then abandoned the Greens. With Nader not seeking votes and convention delegates in Green primaries, caucuses, and conventions, it was difficult for Greens for Nader to win delegates committed to Nader in some states. And both his declaration of candidacy at the end of February and his choice of Camejo as his running mate in June came too late for pro-Nader Greens to maximize support in their respective state parties.

Unable to use the Green's existing twenty-two state ballot lines, Nader had to mount a monumental fifty-state ballot drive. The scale and viciousness of the Democratic campaign to deny him ballot access was probably heightened by the fact that they perceived that they could demonize Nader without alienating the whole Green movement. Nor did it help that in the early months of the campaign Nader tried to deflect the Democratic attacks about "spoiling" the 2004 election by arguing that his campaign would help defeat Bush. That argument simply undercut the rationale for his own independent challenge to both of the corporate-sponsored parties. And it muffled the distinction between his approach of running all-out in all states and Cobb's safe-states approach.

Nader almost went to the Milwaukee convention at the last minute. A number of delegates who voted for Cobb have said this would have changed their vote. Most in the Nader camp at the convention wanted Nader there, but some did not, fearing disrespect from some on the Cobb side in the form of heckling or worse. Nader heard both sides and finally decided to phone in to the Nader/Camejo rally at the convention Friday night before Saturday's presidential nomination vote. Nader's message over the phone hook-up reiterated what he had said in his letters: he would welcome the Greens' endorsement but felt it best that he continue to stay out of the internal politicking and let the Greens make that decision on their own. In a debate Thursday night among the candidates present, Cobb had made the most of Nader's absence. He argued that a Nader candidacy with a Green endorsement as part of a coalition would not build the Green Party. Cobb underscored that claim with the statement: "Ralph Nader is not here. That says something."

After the convention, many Green activists worked for the Nader/Camejo campaign rather than the official Cobb/LaMarche ticket. For these Greens, the Nader/Camejo campaign embodied *independent* Green politics, which they saw as the most effective strategy for resisting the hard right and challenging the bipartisan consensus around militaristic neoliberalism. In New York, for example, the Green Party's state committee budgeted $5,000 to support the national nominee's ballot-access drive with staff and other resources. But many rank-and-file Greens worked to put Nader/Camejo on the ballot as the Peace and Justice candidate instead. In the end they gathered 28,000 signatures for Nader but only 5,000 for Cobb, well short of the 15,000 good signatures required for a ballot line. At the same time Greens used Nader's campaign stops in Binghamton, Buffalo, Rochester, Albany, New Paltz, and New York City to promote the Green Party, which Nader urged voters to support. Working on the Nader campaign strengthened several Green locals and helped instigate new locals in places like Glens Falls. New York Greens found it was possible to build the Green Party by supporting the independent Nader/Camejo campaign.

The same pattern held true in other parts of the country. Tens of thousands of people attended Nader/Camejo campaign events. Local Greens who worked on these events got the sign-up lists for follow-up organizing. Some of the hundreds of Nader/Camejo volunteers are now working with the Greens, particularly in the Greens for Democracy and Independence network initiated by Peter Camejo after the convention.[42] Others are waiting to see if the Greens will commit themselves to political independence and democratize their internal structures. Where the work done on the Nader/Camejo campaign ultimately leads depends in large part on what the Greens do in the next few years on these questions of political independence and organizational democracy.

If Nader had chosen to go for the Green nomination, there is little doubt not only that he would have won it but that the dynamic of the presidential campaign would have been quite different. The Democrats would not have been able to exploit the Green/Nader division to the detriment of both. Instead, a Green/Nader alliance would have created a strong center of opposition to the war, corporate-dominated domestic policies, and the two-corporate-party political system. That clear opposition might have attracted significant sections of the peace movement and other people's movements away from the Anybody-But-Bush current, possibly accelerating buildup of independent opposition to militarism and corporate domination. But even if it had failed to stimulate the growth of a massive opposition movement during the election, the story of the left in the campaign would have changed. It would have been about Nader and the Greens united at the center of opposition to the Bush-Kerry ticket of war and corporate rule—not about everybody but Nader, Camejo, and their followers supporting Kerry as the lesser evil.

The Green Vote Nose-dives

It was the perception among many delegates that Nader's supposed abandonment of the Greens, and not Cobb's support for the safe-states strategy, provided Cobb's margin of victory at the Green National Convention. But in fact, it was Cobb's lesser-evil strategy that got the attention in corporate-media coverage and among progressives who embraced the Anybody-But-Bush strategy in 2004. Soon after the convention a statement by prominent progressives endorsed Kerry in the "swing states" and Cobb in the "safe states."[43] As Cobb had put it in a press release leading up to the Green National Convention, his "strategy will grow the Green Party and not piss off millions of potential Green Party members and supporters."[44] On the second point, Cobb's strategy worked: he did not piss off millions of potential Greens because they never knew he was running.

The Green presidential vote plummeted more than 95 percent, from just short of 2.9 million for Nader in 2000 to just over 0.1 million for Cobb in 2004. Although Cobb claimed that his vote total did not matter much,[45] the number is certainly an important objective standard for measuring support for a campaign. Cobb's total of 119,862 votes was lower in absolute numbers than just about every nonsectarian, independent progressive presidential campaign since the two-corporate-party system solidified after the Civil War, including all the nineteenth-century populist farmer-labor tickets beginning in 1872, the Debsian Socialist Party campaign, the independent Progressive campaigns of Robert LaFollette in 1924 and Henry Wallace in 1948, the 1980 Citizens Party, and the 1996 and 2000 Green Party tickets. The nineteenth-century vote totals were 7 to 15 million compared to more than 122 million in 2004. Cobb's strategy of focusing campaign resources on the safe states did not yield many votes in the safe states. His vote total can only be seen as a humiliating defeat for his safe-states strategy.

Cobb announced that he would run a "smart states" rather than a "safe states" campaign because he was willing to campaign in a battleground state if Greens there wanted him to do so. But the overall message was clear: the Cobb/LaMarche campaign prioritized the defeat of Bush over winning votes for their own ticket. Cobb's vice-presidential running mate, Pat LaMarche, was quoted at her first press conference after the convention as saying she was not even committed to voting for her own ticket if the Bush/Kerry race was close in her home state of Maine.[46] The Cobb campaign quickly put out a statement saying LaMarche had been misquoted. But she kept being quoted along similar lines right up to just before the election. At a campaign stop at Dartmouth College in New Hampshire, for example, *The Dartmouth* reported:

> LaMarche focused on efforts to remove Bush from office rather than promoting herself. She accepts that voting for a Green candidate is not the feasible way to get this done.... Although not technically endorsing Sen. John Kerry for the presidency, LaMarche made it clear she sees him as the lesser of two evils. 'I do not say vote for Kerry, I do not say the K word. So he's not perfect, he's the only solution we have,' she said.[47]

Cobb has claimed that "the Green Party continued to grow in 2004. We ran record numbers of candidates, elected more local officials and registered more Green voters than ever before."[48] But those claims cannot be reconciled with the facts. After years of growth, the number of both candidates and winning candidates was reduced. In the last on-year election in 2002, the Greens ran 561 candidates nationwide and 81 of them won office. In 2004, the Greens ran 433 candidates and 70 of them won office. Because local races are nonpartisan in many places, a better comparison is state and federal candidates, the down-ticket candidates running with the Green presidential candidate at the head of the ticket. Here there was a 121-candidate reduction, from 300 in 2002 to 179 in 2004.[49] As for Green Party registration, after an unbroken trend of steady growth throughout their history, the Greens' party registration totals stagnated during 2004 and early 2005, fluctuating around the 300,000 level.[50]

The Cobb campaign showed little capacity to get on the ballot. Starting with twenty-two established Green Party ballot lines, Cobb was able to get on the ballot in only six more states, all of them in the low end of the range of state petitioning and filing thresholds. Nor was the Cobb campaign able to successfully defend many of the Green ballot lines on election day. The number of state Green parties with ballot lines was reduced from twenty-two at the beginning of 2004 to fifteen after the election.[51] The Nader campaign had to start from scratch and was able to get on the ballot in thirty-five states, despite the Democrats and allied 527 organizations spending an estimated $10 million to $20 million to keep Nader off state ballots through intimidation of volunteers and endless lawsuits.[52] Richard Winger of *Ballot Access News* has said it was the most concerted effort by a major party to deny ballot access to an independent or third-party candidate in U.S. history, surpassed only by the Democrats' campaign in some states to deny ballot access to Earl Browder, the Communist candidate, in 1940.

Political Impact

The most important measure of an election campaign is its political impact. None of the Cobb leadership's postmortems comment on how his campaign affected public opinion on the key issues of the presidential campaign, notably, the bipartisan consensus behind the war in Iraq. All Cobb claims is an image makeover: "A remarkable transformation has taken place in the public's perception of the Green Party.... We've gone from being seen as spoilers to being hailed as saviors,"[53] referring to the Cobb campaign's role in the Ohio recount fight *after* the election.

In fact, the Green presidential campaign had no impact on the political debate of the campaign. But it did affect the dynamic. By bending to the Anybody-But-Bush strategy of the nation's institutionalized liberal leadership, the Greens took themselves out of the 2004 election as a distinct and oppositional voice and served as Exhibit A for the corporate media's claim that the Nader/Camejo antiwar ticket was marginal: not even the Greens supported it.

If the Greens had united behind the Nader/Camejo antiwar, anti-corporate ticket, a potentially massive opposition bloc might have started growing behind their lead. It is a mistake to conclude that, no matter what the Greens did, progressive voters would have followed liberal leaders' direction and backed Kerry's pro-war, pro-corporate candidacy.[55] The Greens could have been the counterforce to the surrender of the left. After all, conventional wisdom considered Howard Dean unbeatable for several months until his support collapsed in the last two weeks before the Iowa caucuses. We do not know what would have happened if, with a united Green Party spearheading the opposition, sections of the antiwar movement had joined behind a united Green challenge to the bipartisan war policies of Bush and Kerry. Such a breakaway might have snowballed, attracting key activists in allied pro-justice movements and changing the whole dynamic of the election campaign and the policy debate. At the least, Green unity behind a resolutely independent candidate would have made the Greens a pole of attraction for the more radical peace and justice activists, particularly among the youth, and laid a strong foundation for future Green electoral insurgencies. As it was the Greens, and the broader left and liberal movements, never gave themselves a chance to find out what they could have accomplished had they stood their political ground instead of collapsing into the Kerry campaign.

Professional Liberals and the Democratic Party

The progressive leadership that led the movements into the Kerry camp was broader than the liberal intelligentsia in the opinion-shaping universities and media. It also included the institutionalized "professional liberals," the paid staff and leaders of the unions and the big environmental, peace, civil rights, women's, gay, and community organizing groups. Selling out to the Democratic Party pays off for the professional liberals in the form of career opportunities and funding. These material benefits flow through social and organizational networks that connect the professional liberals in nongovernmental organizations (NGOs) to their peers in Democratic administrations and the corresponding party organizations that are built from the top down by Democratic patronage and preferment. Corporate funding—grants for the NGOs, universities, and progressive media, and campaign cash for the Democrats—cements it all together, co-opting institutionalized progressivism into the service of the corporate-dominated Democratic coalition.[56]

For the rank and file of the labor, community, people of color, women's, gay, and environmental movements, Kerry and the Democrats offered nothing of substance—not one single progressive program or policy on any front that progressives could rally around. Seeking swing voters, Kerry ran to Bush's right as a war hawk and a deficit hawk, vowing to send more troops to Iraq, to increase forces in the Army and Marines, to increase the military and homeland repression budgets, and to do all that while bringing the federal budget back into balance. His Bush-like sound bites, such as promising "to hunt down and kill the terrorists," made militarism a non-issue in the Bush-Kerry horse race. Given his militaristic priorities and the tax proposals he advanced, a Kerry administration could balance the federal budget only by slashing social spending. Given these parameters, all the professional liberals could offer in support of a vote for Kerry was a defensive apology that Bush would be even worse.

The leaders of the big liberal organizations have been delivering their constituencies to the Democrats for decades. But the Iraq antiwar movement was younger, newer, less institutionalized, and far more dynamic than any other movement going into 2004. Knowing that the Democrats had voted overwhelmingly for Bush's wars and related repressive domestic legislation,[57] the antiwar movement had no rational basis for supporting Kerry's call to escalate the wars on Iraq and terrorism. The peace movement could have been the spearhead of a significant break from the pro-war two-party system in 2004.

The leadership of the biggest antiwar coalition, United for Peace and Justice (UFPJ), decided to focus its efforts on defeating Bush, organizing their one major mobilization in 2004 against the Republican National Convention but not the Democratic convention. The torture at Abu Ghraib and the slaughter in Najaf passed without a significant response. Rather than crafting a focused antiwar message, UFPJ leaders turned the mobilization at the Republican National Convention into a march "against the Bush agenda," as the lead banner and UFPJ spokespeople made clear.

Most of the antiwar intellectuals and leaders with visibility in the movement—including Noam Chomsky, Daniel Ellsberg, Howard Zinn, Naomi Klein, Barbara Ehrenreich, Cornel West, Medea Benjamin, Michael Albert, Carl Davidson, and Tom Hayden—called for a vote for Kerry to defeat Bush. Many of these people, obviously cognizant of the Orwellian nature of their call to vote for peace by voting for pro-war Kerry, tried to have it both ways by issuing statements urging people to vote for Kerry in the competitive "battleground" states and for Cobb in the noncompetitive "safe states."[58] These statements did nothing to move public opinion against the war. But the pro-war corporate media widely reported these statements, using them to dismiss the Nader/Camejo ticket as one that did not even have the support of antiwar leaders.

The Nader/Camejo campaign soldiered on without the Green Party's official support. The Green base was divided, with a major portion of rank-and-file Greens working for the Nader/Camejo ticket. Repelled or disillusioned by the division, some Greens just sat out the 2004 race. Without access to the Greens' twenty-two ballot lines, the Nader/Camejo campaign had to focus nearly all its resources from June until September on ballot petitioning. Excluded again from the presidential debates, Nader and Camejo barnstormed the country focusing their message against the war and the Patriot Act, for reforms to benefit working people, for reforms to make ballot access and elections fair, and for independent politics as the most effective way to fight the right and advance progressive reforms. Nader's 463,647 votes were still far more than the 119,862 that Cobb received on the Green lines, but it was also only one-sixth of the 2,882,782 votes Nader had received in 2000.[59] Nader and Camejo received enough attention and votes to serve as the visible conscience of the peace and other progressive movements, but it was not the massive electoral insurgency against militarism and corporate rule it might have been with the Green Party's support and leadership.

Postelection Demoralization on the Left

The lesser-evil strategy of Anybody But Bush rendered progressive movements demoralized after the election. Not only did they fail to beat Bush, but the self-censorship involved in supporting the pro-war corporate Kerry campaign silenced the voice of the peace and other progressive movements. The professional liberals are blaming the supposedly conservative values of Americans, the tactical mistakes of the Kerry campaign, the sycophancy of the corporate media, everything but their own surrender to the politics of the lesser evil. The more upbeat postelection assessments try to highlight a new progressive institutional infrastructure to support the Democrats, including America Votes, Progressive Majority, Camp Wellstone, Democracy for America, Center for American Progress, Air America Radio, Media Matters, MoveOn.org, and Progressive Democrats of America, groups that are bankrolled in large part by liberal capitalists like currency speculator George Soros, insurance magnate Peter Lewis, and bankers Herb and Marian Sandler, who collectively have pledged to put $100 million into this infrastructure over the next 15 years.[60] But these assessments probably say more about career opportunities for professional liberals than the real prospects for any antiwar, anti-corporate insurgency inside the Democratic Party.

In their rank-and-file majority, Democratic voters were against the war in Iraq and for domestic policies that would benefit working people. But in a case of lesser evilism run amok, Democratic progressives defeated themselves by voting for pro-war corporate Kerry as the "electable" candidate in the primaries, leaving the antiwar candidacies of Dennis Kucinich and Al Sharpton with a combined total of barely 1 percent of the Democratic National Convention's delegates. Kucinich kept his campaign going up until the convention on the promise that he would fight there for antiwar and other progressive platform planks. But then, finding that he could not even muster the 20 percent support required for a platform committee minority report to force a vote of the whole convention on his alternative planks, Kucinich withdrew those proposals at the Democratic Platform Committee meeting. He could have at least made the committee members go on record as to where they stood on his progressive planks by calling for a vote on his proposals. But he instructed his people on the committee to drop his platform amendments without calling for a vote. That was how the progressive remnant of the Democratic Party went down to a crushing defeat and gave up without a fight in 2004.[61]

Not only were the movements dispirited, they were also confused by the defensive campaign around Kerry as the lesser evil. They were unable to recognize serious harms when advanced by the "lesser evil" and consequently they were inert as the congressional Democrats' pushed through the Intelligence Reform and Terrorism Prevention Act of 2004 in December. Seeking to bolster their credentials as "National Security Democrats" and one-up the Republicans' antiterrorism warriors, the Democrats goaded a bloc of reluctant moderate Republicans into passing the bill despite their concerns about its further erosion of civil liberties and its concentration of the intelligence apparatus in the hands of the Pentagon. While the creation of the intelligence czar captured the headlines, the small print in the bill enacted key elements of Bush's proposed Patriot Act II, including steps toward a national ID card with federal standardization of state drivers' licenses and ID cards, expanded FBI powers to conduct secret searches and surveillance, detention without bail for accused terrorists indicted by grand juries, and sharing secret grand-jury information with foreign and domestic law enforcement agencies.

When the new session of Congress convened in 2005, Democrats provided comfortable margins of victory for a string of Republican initiatives: a bankruptcy bill that virtually restores debt peonage; a tort reform bill that closes the state courts to many class-action suits against corporate crimes; and an anticonservation, pronuclear energy bill. When Bush asked in March for authorization to spend $82 billion more for the wars in Iraq and Afghanistan, the Senate approved it 99–0, and only thirty-four Democrats in the House, less than 20 percent of the Democratic caucus, voted against further funding of the occupations.

The Failure of Lesser-Evil Strategies

Compare 1968 to 2004. Nineteen sixty-eight also had an election in which both corporate-party candidates supported an increasingly unpopular war. But in 1968, the antiwar movement came out of the election stronger and energized, not demoralized. The Movement, as it was called, had learned its lesson in 1964. The lesser-evil slogan of Students for a Democratic Society (SDS), "Part of the Way with LBJ," captured the strategy for most of the left in 1964, when Goldwater called for escalation in Vietnam and Johnson promised "no wider war." But after Johnson won the election and escalated anyway, in 1968 the radical currents of the antiwar movement decided to maintain their independence from the corporate-party candidates. There were also liberal tendencies in the peace movement willing to compromise the Movement's "Out Now" demand in order to support Eugene McCarthy, who called for negotiations, or Robert Kennedy, who advocated what would be called "Vietnamization" under Nixon. But in doing so, the liberals were abandoning the clear antiwar demand that motivated most peace activists and their fast-growing sympathizers in the general public.

The radical tendency led protests against the war at the Democratic as well as Republican conventions. They came out of the election bigger and broader, more organized and energized. We now know from Nixon's memoirs, among other sources, that his "secret plan to end the war," which helped get him elected in 1968, was to massively escalate the war with an invasion of North Vietnam and tactical nuclear bombing if North Vietnam did not agree to his terms. Called Operation Duck Hook, the nuclear target folders were drawn up and the deadline for North Vietnam's capitulation set for November 1, 1969. But the massive nationwide October 15, 1969, Vietnam Moratorium, a sort of one-day general strike, convinced him that it would cost him massive domestic rebellion, not to mention the 1972 election, if he carried out his secret plan. The peace movement in the streets, not the Democrats in office, made Nixon back down.[62]

Unfortunately, many of the veterans of 1968 forgot that lesson in 2004. Besides Tom Hayden's quip about "voting with the CIA" as the lesser evil, there was the influential paper by Chicago-based veteran activists Carl Davidson and Marilyn Katz, "Moving From Protest to Politics: Dumping Bush's Regime in 2004." Timed to influence United for Peace and Justice's upcoming June 2003 conference in Chicago, it provided a theoretical rationale for supporting the lesser evil: the left should support the "globalist" imperialists in the Democrats as the lesser evil to the "unilateralist" imperialists around Bush. It advocated a classic Popular Front strategy of the left allying with the liberal wing of the ruling class in order to defeat its right wing.[63]

But the Popular Front strategy has a history of defeat. The left was crushed under the Popular Front strategies followed in Spain, France, and Germany in the 1930s. In the United States, the impetus for progressive reform was lost when in 1936 the labor movement and the Communist Party took the popular movements and the left into the Democratic Party, which could then take them for granted and move to the right.[64]

A peculiarly American version of the lesser-evil strategy has been the practice of fusion where progressives have supported candidates running on both a third-party line and a major-party line. Practiced widely by the populist farmer-labor parties of the late nineteenth century, the populists were repeatedly betrayed by their major-party partners, until they finally self-destructed when they supported the fusion presidential candidacy of Democrat William Jennings Bryan in 1896. Progressives in New York State, where fusion is still legal, have seen the American Labor Party in the 1930s and 1940s, the Liberal Party from the 1950s to the 1990s, and the Working Families Party today repeatedly co-opt potential electoral insurgencies into support for mainstream Democratic and sometimes Republican politicians.

The notion of allying independent insurgencies with progressive Democrats lives on today in what is called the inside/outside strategy, a fusion-type strategy for the majority of states with election laws that outlaw fusion. The idea is to support progressive Democrats and run independents against conservative Democrats. In practice, inside/outside strategists find themselves caught between the loyalty demands of compromise candidates and their own hopes for progressive reform. In order to be acceptable partners with the Democrats, they find themselves compelled to support Democrats who stand opposed to their policy demands. Thus Rev. Jesse Jackson and the Rainbow Coalition, which talked about being a "third force" inside and outside the Democratic Party, ended up completely inside the Democratic Party, supporting candidates like Mondale and Dukakis who advocated policies Jackson and the Rainbow Coalition disagreed with.

The newly formed Progressive Democrats of America (PDA) demonstrates how the inside/outside strategy really means bringing progressives now outside the Democratic Party into it. Kevin Spidel, national field director for Kucinich for President and now deputy national director for Progressive Democrats of America has stated that "the most important thing we do is that inside-outside strategy: Pulling together members of the Green Party, the Independent Progressive Politics Network, the hip-hop community, the civil rights community, our allies in congress, the antiwar community. We are bringing together all the social movements within the Democratic Party under one effective tent."[65]

A March 2005 appeal on behalf of Medea Benjamin of Global Exchange called for support of

> PDA's unique efforts to ... ultimately take over and transform the Democratic Party ... working both inside and outside the Democratic Party.... PDA is not the Democratic Party. They are a group dedicated to transforming the Democratic Party. PDA represents the truest concerns of the largest number of Democrats. It is the voice of the progressive wing and the conscience of the Democratic Party. PDA has

demonstrated great willingness and commitment to work with Greens, Pinks, and other peace and justice activists as it shares in the building of the broad progressive movement.[66]

Popular Front, fusion, inside/outside, and safe states are all species in the same genus of lesser evilism. By relying on the liberal wing of the corporate power structure to defend us from its right wing, the left surrenders its own voice and very identity as an alternative to corporate domination. And history shows, when push comes to shove, that the corporate liberals ally with their conservative counterparts against the people.

The Opportunity Still at Hand

The problems of war, civil liberties, economic justice, and the environment are as much with us after the 2004 election as before. The leadership vacuum for a real opposition to militarism and corporate rule is still there. Whatever its problems and mistakes in 2004, the Green Party is still the major expression of independent progressive politics in the U.S. It is not too late for the Green Party to fill that vacuum.

The Greens in the United States, like Green parties in other countries, have had their strongest base among well-educated people in the service professions, such as teachers, social workers, and the staffs of nonprofit service organizations. The Green parties in other countries built their New Left parties in opposition to the cautious reformism of the traditional Labor, Social Democratic, and Communist parties, as well as the conservative parties. They were reacting to the fact that the Old Left, narrowly focused on bread-and-butter welfare-state reforms, had failed to challenge the system on the issues of militarism, racism, sexism, and ecology. They were also frustrated with the Old Left's near-abandonment of any vision of a new, just, and democratic economic system that moved beyond the exploitation and alienation of capitalism. But the working class in other countries has largely remained attached to the Old Left parties.

The United States has no large labor or socialist party. Without a big party speaking to its needs, the working class is alienated from electoral politics and votes in low numbers. What the Green Party in the United States has the potential to do is unite workers, for whom economic issues are of necessity a leading concern, with the so-called new social movements centered on issues of militarism, ecology, and the liberation of ethnic minorities, women, and gays—which have been the leading concerns of the progressive middle class that has been the base of Green parties in other countries. Thus the Green Party in the United States has the potential to be far more than a 5–10 percent party like other Green parties representing the new social movements. The Greens here could be both a labor and a new social movement party representing a majority of voters.

The potential for this kind of majoritarian bloc was seen in the Camejo campaigns of 2002 and 2003 for California governor, where people of color and low-income people joined the traditional Green voter strongholds in voting for Camejo at rates two times higher than those of white voters and three times higher than those of affluent voters.[67] Likewise the demographic profile of Nader voters shifted from the traditional progressive white-collar base of Green voters in 2000 toward a more blue-collar and nonwhite voter base in 2004.[68, 69] As Nader often said in his postelection antiwar speaking tour, "Sooner or later, the 47 million workers making less than $10 an hour are going to be heard from." Given the complete dependence of the two-corporate-party system on corporate funding, no serious economic justice program will be forthcoming from the major parties. The majoritarian potential of the Nader/Camejo voter core is still there.

Petitioners for the Nader/Camejo ticket found this potential throughout the country. When they petitioned in working-class communities, the reception was friendly. Many people said they would still probably vote for Kerry as the lesser evil, but they knew Nader was on their side and they wanted him as an option on the ballot. It was in the more upscale liberal communities where the traditional Green voter base rubs shoulders with liberal Democrats that petitioners encountered sometimes hostile responses.[70] As discussed above, it is because the professional liberals do receive some material benefits from Democratic administrations that many feel threatened by independent challenges on the left. The future of the Green Party may lie in mobilizing blocs of working-class voters big enough to convince middle-class progressives that their best interests lie with a Green Party now strong enough to win elections.

Election law reforms—especially fair ballot access laws, proportional representation in legislative bodies, and instant run-off voting for single-seat executive offices—will be necessary to realize this majoritarian potential of the Green Party. But it is already clear that the majority of people are with the Greens on the immediate demands, not with the bipartisan consensus of the corporate parties. Noam Chomsky laid this out in his post-election analysis. Reviewing recent public opinion polls, he found that large majorities supported cutting the military budget to fund domestic social programs, including national health insurance (80 percent), public schools, and Social Security. On foreign policy, he wrote:

> A large majority of the public believe that the U.S. should accept the jurisdiction of the International Criminal Court and the World Court, sign the Kyoto protocols, allow the UN to take the lead in international crises, and rely on diplomatic and economic measures more than military ones in the "war on terror." Similar majorities believe the U.S. should resort to force only if there is "strong evidence that the country is in imminent danger of being attacked," thus rejecting the bipartisan consensus on "pre-emptive war" and adopting a rather conventional interpretation of the UN Charter. A majority even favor giving up the Security Council veto, hence following the UN lead even if it is not the preference of U.S. state managers.[71]

These are Green positions, far to the left of the bipartisan consensus of Democrats and Republicans. Although Chomsky did not critically reflect on his own support for Kerry as the lesser evil in 2004 in his article, the lesson to draw from the public opinion polling he cites is that the Greens should forget what the professional liberals say about spoiling elections for the Democrats, go directly to this majority of the people, and mobilize them around the demands they already support. The task of the Greens is to organize them into an independent party and movement, not deliver them once again to a Democratic Party that stands opposed their demands.

If the history of popular insurgencies against old regimes teaches us anything, it is that they are based on hope, not fear; rising expectations, not a demoralizing resignation to the lesser evil; a positive program for a better world, not business as usual to protect us against something worse. It is time for the Greens to declare their unequivocal independence, democratize their party's internal structures, organize the majority that is already with the Greens on immediate demands, and build a self-confident Green movement and party that is ready and able to take power and resolve the very solvable social, political, economic, and ecological problems of our society.

Howie Hawkins
January 2006

Missing Documents and Summary of Contents Not Included

Rachel Odes

Several documents integral to the debate in the Green Party are not included in this collection because their authors refused to grant permission for reprinting. Nonetheless, some of these works fundamentally shaped the discussion represented by the other contributors found in this volume; therefore we include summaries of Ronnie Dugger's "Ralph, Don't Run" and Eric Alterman's "Bush's Useful Idiot," two articles published in *The Nation* and relating to this public conversation about the role of independent politics for progressives and the direction of the Greens. Both are available on the Web and are cited as footnotes.

Ronnie Dugger: "Ralph, Don't Run"
December 2, 2002

The 2000 election fiasco provided occasion for some sober reflection on the political jurisdiction of the Supreme Court and, for some, on the decision to support candidates who chose to position themselves outside the established two-party system. While the blame for George Bush's election was heaped on Ralph Nader and the Green Party even before votes were tallied in Florida, the call for Nader to abstain from an electoral challenge in 2004 did not begin in earnest until 2002, when Ronnie Dugger, the man who nominated Nader at the 1996 and 2000 Green Party conventions, officially warned "Ralph, Don't Run" on the pages of *The Nation* in December of that year.

As became a familiar refrain to Nader supporters in 2004, Dugger argues, "We cannot afford another division in our ranks that will bring about the election of George W. Bush in 2004."[1] He then goes on to enumerate the ways in which Bush was overseeing the creation of a "crypto-fascist" government that trampled on civil liberties and sought to erect an expanding empire that would stop only when the world was reorganized in its own image. Because of this danger, the entire world depended on the unity of American opposition to Bush's reelection, the implication of course being that Nader should not field another candidacy in 2004.

Dugger goes on to explain his defection from being a leading Nader supporter in both 1996 and 2000 to an advocate of abstention in 2004:

> Although I knew that supporting him risked helping elect Republican Presidents in both of those elections, we who supported him and began to forge a third-party politics were acting within our democratic and idealistic rights, believing that the short-run damage to good causes that we were risking was outweighed ethically by the long-run damage to democracy and social justice that the capture of the Democratic Party by major corporations has caused and, if not stopped, will continue to cause.

Dugger's estimation of the calculated "risks" present in any third-party challenge betrays his rethinking of the Nader campaign strategy, a strategy based on placing blame for short-term and long-term failures squarely on the Democrats who refused to act like the opposition to Republican policies that they are so often rumored to be. He goes on to accept some of the blame for Gore's loss in the election, while acknowledging that the candidate himself refused to risk illuminating the corruption of the electoral system even though it would have brought him to the White House, and chastises Nader for refusing to acknowledge his role as an aid to the Republicans.

Eventually, in recounting a heated conversation with Ralph Nader, Dugger comes to the logical end of his argument about the nature of electoral politics in the United States. As he puts it: "The lamentable truth, but the truth, is that the only vehicle with which the voters can beat Bush for President is the Democratic Party. There is no other." So, despite the history rife with betrayals, failures, and disappointments, Dugger concludes, the year 2004 represents the time when the Republicans will have gone so far to the right that there is no choice but to accept that the Democrats are the sole road of opposition.

Dugger elaborates on his understanding of the current situation and defends his position advocating a campaign for a progressive Democrat in the primaries with this history:

> Certainly the [Democratic] party has sold out to corporations, including military contractors. Greens—indeed most progressives, and Senator John McCain as well—know and say that both parties have sold the people and the government to the highest bidder. That is what drove so many of us to Nader. But there is more difference between the Republicans and Democrats than Nader concedes. The majority of House Democrats and almost half the Democratic senators rejected Bush's request for blank-check authority to wage war against Iraq. Democrats in the Senate have blocked judicial nominees who would make the federal courts dramatically more right-wing. And Democrats in the House and Senate remain significantly better than the Republicans on the major domestic issues and significantly more committed to protecting civil rights, civil liberties, and abortion rights. That, along with fear of electing Republicans by voting third-party—not ignorance of the issues, as some of my less thoughtful Green friends suggest—is why overwhelming majorities of Black and Latino voters, and significant majorities of women, continue to vote Democratic....
>
> This does not mean that any of us—least of all Ralph—should pronounce ourselves satisfied with the Democratic Party of 2002. Emphatically to the contrary, the Bush disaster and the corporate scandals provide a historic challenge and a chance to return the Democratic Party to what it should be. Attempting to do this by electing Bush to a second term is an option that is neither rational nor safe. Our job is to resist Bush, not to elect him....
>
> The months ahead should be devoted to building nonviolent resistance to Bush's policies and his election. We need to build at once an Internet-based communications network (not an umbrella organization) among progressive, populist, labor, youth, civil rights, women's and religious organizations and individuals. The resistance must take many forms: local protests, sit-ins, teach-ins and, yes, marches on Washington, perhaps even Martin Luther King Jr.'s 1968 idea of a people's encampment in the city, in 2004—all the tactics that we know matter in building an opposition force and making that opposition heard. And we may hope that in the midst of the pressures and dynamics of the next year and a half, we will focus a substantial portion of our energies on securing the Democratic nomination for a true progressive.

These grassroots efforts, Dugger argues, are what could help shake the corporate-controlled, corrupted, conservative elements that seemed to have such a firm grip on the helm of Democratic Party politics. Initially, this progressive opposition could orient its demands toward changes in the Democrats' platform, finally giving voice to those who sought an opposition to Bush's tax cuts and aggressive foreign policy. Such activists could then mobilize behind candidates like Dennis Kucinich and Al Sharpton, who stood as marks on the moral compass of a party that had been so severely misdirected.

By 2002 it was time for the left to organize on the basis of unity, repairing the rifts that had been caused by Nader's run in 2000. The steps required for a show of force in 2004, Dugger writes, begining at the local level—"taking over the moribund Democratic Party infrastructure" precinct by precinct. With the enthusiasm Nader generated among a new layer of voters and the hope he brought to young people engaging with the electoral process for the first time, Dugger thinks the demands he saw as so critical for the Democrats to represent might just gain a hearing. He concludes:

> Each Nader person has to decide for himself or herself which course is better for 2004: supporting Nader again or converging with Democratic progressives in the Democratic primaries. There are no guarantees. Both courses have grave inherent risks. The first runs the high risk of electing Bush; the second, of ending up with yet another corporate puppet as the Democratic nominee. But apart from the Bush policy and practice of aggressive warmaking, the disgrace of the corporate and financial systems since the collapse of Enron provides progressives with their best political opportunity since 1932. We should now launch a two-year drive for the moral recovery of the Democratic Party and, hence, of the United States. Bush, riding war and the patriotic psychosis he is using our White House to foment, may win whatever we do. But we should not be for Nader knowing that it will help elect Bush. In the emergency that has materialized as if in a nightmare, we may not do that. We no longer have the right.

Eric Alterman: "Bush's Useful Idiot" September 16, 2004

Eric Alterman, a regular columnist for the *The Nation*, was a vocal opponent of Ralph Nader's 2000 presidential run, and was even more vociferous in his opposition to Nader's 2004 bid. Using the facts of the devastation wreaked by the Bush administration on Americans fighting in Iraq, cuts in health care, and environmental destruction, Alterman sums up his take on the political crisis facing the country by proclaiming that "the devastating evidence of Nader's myopia is everywhere around us."[2]

Repeating and escalating pervasive attacks on Nader's character, Alterman compares Nader's goal of growing the Green Party by running for president to George Bush's cynical use of "nation building" as a justification for war on Iraq. He also likens the tarnish on Nader's progressive reputation to the betrayals of former leftists David Horowitz and Christopher Hitchens. Further, Alterman echoes the accusations lobbed at Nader of accepting Republican legal counsel and petitions gathered by politically objectionable forces.

Alterman then summarizes the large-scale defections from the broad political coalition that supported Nader's run in 2000, citing that

> among the seventy-four members of the "113-person Nader 2000 Citizens Committee" who've signed a statement urging support for Kerry/Edwards in all swing states this year are: Phil Donahue, Jim Hightower, Susan Sarandon, Noam Chomsky, Barbara Ehrenreich, Howard Zinn, and Cornel West. Indeed, Nader is without a single high-profile supporter anywhere this time around. And he has added to his list of enemies what he terms the "liberal intelligentsia": those he defines as concerned with issues but willing to accept the "least-worst option."

These allies did do substantial damage to Nader's ability to mobilize forces at the grassroots level, and former supporters like Michael Moore with long-term progressive credibility used any public platform available to argue against those who even considered voting for or working to support Nader or the Greens. Alterman continues:

> [H]e is actively hated by the leaders of the dispossessed to whom he professes his allegiance. On June 22, for instance, Nader met with members of the Congressional Black Caucus in a session that ended with shouting, cursing and several members walking out in a state of fury. When it was over, Texas Representative Sheila Jackson Lee told CNN, "This is the most historic election of our lifetime, and it is a life-or-death matter for the vulnerable people we represent. For that reason, we can't sacrifice their vulnerability for the efforts being made by Mr. Nader."

Accusing Nader of operating on the dubious assumption that "things need to get much worse before they could begin to get better," Alterman then goes on to incriminate supporters of Nader's 2000 campaign who were themselves victims of Bush's reactionary judicial appointments—citing himself as a voice of sanity who knew even then how bad Bush was going to be for American workers like those subject to the politicized decisions of the National Labor Relations Board. Of supporters of Nader's 2004 presidential bid, Alterman asks, "What in God's name will convince [them] to abandon his lemming-like march?" He considers such individuals to be oblivious to atrocities perpetrated by the likes of Bush, Cheney, Ashcroft, and Rumsfeld, since ignorance, Alterman believes, is the only explanation for pursuing Nader's strategy of building a political organization outside the purview of the Democrats.

Alterman's argument ends with an expression of fear for the outcome of an election where Nader proves to be a factor. His poll numbers, on Alterman's writing, were "higher than the 2.74 percent of Americans who provided the votes for his 2000 kamikaze mission—high enough to tip key states toward the single worst President in American history."

CHAPTER ONE

Green Independence?
The Debate Begins

Run, Ralph, Run!

By Howie Hawkins
Unpublished letter to The Nation
November 14, 2002

Ronnie Dugger's proposal ("Ralph, Don't Run," November 14, 2002) for populists and progressives to enter the Democratic Party is as old as the Populist/Democratic fusion campaign for William Jennings Bryan that killed nineteenth-century populism. Now he wants the Greens to commit suicide by making the same mistake.

The overwhelming majority of Democrats in Congress voted for Bush's tax cuts, his military buildup, his assaults on civil liberties, and his regulatory and tax favors to corporate interests. But now, according to Dugger, we should rely on these same Democrats to provide the resistance!

Cynthia McKinney, a Democratic Congresswoman who did resist, is what the Democrats do to their progressives these days. When the right (including Georgia's Democratic senator, Zell Miller, and the Democratic Leadership Council) targeted her for defeat, she was abandoned by the state and national Democrats, from Andrew Young and Maynard Jackson to Terry McAulliffe and Bill Clinton.

We can't fight the far right by supporting the moderate right. The left did that in Germany in the 1930 elections, and the moderate right they helped to elect soon handed power over to Hitler.

The Democratic Party has been the graveyard of every progressive insurgency since the Populists died there in 1896. Reforming the Democrats has been the dominant strategy of liberals, progressives, and even most radicals since 1936. Inside the Democratic Party, the left lost its independent voice. Its analyses and policy proposals disappeared from public debate. The left ended up doing the trench work for candidates who were bankrolled by and indentured to the dominant corporate wing of the party.

Dugger's strategy has already been tried and tried—by the Communist Party and the labor movement since 1936, by the right wing of the Socialist movement led by Michael Harrington, by the mainstream civil rights, women's, peace, and environmental organizations since the 1960s, and by the many liberal presidential contenders like George McGovern, Fred Harris, Ted Kennedy, and Jesse Jackson in the 1970s and 1980s.

As for 2004, by front-loading the primaries to make them virtually a national primary requiring megabucks for a media campaign, the Democratic leadership has all but guaranteed that no Sharpton or Kucinich is going to upset their coronation of a corporate Democrat for the presidential nomination.

Dugger wants to take over the Democratic infrastructure from the precinct level in order to influence the nomination and platform. But he's aiming at an empty shell with little power. The real Democratic infrastructure is the money-raising and media-buying infrastructure.

Duggeristas can win all the precinct chairships they want and it won't mean a thing. When McGovern stole the nomination from the Democrats' corporate wing, they still defeated him by putting their money and media behind Nixon. The winner of the presidential primaries will write the platform, not delegates to the convention. The Democratic precinct infrastructure, such as it is, is for mobilizing votes in general elections, not for primaries or for debating platform planks. Candidates' campaign organizations have largely supplanted mobilization by precinct organizations in most places anyway.

What is there to show for decades of attempts to reform Democratic politics? The left marginalized itself by disappearing into the Democratic Party. And the Democratic Party has moved steadily to the right as it took the votes on the left for granted. The Democrats have retreated on economic class issues since World War II and on racial justice issues since the 1970s. They never had a serious energy and environmental program and have always supported the militaristic "bipartisan foreign policy" to make the world safe for corporate profiteering.

Every presidential cycle we hear this same refrain: The Republican (Goldwater, Nixon, Reagan, Bush...) is practically a fascist, so we've got to unite behind a Democrat to defeat him. Well, when we did get a Democrat, we got Johnson and Vietnam, then Carter and the initiation of the regressive tax, budget, and deregulatory policies we call Reaganism, and finally Clinton and the completion of Reaganism.

There's a class basis for the bipartisan policy of austerity for workers at home, imperialism abroad, and lip service for the environment. Both major parties are corporate parties. When progressives enter the Democratic Party, they are entering into a coalition with corporate forces who have no interest in empowering workers, retreating from empire, or investing in an ecological transformation of our economy and technology. The best way to fight the right is to build independent political organization and action by the "plain people," as the original Populists put it. It is far easier to build that political party independently than it is to try and take over the Democratic Party. Inside the Democratic Party, activists' energy is spent on the internal struggle and the left's program never reaches the public.

Ralph Nader has a far better chance of winning the presidency in 2004 than Dugger does of realizing his fantasy of persuading the Democrats to "fight for instant-runoff voting" (and open the door wide for the Green Party) in return for the support of Greens in 2004. The Democrats will take votes on their left for granted as always ... unless Ralph runs again.

The point of such a campaign is to try and win the office, not influence the Democrats. What the left needs is a Nader/McKinney ticket heading up Green Party slates for all offices, not another self-defeating attempt to fight the right by supporting the moderate-right Democrats against the far-right Republicans.

Run, Ralph, Run!

Appeal to Ralph Nader

From Green Gubernatorial Candidates
December 2002

Dear Ralph,

The Green Party is presented with a crucial opportunity in the 2004 elections. The threat of war, corporate crime, and the continued corrupt domination of money over our electoral system continue to attract people to our party. The 2004 campaign could be exceedingly important in consolidating the Green Party on the national level.

For more than three decades you have been an exemplary civil servant in defense of consumers, civil liberties, civil rights, and democracy. Your willingness to champion the cause of the Green Party by running as its presidential candidate at a time when the party was new and unorganized was an enormous help to the party's growth.

Your willingness to put your long-standing reputation and the great admiration that millions of people throughout the world have for you at the service of this small party shows an exemplary commitment to higher goals at the sacrifice of personal gain or benefits.

Your year 2000 message against corporate crime and abuse and your call for opening the electoral process to new voices have proven correct and are now reluctantly accepted by many who criticized you at the time.

The Green Party is attracting large numbers of youth. It is starting to gain support among people of color. The sharp rise in the Latino vote in California and Iowa for the Green Party is but one sign of what is possible. Women, unionists, and environmentalists who watch their hopes and rights betrayed by the Democratic Party are increasingly joining in protest by voting Green.

As we approach the 2004 presidential campaign, the Green Party faces a critical time. We will need a candidate who can educate for peace, nonviolence, and the rule of law.

Being a diverse party that welcomes controversy, the Green Party will undoubtedly discuss the focus and choice of presidential candidates in a spirited manner.

We, the undersigned, who ran as gubernatorial candidates for the Green Party in 2002, request that you enter the race for the nomination of the Green Party for president in 2004. We know that once again we are asking a huge personal sacrifice from you, but we also know you will be able to bring the Green message to tens of millions of Americans. We believe this time around, the possibility of your inclusion in televised debates will increase and may succeed.

We see one more presidential campaign by you as a major organizing opportunity for the Green Party. It will help the party win elections at the local level, as your candidacy will attract mass media exposure. We believe few people can articulate the need for change and democracy in America as well as you, and certainly no one with the standing you have today in America.

Please give our request your careful consideration.

Sincerely,

Stanley Aronowitz, Candidate for Governor, New York
David Bacon, Candidate for Governor, New Mexico
Peter Camejo, Candidate for Governor, California
Doug Campbell, Candidate for Governor, Michigan
Jonathan Carter, Candidate for Governor, Maine
Nan Garrett, Candidate for Governor, Georgia
Jay Robinson, Candidate for Governor, Iowa
Jill Stein, Candidate for Governor, Massachusetts

The Avocado Declaration

Initiated by Peter Miguel Camejo
January 2004

Introduction

The Green Party is at a crossroads. The 2004 elections place before us a clear and unavoidable choice. On one side, we can continue on the path of political independence, building a party of, by, and for the people by running our own campaign for President of the United States. The other choice is the well-trodden path of lesser-evil politics, sacrificing our own voice and independence to support whoever the Democrats nominate in order, we are told, to defeat Bush.

The difference is not over whether to "defeat Bush"—understanding that to mean the program of corporate globalization and the wars and trampling of the Constitution that come with it—but rather how to do it. We do not believe it is possible to defeat the "greater" evil by supporting a shamefaced version of the same evil. We believe it is precisely by openly and sharply confronting the two major parties that the policies of the corporate interests these parties represent can be set back and defeated.

Ralph Nader's 2000 presidential campaign exposed a crisis of confidence in the two-party system. His 2.7 million votes marked the first time in modern history that millions voted for a more progressive and independent alternative. Now, after three years of capitulation by the Democratic Party to George Bush they are launching a preemptive strike against a 2004 Ralph Nader campaign or any Green Party challenge. Were the Greens right to run in 2000? Should we do the same in 2004? The Avocado Declaration, based on an analysis of our two-party duopoly and its history, declares we were right and we must run.

Origins of the Present Two-Party System

History shows that the Democrats and Republicans are not two counterpoised forces, but rather complementary halves of a single two-party system: "One animal with two heads that feed from the same trough," as Chicano leader Rodolfo "Corky" Gonzalez explained.

After the Civil War, a peculiar two-party political system has dominated the United States. Prior to the Civil War, a two-party system existed which reflected opposing economic platforms. Since the Civil War, a shift occurred. A two-party system remained in place but no longer had differing economic orientations. Since the Civil War the two parties have shown differences in their image, role, social base, and some policies, but in the last analysis they both support essentially similar economic platforms.

This development can be clearly dated to the split in the Republican Party of 1872 where one wing merged with the "New Departure" Democrats that had already shifted toward the

Republican platform, which was pro-finance and industrial business. Prior to the Civil War, the Democratic Party, controlled by the slaveocracy, favored agricultural business interests and developed an alliance with small farmers in conflict with industrial and some commercial interests. That division ended with the Civil War. Both parties supported financial and industrial business as the core of their programmatic outlook.

For over 130 years the two major parties have been extremely effective in preventing the emergence of any mass political formations that could challenge their political monopoly. Most attempts to build political alternatives have been efforts to represent the interests of the average person, the working people. These efforts have been unable to develop. Both major parties have been dominated by moneyed interests and today reflect the historic period of corporate rule.

In this sense United States history has been different from that of any other advanced industrial nation. In all other countries, multiparty systems have appeared, and to one degree or another these countries have more democratic electoral laws and better political representation. In most other countries there exist political parties ostensibly based on or promoting the interest of noncorporate sectors such as working people.

Struggles for Democracy and Social Justice

In spite of this pro-corporate political monopoly, mass struggles for social progress and to expand democracy and civil rights have periodically exploded throughout United States history.

Every major gain in our history, even pre–Civil War struggles—such as the battles for the Bill of Rights, to end slavery, and to establish free public education—as well as those after the Civil War, has been the product of direct action by movements independent of the two major parties and in opposition to them.

Since the Civil War, without exception, the Democratic Party has opposed all mass struggles for democracy and social justice. These include the struggle for ballot reform, for the right of African Americans to vote and against American apartheid ("Jim Crow"), for the right to form unions, for the right of women to vote, against the war in Vietnam, the struggle to make lynching illegal, the fight against the death penalty, the struggle for universal health care, the fight for gay and lesbian rights, and endless others. Many of these struggles were initiated by or helped by the existence of small third parties.

Division of Work

When social justice, peace, or civil rights movements become massive in scale, and threaten to become uncontrollable and begin to win over large numbers of people, the Democratic Party begins to shift and presents itself as a supposed ally. Its goal is always to co-opt the movement, demobilize its forces and block its development into an alternative, independent political force.

The Republican Party has historically acted as the open advocate for a platform which benefits the rule of wealth and corporate domination. They argue ideologically for policies benefiting the corporate rulers. The Republicans seek to convince the middle classes and labor to support the rule of the wealthy with the argument that "what's good for General Motors is good for the country," that what benefits corporations is also going to benefit regular people.

The Democratic Party is different. They act as a "broker," negotiating and selling influence among broad layers of the people to support the objectives of corporate rule. The Democratic Party's core group of elected officials is rooted in careerists seeking self-promotion by offering to the corporate rulers their ability to control and deliver mass support. And to the people they offer some concessions, modifications on the platform of the Republican Party. One important value of the Democratic Party to the corporate world is that it makes the Republican Party possible through the maintenance of the stability that is essential for "business as usual." It does this by preventing a genuine mass opposition from developing. Together the two parties offer one of the best frameworks possible with which to rule a people that otherwise would begin to move society toward the rule of the people (i.e., democracy).

An example of this process is our minimum-wage laws. Adjusted for inflation, the minimum wage has been gradually declining for years. Every now and then the Democrats pass a small upward adjustment that allows the downward trend to continue but gives the appearance that they are on the side of the poor.

Manipulated Elections

Together the two parties have made ballot access increasingly difficult, defended indirect elections such as the electoral college, insisted on winner-take-all voting to block the appearance of alternative voices, and opposed proportional representation to prevent the development of a representative democracy and the flowering of choices. Both parties support the undemocratic structure of the U.S. Senate and the electoral college, which are not based on one person, one vote, but instead favor the more conservative regions of the nation.

Elections are based primarily on money. By gerrymandering and accumulating huge war chests—payoffs for doing favors for their rich "friends"—most officeholders face no real challenge at the ballot box and are reelected. In the races that are "competitive," repeatedly the contests are reduced to two individuals seeking corporate financial backing. Whoever wins the battle for money wins the election. Districts are gerrymandered into "safe" districts for one or the other party. Gerrymandering lowers the public's interest and involvement while maintaining the fiction of "democracy" and "free elections." The news media go along with this, typically focusing on the presidential election and a handful of other races, denying most challengers the opportunity to get their message out to the public.

Corporate backing shifts between the two parties depending on short-term, even accidental, factors. In the 1990s, more endorsements from CEOs went to the Democrats. At present the money has shifted to the Republican Party. Most corporations donate to both parties to maintain their system in place.

No Choice, No Hope

The Democratic Party preaches defeatism to the most oppressed and exploited. Nothing can be expected, nothing is possible but what exists. To the people they justify continuous betrayal of the possibility for real change with the argument of lesser evil. It's the Republicans or us. Nothing else is possible.

Democracy Versus Cooptation

Democracy remains a great danger to those who have privilege and control. When you are part of the top 1 percent of the population that has as much income as the bottom 75 percent of the people, democracy is a permanent threat to your interests. The potential power of the people is so great that it puts sharp limits on what corporations can do. The ability of the Democratic Party to contain, co-opt, and demobilize independent movements of the people is a critical element in allowing the continued destruction of our planet; abuse, discrimination, and exploitation based on race, gender, sexual preference, and class; and the immense misdistribution of wealth.

As we enter the twenty-first century there is no more important issue than saving our planet from destruction. The world economy is becoming increasingly globalized. Corporate power is now global in nature and leads to massive dislocations and suffering for most people. The planet is overpopulated and the basis of human life declining. The greatest suffering and dislocations exist in the third world, but there is also a downward trend in the United States as globalization leads to a polarization of income and wealth. This shift is making the United States each day closer to a third-world country, with an extremely wealthy minority and a growing underclass. This polarization adds further fear of democracy for the elite.

The Growing Shift Against the Rule of Law

The shift away from the rule of law has accelerated in recent years. This process will be a factor in the 2004 presidential elections, especially if a Green candidate is involved in the race. The shift away from our Constitution is proceeding with the complicity of both parties and the courts. The changes are made illegally through legislation rather than the official process by which the Constitution can be amended because to do otherwise would awaken a massive resistance. A similar process is under way regarding the rule of law internationally.

The reason given for these steps since September 2001 is the terrorist attack within the borders of the United States—an attack made by forces originally trained, armed, and supported by the United States government. The so-called "war on terrorism" does not exist. The United States government has promoted, tolerated, and been party to the use of terrorism all over the world. The United States has even been found guilty of terrorism by the World Court.

The terrorist attacks against U.S. targets are important, but they need to be countered primarily in a social and political manner—a manner which is the opposite of that taken by the USA PATRIOT Act and the occupations of Afghanistan and Iraq. On the contrary, by aggravating inequality and injustice, disrespecting the rule of law and its military interventions and occupations, the present policies of the U.S. government add to the dangers faced by U.S. citizens throughout the world and in the United States. Especially dangerous are the promotion of nuclear, chemical, and bacteriological weapons and the open declarations of the intention to once again use nuclear weapons.

This recent shift, while rooted in bipartisan policies over the last decades, has been accelerated by the present Republican administration. Its ability to carry out these actions has depended on the Democratic Party's support and its ability to contain, disorient, and prevent the development of mass opposition.

Amazingly, in December of 2003 General Tommy Franks, the recently retired head of U.S. Central Command, was quoted as stating that he thought the people of the United States may prefer a military government over our present Constitutional republican form if another terrorist attack occurs. Such a statement is so far off base one must wonder why it is being made. The people of the United States are solidly opposed to any consideration of a military dictatorship in the United States. In fact, polls have repeatedly shown they favor increasing our democratic rights such as limiting campaign contributions and allowing more points of view in debates.

Never in our history have top military leaders or ex-military leaders spoken openly of ending our Constitutional form of government. No leader of the Democratic Party has protested Franks's comments. How many officers in the armed forces have such opinions? If there are any they should be immediately removed from the military.

Democrats: Patriot Act and Unequivocal Support for Bush

The Democratic Party leadership voted for the USA PATRIOT Act. In the United States Senate only one Democrat voted against the Patriot Act. Democrats considered "liberal" such as Paul Wellstone and Barbara Boxer voted for the USA PATRIOT Act. Huge majorities have repeatedly passed votes in the Congress against the United States Constitution. In one case only one Congresswoman, Barbara Lee, voted against the abrogation of the Constitution's separation of powers as stated in Article 1, Section 8. Democratic Party politicians, when called upon to support the Republican Party and their corporate backers, repeatedly comply and vote against the interest of the people and against the Constitution they have sworn to uphold.

The Democratic Party leadership as a whole gave repeated standing ovations to George Bush as he outlined his platform in his January 2002 State of the Union address, a speech that promoted the arbitrary decision to occupy sovereign nations through military aggression in violation of international law. The ovations given the Republican platform by the Democratic Party were done on national television for the people to see a unified political force. The effect is to make people who believe in peace and support the U.N. charter, the World Court, and the rule of law feel they are isolated, powerless, and irrelevant.

A resolution was passed in March of 2003 calling for "unequivocal support" for George Bush for the war in Iraq. It had the full support of the Democratic Party leadership. Even Democratic "doves" like Dennis Kucinich would not vote against the resolution. Only a handful of congressional representatives (eleven) voted against the motion to give "unequivocal support" to George Bush.

The Role of the Democratic Party

The Democratic Party with its open defense of the Republican platform and its attacks on our Constitution and the rule of law internationally would be of little value to those who favor the present policies if it allowed the development of a mass independent opposition. The failure of such forces to exist in sufficient strength permits the Democrats to be more open in their support for antidemocratic policies.

Nevertheless some voices outside the Democratic and Republican parties are beginning to be heard. Massive antiwar street demonstrations, and the voice of a new small party, the Green Party, have gained some attention and respect. In no case did the Democratic Party as an institution support, call for, or help mobilize popular forces for peace and respecting international law. Yet large numbers of its rank and file and many lower-level elected officials against their party participated and promoted antiwar protests.

Many lower elected officials among the Democrats and even some Republicans who defend the Constitution of the United States are voting to oppose the USA PATRIOT Act at the local level. Even many middle-level Democrats have conflicting views and sometimes take progressive stances in concert with the Green Party's platform. These individuals live in a contradiction with the party they belong to. While we can and should join with them behind specific issues, we do not adopt their error of belonging to a party that is against the interest of the people—that is, pro-corporate—and against the rule of law.

Democrats Attack the Green Party

The Democratic Party allows its lower-level representatives to present themselves as opposed to the war. Some of its leaders have begun to take on an appearance of disagreeing with "how" the policies of Bush are being implemented. The Democratic Party has unleashed a campaign to divide and conquer those opposed to the pro-war policies. On one hand it tries to appear sympathetic to antiwar sentiment, while on the other it tries to silence voices opposed to Bush's policies.

Soon after the 2000 presidential election, the Democrats began an attack on the Green Party on the grounds that since there is no runoff system, that is, since the Democrats in partnership with the Republicans do not allow free elections, the Green Party's existence and its candidate for president, Ralph Nader in 2000, should be declared responsible for George Bush becoming president.

Progressive Democrats Join the Attack

This campaign against the Greens has been heavily promoted by the corporate media. It has achieved success in part because of the support it has received by the more liberal wing of the Democratic Party and some of the "progressive" journals controlled by liberal Democrats, such as *The Nation* and *Mother Jones*.

Their political message is simple and clear: "No voice truly critical of the platform of the Republicans may be permitted; only the Democrats must appear as 'opponents' to the Republicans." They have no objection to rightist, pro-war third-party candidates entering the race and promoting their views. They only oppose a voice for peace and the rule of law like that of Ralph Nader in 2000.

Never in the history of the United States has a magazine claiming to favor democracy run a front-page article calling on an individual not to run for president—until *The Nation* did so against Ralph Nader running for president in 2004. The fact that polls show 23 percent of the people favor Nader running (extrapolated to the total voting population this would represent about 40 million people) and 65 percent favored his inclusion in debates is of no concern to *The Nation* as it seeks to silence the only candidate who in 2000 opposed the premises of George Bush's platform.

The Conspiracy Against the Voters

The Nation's editorial board is free to campaign for the Democratic Party and urge people to vote for the Democrats in spite of their support for the USA PATRIOT Act, their votes for unequivocal support to George Bush, etc. That is their right. But they want something else. They want the Greens to join with them in a conspiracy to deny the voters a choice.

All voters are fully aware there is no runoff in a presidential race. Many who support the platform of the Greens will vote against their own principles by voting for the Democratic Party. Each voter will make that decision. But *The Nation*, along with many others, is calling on the Greens to disenfranchise voters who disagree with *The Nation*'s preference for the Democratic Party. It wants these voters to have no choice and be unable to express their electoral wish. *The Nation* and those it represents want to silence the voices of these voters, not to allow it to be registered, as a way to try and force them to vote for their party, the Democrats.

The passage of the USA PATRIOT Act, the undemocratic electoral laws, the manipulation of electoral campaigns by the corporate media, and the campaign to silence the Greens are all part of the same campaign against democracy. They are just another example of how the two-party system is set up to repress and silence those who favor democracy.

Lesser Evil Leads to Greater Evil

The effectiveness of the "lesser-evil" campaign has penetrated within the Green Party, where a minority supports the concept that the Green Party should not run in 2004. Behind this view is the concept that politics can be measured in degrees, like temperature, and that the Democrats offer a milder and thus less-evil alternative to the Republican platform. This view argues that to support the "lesser evil" weakens the greater evil.

Such a view fails to grasp the essence of the matter. Political dynamics work in exactly the opposite way. To silence the voice of the Green Party and support the Democrats strengthens George Bush and the Republican Party because only the appearance of forces opposed to the present policies, forces that are clearly independent of corporate domination, can begin to shift the relationship of forces and the center of political debate. Despite the intention of some of its promoters, the anti–Green Party campaign helps the policies pursued by Bush as well as his reelection possibilities.

Although some claim that George Bush's policies represent only a small coterie of neoconservative extremists, the reality is otherwise. Bush and his friends serve at the will of the corporate rulers. His standing with the American people can be crushed in a moment if the corporate rulers so choose—just by the power of their media, which today is concentrated in the hands of a half dozen giant conglomerates.

It is in the interests of the corporate effort toward a new colonialism to have Bush reelected in 2004, thereby legitimatizing his government before the world. In order to safely achieve that, the voices that truly oppose Bush's policies need to be silenced.

Opposition Is Rising

Opposition is rising against Bush. The massive overwhelming majority of the world is against Bush's war policies. The resistance to the occupation in Iraq and Afghanistan, and the inability of the U.S. media and government to prevent the world from hearing the truth about these events, is weakening Bush's standing. The corporate interests and their media apparently want to make a great effort to get Bush elected, but if this becomes too difficult, the Democratic Party will be prepared to appear as an "opposition" that will continue the essence of Bush's policy with new justifications, modifications, and adjusted forms.

The only force that could upset the general direction of the bipartisan policies put in place over the last few years would be a destabilizing mass development inside the United States, along with world public opinion. This occurred during the war in Vietnam and forced a reversal of U.S. policy.

In the case of Vietnam, the Republicans under Eisenhower initiated the direct U.S. intervention by sponsoring the Diem regime in the south of Vietnam when the French withdrew in the mid-1950s. With U.S. encouragement, his regime refused to abide by the peace accords and hold talks and elections to reunify the country. The Democrats under Kennedy sent ground troops in the early sixties. The U.S. force expanded massively from 16,300 under Kennedy to more than half a million by 1967 under Lyndon Baines Johnson, Kennedy's vice president, who won reelection in 1964 as the supposed "peace" candidate.

The rise of a massive uncontrollable opposition within the United States and around the world became a critical brake on the pro-war policies. An entire generation was starting to deeply question the direction of the United States in world affairs. The Democrats and Republicans, reflecting the opinion of the major corporate leaders and strategists, decided they had no choice but to pull back and concede military defeat in Vietnam because the developing division in U.S. society threatened to result in the emergence of a massive independent political force. This change in policy was carried out under Republican Richard Nixon.

Saving Bush from a backlash is now on the agenda, and the positions of the Democratic Party help Bush in several ways.

First, they seek to prevent even a small but independent critical political development, that is, they try to silence the Green Party, and they orient those opposed to the new colonialism to stop demonstrating and focus instead on the electoral campaigns of their party.

Second, they seek to convince the people that what was wrong with the invasion of Iraq was just that the United Nations—meaning the undemocratic Security Council dominated by the wealthiest countries—did not lend it political cover, or that NATO was not the military form used, or that the U.S. did not include France and Germany in stealing Iraq's resources, or that not enough troops are being used or some other question about how things are being done rather than what is being done.

They promise that all will be well if the Democrats can take charge and handle the matter better. With this orientation the Democrats free the hands of corporate America to give their funding and support to Bush. With the exception of a relatively few isolated voices, they offer not real opposition, but only nuances.

And those isolated voices of opposition within the Democratic Party (Kucinich, Rev. Al Sharpton and Carol Moseley-Braun), no matter how well intentioned, have a negative consequence: they give legitimacy to the Democrats as the "opponents" of the Republicans.

These exceptions to the general rule are allowed on condition that after the primary campaigns these individuals will urge a vote for the Democratic nominee. This must be done no matter how different that nominated candidate's positions are from the positions taken during the primary campaign. The cover for their political sellout is the winner-take-all system that allows them to posture as just "opposed to Bush" as they support the very party that has supported Bush.

Those are the dues you have to pay to "play" in that game; otherwise you will be eliminated and driven out of the House, the Senate, or a governor's office.

For the Green Party there is nothing more important or effective, long-term and short-term, in the efforts to stop Bush than to expose how the corporate interests use their two-party system and the role of the Democrats in that system. We must let all Americans who question the policies of Bush, who favor the rule of law, peace, and our Constitution and Bill of Rights see the Democratic Party's hypocrisy, how they support the war and the USA PA-TRIOT Act.

Democrats Help Institutionalize Bush's Platform

It is transparent that the Democrats' objective is to help institution-alize the USA PATRIOT Act and its break with our Constitution and Bill of Rights. They do this by proposing amendments and ad-justments to the law that will disorient, divide, and weaken the op-position to the USA PATRIOT Act, and give the appearance that public concerns have been addressed.

The Democrats are making interesting suggestions for how to pursue the war effort. Some are calling for a more extensive commit-ment and the sending of more troops to suppress any resistance to U.S. domination in Iraq and Afghanistan. Others are suggesting more flexibility in forming alliances with European nations that had made capital investments to exploit Iraq's oil wealth under the Sad-dam Hussein dictatorship. These proposals are all aimed at continu-ing the denial of self-determination for the people of Iraq, which means continuing war and continuing violation of international law.

The Democrats and Republicans both supported Saddam Hus-sein and the Baathists in Iraq before 1990 when it served their in-terests. Now they argue with each other over how best to oppress the Iraqis as they try to fool the American people into thinking they are actually trying to bring the Iraqis democracy and freedom.

Self-Correcting Mechanism

The role of these two parties is not a conspiracy. Boxer, Wellstone, and many other Democrats did not vote for the USA PATRIOT Act consciously seeking to assist Bush. Being Democrats, they became part of a system that will have them removed if they do not follow the rules of support when corporate America insists. To rise in the Democratic Party there is a process that results in compliant people unable to question, who remain silent before betrayals or criminal acts. Cynthia McKinney is an example of a Democrat who refused to go along, stepped across the line within the Democratic Party, and was driven out of office by the combined efforts of both the

Democratic and Republican parties and the corporate media.

The Fourth Amendment to the Constitution prohibits searches without probable cause and a judge's order. Voting for a law that abrogates this amendment, as the USA PATRIOT Act does directly, is an illegal act. The Democrats and Republicans who voted for this law were fully aware of what they were doing. It is an insult to the intelligence of people like Wellstone and Boxer to say that they didn't fully understand the choice they were making. The Green Party differs; it defends the Fourth Amendment and seeks to defend the Constitution and respect for the law which provides the only method by which the Constitution can be amended, requiring the consideration and vote of the states.

It should be said that there are many issues where Greens agree with Democrats like Boxer and Wellstone, and even admire positions they have taken and efforts they have made. But to go into denial and refuse to recognize the obvious—that the Democrats have joined in passing and promoting the USA PATRIOT Act against the Constitution with the support of people like Boxer—is to deny the true framework we face politically in our nation.

The self-purging process of the Democratic Party is an ongoing balance between allowing, even welcoming, voices of opposition in order to co-opt them and not allowing those voices to form a serious challenge, especially any challenge that favors the development of political formations not dominated by corporate money.

Success of the Democratic Party

The Democratic Party should be seen historically as the most successful political party in the history of the world in terms of maintaining stability for rule by the privileged few. There is no other example that comes near what the Democratic Party has achieved in maintaining the domination of money over people.

Through trickery, the Democratic Party co-opted the powerful and massive rise of the Populist movement at the end of the nineteenth century using precisely the same lesser-evil arguments now presented against the Green Party.

They blocked the formation of a mass Labor Party when the union movement rose in the 1930s. They derailed, co-opted, and dismantled the powerful civil rights movement, anti–Vietnam War movement, and women's liberation movement. They have even succeeded in establishing popular myths that they were once for labor, for civil rights, and for peace. Nothing could be further from the truth.

One quite popular myth is that Franklin Delano Roosevelt was pro-labor. Continuing the policies of Woodrow Wilson who oversaw a reign of anti-union terror, including blacklisting and deporting immigrant labor organizers, FDR's administration sabotaged union drives every step of the way. When workers overcame their bosses' resistance and began winning strikes, FDR turned on them and gave the green light for repression after police killed ten striking steel workers in 1937. As FDR said himself, "I'm the best friend the profit system ever had." After WWII Truman used the new Taft-Hartley Anti-Labor Act to break national strikes more than a dozen times.

The Democrats have not abandoned "progressive" positions they once held, as some Democrats repeatedly claim, but have simply shifted further to the right as world globalization has advanced, leading to the lowering of democratic rights and the growth of wealth polarization within the United States.

If a massive opposition develops, if the Greens begin to win races and their following grows, the corporations will put more money behind the Democrats, the media will become more sympathetic to the Democrats, promote their more "progressive" voices. The media would also become more critical of the Republican lack of sensitivity, all in an effort to maintain the two-party system. That is, a shift toward the Democrats will occur if the Democrats cannot control the people.

The two-party system is a self-correcting mechanism that shifts back and forth between the two parties, and within different wings of those parties, to maintain corporate political control. Loyalty to the two-party system is inculcated in the educational system, and our electoral laws are rigged to discriminate against third parties.

Green Voice Must Be Heard

Those who call for a "lesser evil," which is still a call for evil, will unfortunately succeed. The call for a "lesser evil" is what makes possible the greater evil. Those voices who say Ralph Nader should not run, that the Greens should consider withdrawing, that the

Greens should not campaign in states where the vote is close are unconsciously helping Bush's reelection by weakening the development of an opposition political movement which could shift the balance of forces. Nothing is more important than the appearance of candidates and mass actions that tell the full truth, that call for the rule of law and respect for the Bill of Rights, and speak out for peace and social justice.

There is nothing more threatening to the rule of the corporations than the consolidation of a party of hundreds of thousands of citizens, especially young people, that fearlessly tell the truth to the American people. Only such a movement can in time become millions, then tens of millions and eventually win. But it is also the best strategy for the short term, to force a shift away from the direction being pursued today.

Short Term Versus Long Term

The idea that there is a conflict between the short term and the long term is a cover for capitulation. It has been the endless argument of the Democrats against challenges to their policies. When independent movements appear, the Democrats call on people to enter the Democratic Party and work from within. There is no time to go outside the two-party framework, they argue. This argument was made a hundred years ago, fifty years ago, twenty-five years ago, and of course remains with us today. Millions have agreed there's no time to do the right thing. Very powerful groups, like the AFL-CIO, have followed this advice. As a result, the number of workers in unions has dropped from 37 percent of the workforce to 12 percent as they politically subordinated themselves to the pro-corporate Democratic Party.

Rather than success, these movements have found the Democratic Party to be the burial ground for mass movements and of third-party efforts that sought to defend the interests of the people throughout American history.

If we follow the advice of the "left" Democrats who call on Greens to return to the Democratic Party, the Green Party will collapse like the New Party did for fear of confronting the Democrats.

The exact opposite is needed. We need to encourage those Democrats who are opposing the policies of their party to follow the lead of Congressman Dan Hamburg and break with the Democrats and join with us in developing an alternative force, fighting for democracy, social justice, and peace.

All people who believe in democracy need to call on *The Nation* and others to stop their campaign against the Greens, a campaign at the service of corporate America. Instead they should join with the Greens in a battle for democracy in the same manner in which many progressive Democrats in San Francisco rejected their party's nomination for mayor and joined with the Greens to create a progressive alternative. We need to suggest to "progressive" Democrats that they should concentrate their attacks on the leadership of their party and its support for George Bush's policies, and not on the Greens for telling the truth and actually fighting for the ideals many of these Democrats claim to hold.

The Year 2004

The year 2004 is a critical year for the Greens. The campaign of the Democrats will be powerful and to some extent effective. Some will abandon us, but others will be attracted by our courage and our principled stance. In California, the Green registration continues to rise even as the campaign against the Green Party grows. We may very well receive a lower vote than in 2000. But if we do not stand up to this pressure and hold our banner high, fight them, and defend our right to exist, to have our voice heard, to run candidates that expose the two-party system and the hypocrisy of the Democratic Party and its complicity with the Republicans, we will suffer the greatest lost of all.

The Green Party

The Green Party can and will win the hearts and minds of people when they see us as reliable and unshakable, if we stand our ground. In time this leads to respect and then support. Those Greens who agree with the Ten Key Values but have disagreements with this Avocado Declaration need to be respected. We need to allow an open and honest debate as an essential part of our culture.

Truth can only be ascertained through the conflict of ideas. Thus democracy is essential for society but also for our internal process. The present discussion around the 2004 elections is one that will not end but will be with us for a long time. It finds expression in many forms because it is the most *fundamental issue* of American politics in our epoch. Are we willing to stand up to the rule of corporate domination and its central political agent that has deceived and betrayed our people, the Democratic Party?

The Green Party Must Be a Pluralistic Organization

The Green Party seeks to bring all those who agree with its Ten Key Values into one unified political party. It welcomes diversity, debate, and discussion on issues of strategy, tactics, and methods of functioning. By its nature, a healthy organization that fights for the interests of the people will always have internal conflicts, sharp differences, personality difficulties, and all other things human. This is not only normal, it is healthy.

The Greens do not consider themselves a substitute for other movements or organizations, such as peace organizations and other specific issue groups that seek to unite people of all political persuasions around a specific platform. We welcome diversity with other groups that seek to move in the same direction with us but are not agreed to join us. We will try to work with such organizations where common ground exists. Thus the Avocado Declaration includes a call for the Greens to accept diversity and maintain unity as we seek to build an effective mass organization.

Let those that agree with the Avocado Declaration help protect and build the Green Party as a vehicle for democracy, freedom, liberty, and justice for all.

The Green Party and the 2004 Elections: A Three-Dimensional Plan

By John Rensenbrink and Tom Sevigny
Green Horizon Quarterly, *May 1, 2003*

This message is an attempt to bring together in a single vision various ideas, points of view, and practical recommendations that have been made by many different people in the rapidly intensifying debate over what the Green Party of the United States should do in the 2004 national elections.

We think everyone would agree that it would be foolish to enter the national races, especially the one for president and vice president, without strategically weighing all the options. We cannot afford to have a knee-jerk reaction and blindly enter any race, certainly not the one for president in this fateful time.

After making two observations about the evolving situation facing the Green Party, we present a "Three-Dimensional Plan." It will enable the Green Party to avoid grave dangers, build our party, and move forward with confidence, strength, and unity.

We take pains to point out that we propose this not in our capacity as holders of official positions within the national Green Party (Tom as a cochair of the Steering Committee and John as member of the Presidential Exploratory Committee). We propose this plan simply as concerned members of the Green Party.

Setting the Context: Some Observations Regarding the Situation

Two things especially rivet one's attention as we look toward the 2004 elections.

First, the prospect of a Green Party run for the presidency is producing a gathering storm of debate within and without the party, peppered with near-panic declarations, threatening to engulf the party in fractious internal contestation. One longtime and savvy leader of the Greens describes the situation as "a dark and scary tunnel." But outside the party this debate is also rising to a flood of concern, advice, and anguished pronouncements—not only from Democrats or from those erstwhile Republicans who detest Bush, but especially from the peace and environmental movements. Great fear is expressed that the Green candidate for president will prevent the defeat of George Bush and his despised cronies. One commentator online entitles his article "Bush Presents Colossal Dilemma for Greens in 2004" (Earl O. Hutchinson).

One can't help smiling a little—it's as if "the movements" have finally discovered the Green Party! However, we believe they make a solid point—and that in any case they reflect the feelings and considered opinions of millions of voters. The Green Party cannot and must not just shrug our shoulders and pretend this outpouring does not exist or is simply misguided. We could self-destruct if we did that. Second, a widespread belief has taken hold among many sections of the electorate that the Green Party's campaign for the presidency in 2000 either caused, or in any case paved the way for, Bush's becoming president.

Quite aside from the virulence of the attack on the Green Party and our candidate Ralph Nader (and from some quarters it was and is very, very nasty), there exists a strong residue of opinion among millions of voters that Ralph and the Greens spoiled Gore's bid for the presidency.

Whether or not they are right about this (we don't believe they are), and quite aside from whether or not they are right that Gore would not have been as bad as Bush, their opinion has settled into a solid view.

The Green Party can dismiss this—and we have read countless e-mails, preaching to the choir, detailing that this view is mistaken and wrong. But that will not make it go away. The point is, it will *not* go away. We must face this. We must find a positive and creative way forward.

In fact, let's find a way to use these negatives to our advantage.

With this in mind, we urge the following "Three-Dimensional Plan" for 2004.

A Three-Dimensional Plan for 2004

The plan has three fully integrated components. Together they offer a winning strategy for 2004.

The three components are:

First, the Green Party runs 4–6 candidates for Congress (House of Representatives) in 2004 in carefully selected districts, fully focusing the energies and resources of the party to get them elected.

Second, the Green Party runs homegrown Greens for president and vice president in a vigorous campaign that includes, at the beginning, the stated intention to be ready to (a) give their support to the Democratic ticket late in the campaign if the race between the R and D candidates is very close; or (b) if the race between the D and the R candidates is very close, to concentrate only in states where the outcome between the D and the R candidates is not in doubt.

Third, the Green Party invites nationally known figures, especially Ralph Nader and Cynthia McKinney, to throw the weight of their presence and resources in support of the congressional candidates and the homegrown Green candidates for president and vice president. This third component could include a campaign for the U.S. Senate in Connecticut by Ralph Nader.

What This Plan Accomplishes

1. It transcends the spoiler argument and "spoiler effect" altogether and removes it from the campaign.

2. It opens the door for the Green message to be heard on its merits.

3. It grooms national candidates for 2006 and 2008—both the homegrown candidates for president and vice president and the congressional candidates. It gives them experience and national exposure.

4. It enables the Green Party to "run against Congress"—doing what Harry Truman did so effectively in 1948 when he ran, and won, on the slogan of the "do-nothing Congress." This has enormous potential for us—it could even result in having a Green in Congress as we begin the year 2005. Maybe more than one! We can all join in on this—Ralph and Cynthia, our presidential and vice presidential candidates, all the tendencies and wings within the party—as well as many celebrities who would be able to support us enthusiastically, whereas now they are hesitant, given the rising pressure to defeat Bush at all costs. We could go a long way with this and find it very exciting and satisfying to boot. Congress has been an enormous failure in the past two years and deserves to be run against. We think most voters agree and would give our campaign a big hearing.

5. By running against Congress, we can make our case against the Democrats even stronger. We can use their blank check for war, their support of the Patriot Act, etc., in a much more effective way than we could by putting our big efforts into running a high-profile presidential candidate as we did

last time. The Democrats in Congress could have stopped Bush; they decided to go along with him. We are free to make that point, again and again, effectively.

6. It unifies the party, transcending what could otherwise become a very bitter debate and harmful infighting within our party.

7. The plan enables us to change from what would otherwise be a defensive posture in the campaign, always having to expend energy and time reliving and explaining the past, to a positive and forward-looking posture.

8. It helps our party grow, whereas the present prospect is of a party saddled with baggage from the past, divided within itself, uncertain about its future, and on the outs with millions of voters who could otherwise be on our side. With this plan, we surmount the negatives, surprise our critics, and take a new leap forward.

For a Green Presidential Campaign in 2004
By Howie Hawkins
Presentation at Regional Green Meeting, June 28, 2003

Progressives are running scared today. They are scared of Bush and are demanding that the Greens not run a candidate and back a Democrat, or that the Greens backhandedly support the Democrat by not campaigning in the swing states.

To be sure, Bush is scary. Constitutional rights restricted. Unilateral presidential war powers. War budget hiked. International treaties abrogated. Tax cuts for the rich. Worker safety and environmental regulations gutted. Pandering to corporate interests in the midst of a corporate crime wave. An anti-consumer bankruptcy bill. Invasions of Afghanistan and Iraq, with threats of future invasions or proxy wars for regime change in Iran, Syria, Saudi Arabia, North Korea, Venezuela, Cuba, and who knows where else.

But the Democrats are scary, too. The majority of congressional Democrats have let Bush have his way on every one of these issues.

If the Democratic Party won't resist Bush's policies in Congress, why should progressives support them for the presidency? The Democrats didn't even resist Bush when he stole the Florida vote in 2000. We now know that Gore won Florida handily from the recount done by the media consortium that included the *Wall Street Journal*, *New York Times*, and *Los Angeles Times*. But the Democrats, far more interested in preserving the system's legitimacy than fighting its racism, refused to make an issue of how the Republicans cut Blacks from the voter rolls through computerized racial profiling.

The Congressional Black Caucus gave the Democrats a second chance after the Supreme Court selection of Bush, when it appealed to Senate Democrats to object to accepting the Florida electors. The objection of just one Democratic senator would have forced an investigation of the racial voter profiling and a recount of the Florida vote. But not one of them—not Wellstone, not Kennedy, not Feingold, not Boxer, not Clinton, not Kerry—not one of the Democratic liberals objected.

And the Greens are supposed to stand down and leave it to the Democrats to fight Bush?

Yes, a Democrat might beat Bush. But no Democrat is going to beat Bushism.

Just as electing Clinton did not beat Reaganism, but took Reaganism far beyond what Reagan and Bush Sr. could accomplish, so electing a Democrat will not defeat Bushism to change the basic foreign and domestic policies of the U.S.

What was called Reaganism (to scare us into voting Democratic) was really a bipartisan consensus around neoconservative militarism and neoliberal economics. That bipartisan consensus was initiated under Carter, supported by the majority of congressional Democrats during the Reagan and Bush Sr. administrations, carried far beyond what Reagan and Bush Sr. could do by Clinton, and is now being taken even further by Bush, again with the support of the majority of congressional Democrats.

These policies were initiated under Carter, who increased the military budget beyond Ford's projections and got the U.S. into covert military operations in Afghanistan with the hope, successful as it turned out, that it would provoke the Soviets to invade. The

U.S. began in 1978 training the Islamic fundamentalists who we now know as Al Qaeda. Bush's military occupation of Afghanistan and Iraq is the Carter Doctrine in practice, which stated in essence that the U.S. would go to war for oil in the Middle East.

Neoconservative militarism is the post-Vietnam foreign policy of the corporate rulers as they reasserted their post-World War II policy of dominating the capitalist world. With the fall of the Soviet bloc, Bush Sr. declared a New World Order in which the U.S. would dominate the whole world and make it safe for capitalist exploitation. The Clinton administration continued this policy through NATO expansion and its intervention in the Balkans without UN authorization, as well as the complex of trade and credit policies administered by the IMF, World Bank, WTO, and numerous corporate-managed trade agreements on the model of NAFTA.

Both parties are just as committed to economic policies of neoliberal austerity. Again, these polices were initiated under Carter, who slashed social programs to increase the military budget and reassert U.S. interventionism with the development of the Rapid Deployment Force, adopted monetarism as fiscal policy with the appointment of Volker to the Fed, and began the attack on organized labor by refusing to support the common situs picketing law he had pledged the AFL-CIO he would support.

Neoliberal austerity became the post-Keynesian economic policy of the corporate rulers as they ran into the internal limits to profits and growth under the Keynesian welfare/warfare state.

The new ruling-class consensus is the austerity/warfare state of neoliberal economics and neoconservative empire.

And that ruling-class consensus is the pro-war, pro-corporate bipartisan consensus.

What is now called Bushism is not a radical departure but a continuation of this bipartisan consensus, with the majority of Democrats in Congress voting for Bush's key programs: the tax cuts, war budgets, war powers, and USA PATRIOT Act.

Worried about Bush's global empire building? Empire building is a bipartisan geopolitical strategy of using military basing and control of oil in the Middle East and Central Eurasia to keep Western Europe, Russia, China, and Japan from challenging U.S. hegemony. This geopolitical strategy is as prevalent in the pronouncements of Democratic national security advisers like Zbigniew Brzezinski as in those of their Republican counterparts like Henry Kissinger. The Bush administration's particular intellectual framework for empire coming out of the Project for a New American Century is authored by Democrats as well as Republicans, such as Clinton's CIA director, James Woolsey, and Paul Wolfowitz, the former aide to the late senator Scoop Jackson (D-WA). The Clinton administration's imperialist motives for supporting Star Wars were stated quite openly in the Air Force's "Vision for 2020": "dominating the space dimension of military operations to protect U.S. interests and investment."

Indeed, the Democrats' unadulterated support for empire goes back before Carter, before Kennedy and Johnson's Vietnam War, to another Democratic administration, that of Truman, with Dean Acheson's Cold War strategy of building alliances of U.S. satellites to contain the Soviet bloc and make the "free" world safe for corporate exploitation. With the demise of the USSR's own empire, the U.S. geopolitical strategy switched "from containment to enlargement," as Clinton's first national security adviser, Anthony Lake, declared in a 1993 speech of that title, adding in words that sound like Wolfowitz's that U.S.-led alliances would accomplish this by "diplomacy where we can; force where we must."

Worried about Bush's militarism? Remember that the post-Vietnam hikes in military spending were initiated by Carter, taking them above the levels Ford had projected, and that the post–Cold War military spending hikes were initiated by Clinton, taking them well above Bush Sr.'s projections. Bush Jr.'s further hikes have been supported by the majority of congressional Democrats. The current mantra among the Democratic Party political consultants and pollsters is that the Democratic presidential candidate must be as "strong on national security" as Bush to be competitive in the 2004 election.

The Clinton foreign policy team was frustrated by the military's cautious Powell Doctrine. As Clinton's secretary of state and then UN ambassador, Madeline Albright, angrily told Colin Powell, now Bush's secretary of state and then chairman of the Joint Chiefs of Staff, "What's the point of having this superb military that you've always been talking about if we can't use it?"

What about Bush's unilateralism? Wouldn't Democratic imperialism be a little softer, more "globalist"? Not hardly. It was Clinton's secretary of state and Brzezinski protégé, Madeleine Albright, who told the UN Security Council in 1994 regarding Iraq: "We will act multilaterally when we can, unilaterally when we must." And thus under Clinton the U.S. bypassed the Security Council to impose regime change by military force on Iraqi Kurdistan, Kosovo, and Serbia.

How about Bush's domestic repression? The Clinton/Reno anticrime and antiterrorism bills instituted more than fifty new death penalties, emaciated habeus corpus, militarized domestic policing, gutted Posse Comitatus, legalized FBI and CIA domestic political spying, expanded the drug war, and subsidized expansion of the prison-industrial complex. The Clintonites sent in Delta Force to make sure the heads of anti-WTO demonstrators were cracked in Seattle. The post–September 11 detention of thousands without trial, any kind of hearing, or access to lawyers was done under the statutory authority of Clinton's Anti-Terrorism and Effective Death Penalty Act of 1996. The USA PATRIOT Act just expanded this repressive authority further, again with the votes of the majority of congressional Democrats.

Well, maybe the Democrats aren't as extreme as Bush on domestic economic policy? Here again there is a basic bipartisan consensus. Carter initiated the neoliberal turn as the bipartisan consensus switched from military Keynesianism to military neoliberalism. Though neoliberalism is cloaked in the egalitarian-sounding rhetoric of free markets, the reality is state enforcement of greater inequality: welfare for the corporate rich (investment incentives in theory) and hardship for workers (to motivate higher productivity in theory).

Today's corporate scandals are a legacy of Clinton's financial deregulation, media monopolization a legacy of his deregulatory Telecommunications Act, the loss of two million jobs a legacy of NAFTA and the other trade deals Clinton made that are sending U.S. manufacturing and backroom service jobs to cheap labor markets overseas. Bush's biggest contribution to the neoliberal agenda has been his tax cuts for the rich, which the Democrats enabled by declaring it a "victory" to pare down their size somewhat.

This bipartisan consensus is forged by the corporate ruling class through its media ownership and financing of publications, broadcasts, think tanks, and its two political parties, Democratic and Republican. To be sure, there are tactical differences within this consensus. No doubt the ruling class is split about Bush. Many of them are worried about the economic irrationality of the latest tax cuts, the destabilizing consequences throughout the Middle East and Europe of the military occupation of Afghanistan and Iraq, and Bush's pandering to the domestically destabilizing social agenda of the Christian fundamentalists. And this faction of the corporate rich will support a Democratic version of the bipartisan consensus, the Slick Soft-Right of a Clinton rather than the Crude Hard-Right of a Bush Jr.

But that is their fight, not ours!

Our fight is to get our alternatives into public debate in the 2004 election: cooperative security instead of the U.S. as global occupation force; renewable energy instead of oil imperialism; economic security through national health care, guaranteed income above poverty, jobs for all at living wages, fair trade and progressive taxes instead of the neoliberal regime of motivating the poor with hardships to work harder and the rich with corporate welfare to invest; economic production in an ecologically sustainable balance with nature instead of endless growth through environmental marauding by the military-industrial complex; repealing repressive laws to restore civil liberties and dismantle the prison-industrial complex instead of Patriot Acts and drug wars; a multiparty system founded on proportional representation and public funding of public elections instead of a state-sanctioned, corporate-financed two-party system with two right wings.

Our fight is to get as many votes as we can for the Green Party candidates for the presidency, House, and Senate. The more votes we get, the more seriously our alternatives will be taken by the public and the more we will be able to further organize and mobilize around them.

One thing is certain. These alternatives will not be heard without a Green campaign. We will not have the vehicle needed to organize people around real alternatives. If the left tails the lesser-evil Democrat again, which has been the dominant strategy of what passes for a left in the U.S. since most of it collapsed into the New Deal coalition in 1936, the whole debate will shift further to the right again.

Let us clear up some fantasies about Sharpton and Kucinich. The other candidates are clearly pro-war, pro-corporate candidates. But Sharpton and Kucinich sound progressive.

Sharpton, as we in New York know, is playing for patronage. That is what he did with his senatorial and mayoral campaigns. He wants to be the Black political broker for patronage to the Black political class. We know from his history that he will more likely support a Republican to spite Democrats who snub him than a Green. We should definitely keep the door open to his supporters and even to Sharpton himself, but let us not be naïve about what his objectives are in the Democratic presidential primaries.

Kucinich sounds like Nader on his policy proposals. But he is not running for president. He is running to build his national stature and fund base to get ready to run for U.S. Senate from Ohio. He will pull out no later than Super Tuesday next March 2 in order to file in Ohio in time to run for reelection to Congress in 2004.

But Kucinich is not like Nader in that he opposed independent politics and the Green Party.

"I have no interest in a third-party candidacy. None," says Kucinich. "I want to do it the other way—bring third-party candidates into the [Democratic] Party and get support in the primaries" (Ruth Conniff, "The Peace Candidate," *The Progressive*, April 2003).

Kucinich recently told the *Cleveland Plain Dealer*: "The Democratic Party created third parties by running to the middle. What I'm trying to do is to go back to the big tent so that everyone who felt alienated could come back through my candidacy." (*CounterPunch*, April 2003).

The second quote is particularly important to think about. He does not say take the Democratic Party away from its corporate rulers. Rather he wants to bring the wayward Greens into coalition with the Democratic Party's corporate rulers in a "big tent." The whole point of the Greens as an *independent* party is our independence from the corporate rulers. We want to build a coalition of all of the popular constituencies that are exploited and oppressed by the corporate rulers. That's a big enough tent to win elections. But it's a different tent than the one Kucinich wants to build.

Inside the Democratic Party, the left enters into coalition as subordinate partners with the very corporate rulers who are violently committed to maintaining the system the left presumably wants to transform.

When the left supports the Democrats, it commits suicide and disappears. The left surrenders its voice in the election to the Democrats, who will then triangulate right to cut into the Republican vote. The left surrenders its very identity as an alternative for a different world by supporting a (hopefully) lesser-evil administration of the status quo.

We cannot rely on the Slick Soft-Right Democrats to fight the Crude Hard-Right Republicans. The Democrats haven't done it during the first two and half years of the Bush administration. There is no good reason to start relying on them now. The best defense against the Hard Right is not defensive support for a Softer Right, but a strong offensive around a real campaign for a progressive alternative.

The minute the Greens fail to mount a serious campaign (whether by openly supporting a Democrat as the lesser evil or doing it backhandedly by staging a "strategic" campaign of not competing in swing states) is the minute the public will stop taking the Greens seriously. What little leverage Kucinich and Sharpton may now have to push the debate to the left will vanish as the Democrats are then free to take votes to their left for granted.

Cynthia McKinney is the future of progressives in the Democratic Party. She is the poster child for what Democrats do to their progressives. When the Democratic Leadership Council and the AIPAC (American Israeli Public Affairs Commission) targeted her for defeat because she had the temerity to call for justice for Palestinians, the Democratic leadership ran away from her, from Maynard Jackson, Andrew Young, and John Lewis in her home town of Atlanta to Jesse Jackson Sr., Terry McAuliffe, and Bill Clinton nationally. They let a Republican judge who supported right-wing fundamentalist Alan Keyes in the 2000 Republican primaries re-register as a Democrat and beat McKinney with Republican votes in Georgia's open primary system.

The spoiler argument against a Green run for president is garbage. The Democrats spoiled the election by, first of all, offering a phony alternative to the Republicans. And then the Democrats spoiled their own election by not fighting for what they had won in

Florida. Contrary to the "Nader elected Bush" refrain of the Any-body-But-Bush Democrats, Nader probably helped Gore beat Bush in the popular vote. Analysts as different as Alexander Cockburn on the left and Al From, chair of the Democratic Leadership Council, on the Democratic right, note that exit polling data show that Gore did better with Nader in the race than he would have without Nader. While From uses this data to preposterously counsel Democrats to ignore their left and run to the right, Cockburn's explanation is obviously more persuasive: Nader's campaign forced Gore to articulate some populist, anti-corporate themes that brought many disillusioned Democrats back into the fold. Without Nader in the race, these Democrats would not have voted, and many of Nader's voters would not have voted either.

A Green campaign in 2004 doesn't have to win the presidency to define the debate, move it to the left, and begin to undermine Bushism, which is to say, the bipartisan policy consensus. Truman made his remarkable comeback to beat Dewey by stealing Wallace's thunder and campaigning on the Progressive Party's economic and social agenda. Perot's 19 percent in 1992 made budget balancers out of both corporate parties and set the course for federal budget policies in the 1990s. To define the debate, the Green campaign just has to be serious about getting every vote it can in every state.

At the least, that kind of campaign makes the Greens a threat to "spoil" the Democratic side of the two-party charade and thus compels attention to our campaign. Much better would be a double-digit vote percentage, which could leverage some reforms during the next administration and lay the foundation for further gains at all levels in future elections.

Nothing would be more dispiriting for progressives than a self-defeating, defensive campaign for a pro-war, pro-corporate Democrat. And nothing would be more inspiring than an all-out Green presidential campaign for what we believe in. That kind of Green campaign could be a rallying point for progressives and social movements and begin to turn the tide against the pro-war, pro-corporate bipartisan consensus.

A Green Party "Safe States" Strategy

By *Ted Glick*

ZNet, *July 1, 2003*

Within and outside of the Green Party there is much discussion about whether or not the Greens should run a presidential candidate in 2004. Some of the external opposition to it is from some of the same people who were opposed to the Nader/LaDuke campaigns in 1996 and in 2000. But other opposition, or serious questioning, comes both from within the Greens and from progressives who have supported, or who continue to support, Green candidates in the past and present.

It's no mystery as to why this is the case: the militaristic and repressive response of the Bush administration following the September 11, 2001, attacks, the dangerous reality of what can only be described as twenty-first-century corporate warmongers and fascists in positions of power within the White House, Pentagon, Justice Department, and elsewhere within the Bush regime. The September 11 attacks are being used by them to attempt to significantly strengthen and expand an already oppressive and repressive, corporatized political and economic system.

What they have done and what they intend to do are qualitatively and quantitatively beyond anything we have experienced in this country for many decades.

In this context, it has to be admitted that, on the surface, the "anybody but Bush" argument (Lieberman, Graham, Edwards, Daschle, Kerry) has validity.

However, I think it would be a huge mistake for the Green Party not to move forward with its plans to nominate a candidate, for a number of reasons.

The fact is that the Green Party is the leading national "third party" formation. It has earned this through its work over many years throughout the country. For those of us who understand clearly that the Democratic Party[1] is part of the problem and in no way part of the solution, there is a serious risk that a decision by the national Greens to not run a presidential candidate could jeopardize its prospects for the future.

Although the analogy is not exact, there is a potential parallel with the decision of the Populist Party in 1896—a "third party" that was much stronger than the Greens—to support the Democratic Party candidate, William Jennings Bryan. That decision led to internal divisions and demoralization within Populist Party ranks that led to its virtual disappearance by the turn of the century.

The need for a progressive alternative to the Democrats and Republicans is too great for such a risk to be taken, *especially* because of the dangerousness of the Bush regime. Think about it: what if the Greens decided to make no effort to field a presidential candidate and then, with no candidate on the ballot in November 2004, Bush still wins? We will have a doubly demoralized progressive movement, demoralized because Bush has won but also demoralized because we will have suffered through months of political campaigning where, almost certainly, the national political debate between the Republicans and the Democrats moves the "political center" even more to the right. Talk about political torture!

As we saw in 2000, a serious Green Party presidential campaign can bring progressive ideas, energy, and visibility into the political arena that is badly needed. Remember all those super-rallies across the country in the fall of 2000? What if it comes down to a Bush–Lieberman race, or Bush–Edwards, Bush–Daschle, or Bush–Kerry?

All of those Democrats, all seen as the leading contenders at this point in the game, supported the war on Iraq and voted in October, along with candidate Bob Graham, to give Bush authorization to decide on his own about going to war. All of them, to a greater or a lesser degree, have gone along with the Bush regime's quest for empire conducted under the guise of a "war on terrorism." None of them can be expected to seriously challenge the dangerous direction of U.S. foreign policy. In certain respects, a couple of them are even more aggressive than Bush.

What about Sharpton or Kucinich, or (in another category) Moseley-Braun? Well, if one of them got the Democratic nomination, it would be a political development that the Green Party would need to seriously consider. Such a development would be the political miracle of U.S. history. And because it is so unlikely, the Democratic Party and the corporate media being what they are, it's really not something the Greens have to worry about at this point in time. Finally, what about "dark horse" Howard Dean? A Dean candidacy would mean a more progressive approach on the part of the Democrats, but let's not forget the usual dynamic of a liberal primary campaign turning into a centrist general election campaign. Given Dean's need for that corporate and fat-cat money if nominated, it's a certainty that there would still be a big political space to his left, one the Greens could once again fill.

A "Safe States" Strategy

But the filling of this political space by the Greens has to be done in a certain way, in my humble opinion. It's what I call the "safe states" strategy.

Everyone knows that a Green Party presidential candidate will not win in 2004. But a presidential campaign can help to build the party, give it visibility, attract new members, keep or attain ballot status in a number of states. And if it pulled out 5 percent or more of the popular vote it would mean millions of dollars for party-building leading into 2008.

The best way to do all of these things is to explicitly focus the campaign[2] only in those "safe states" where past voting histories and current polling indicates that either Bush or the Democrat is very likely to win. Let's remember that our presidential election is in some respects not a "national" election; it's fifty separate state elections to choose representatives to the electoral college. If it truly was a national election Al Gore would have been elected president in 2000, even with Jeb Bush and Katherine Harris's criminal activity of throwing legal voters off the Florida voting rolls.

By running this kind of campaign in 25–35 or so almost-certain "safe states,"[3] the Greens cannot be accused, at least accused in good faith, of just being spoilers out to deny the Democrats the presidency. Indeed, by running such a campaign, the Greens and their presidential candidate are saying in no uncertain terms that although both the Republicans and Democrats are problematic, the Bushites represent such a particular danger right now that we have modified our campaign accordingly.

This will gain us the respect of some of our allies in the Democratic Party who are pretty much with us on the issues but, in part because of the winner-take-all nature of our electoral system, are unprepared to move outside it right now. It could well mean more votes from these allies for local Green candidates in states where such candidates are running.

It should increase the popular vote for the Greens toward 5 percent as the argument can be made in the "safe states" that voters should not waste their vote by voting for the Democrat or Republican but should instead vote for the candidate they know is closest to their own views.

And it is possible that such a strategy will actually increase the likelihood that the Democrat, whoever he is, defeats Bush and/or that the Democrats win at least one house in Congress. A Green presidential candidacy will motivate possible nonvoters to come out and vote. This will add to the vote totals of some local and congressional Democratic candidates where there is no significant Green opposition. It will put pressure on the Democratic presidential candidate to use more populist-sounding, anti-corporate language, as was the effect of the Nader 2000 candidacy on Al Gore, which then increased his standing in the polls and helped lead to his popular-vote victory.

What about if the Bush campaign is so politically overwhelming that there are very few "safe states"?

I don't think this is likely. There are too many negatives, from the economy to the exploding national debt to growing armed resistance in Afghanistan and Iraq, to expect that the Bushites will be able to win a landslide victory. Things have been close at the national level between the D's and R's for a long time, and that is the likely scenario again.

However, if the race does look so bleak, it is very unlikely that a Green Party decision not to run a presidential campaign would be able to have much of an effect as far as preventing a Bush victory. Indeed, in such a case, an argument could be made that it's even more important to have an independent progressive voice out there because such a situation could result only if the Democrats truly messed up royally, were so internally divided or "off message" that they alienated a large chunk of their base.

The bottom line: it is not sound politics for progressives to say that the Bushites are so bad that we have to support whomever the Democrats nominate. Think Joe Lieberman! Indeed, the major contribution progressives can make to getting Bush out of office may well be the Green Party "safe-states" strategy articulated here.

Is there risk to this strategy? Of course. But there is also risk to another support-the-Democrats strategy. There is risk that without an effective "left prod," the Democrats will blow it again. There is definitely a risk that we could jeopardize the viability of the shoots and seedlings of a viable progressive party that the Greens represent.

In 2003 and 2004, just like other years, let's use our brains and be the independent, critical thinkers we like to think we are.

Green Party 2004 Presidential Strategy
By David Cobb
Presented at the National Committee meeting in
Washington, D.C., July 2003

The Green Party is the electoral arm of a growing worldwide movement for peace, social justice, ecology, and democracy. The fundamental question facing us is one of sovereignty. Who shall rule—"We the People" by shared public decision-making or un-elected and unaccountable corporate executives in private board-rooms?

The seriousness of the question cannot be understated. Unre-strained corporate power is literally destroying the earth and creat-ing an unjust and ultimately unsustainable world with the plunder. Against this somber backdrop the Green Party must consider how we can continue to grow and evolve beyond our current role as the party of opposition to the party of transformation of politics, cul-ture, and economics.

Growing Our Party

I propose that the Green Party run a strategic presidential cam-paign in 2004 that builds the party at the local, state, and national levels. I commit that all actions of a Cobb Green Party campaign will work toward that end. If I seek the Green Party nomination for president, I make the following pledges:

- I will publicly support the Green Party platform as adopted at the Green Party National Convention.

- I will immediately share all volunteer lists generated during my campaign with the respective local and state Green Party.

- I will share (at no cost) all donor lists generated during my campaign with the Green Party National Committee by January 2, 2005.

- I will coordinate all hires at the national level with the Green Party National Committee, and at the state and local level with the respective state and local Green Party.

- I will hire Green Party activists to work on my campaign at the national, state, and local level.

The Green Party presidential campaign must be run to increase Green Party membership, build and strengthen our internal infrastructure, help local candidates and initiatives, create state and local chapters where they do not yet exist, and hone our skills as citizen organizers so that we continue to thrive and provide voters a true choice.

The Strategy

The Green Party stands at a crucial moment in our history. The unelected Bush regime has deeply divided the American people. It is unacceptable to claim that there is no difference between the Democratic and Republican parties. If we want our party to grow, we must demonstrate to the American people (and especially progressive voters) that we hear their concerns of the danger Bush poses.

I propose the following strategy for the Green Party presidential campaign in 2004:

1. We consistently articulate instant runoff voting (IRV) as the only solution to the question of Greens as "spoilers."

2. The candidate should publicly state that if Dennis Kucinich or Al Sharpton wins the Democratic Party nomination, we

will withdraw from the race. *We* know that the DNC leadership and their corporate funders will never allow a Kucinich or Sharpton nomination. By publicly making this statement we demonstrate our willingness to work across party lines with genuine progressives, and when Kucinich and Sharpton are rebuked by the Democratic Party leadership (as were Jesse Jackson and Jerry Brown), it will continue to illustrate that the Democratic Party is not the progressive party in the U.S.

3. The candidate should publicly state that if Joseph Lieberman wins the Democratic Party nomination our presidential campaign will be run so as to prevent his election. We will not back away from an absolute rejection of such a corporate conservative candidate.

4. The candidate should publicly state that if a marginally "moderate" (but still woefully inadequate) candidate wins the Democratic Party nomination, we will follow a *strategic-states plan* for our campaign. Most of our resources should be focused on those states where the electoral college votes are not "in play."

The Green Party can run a strong campaign in 2004 that grows our party, garners millions of voters, and culminates with George Bush losing the election. The Green Party has grown larger, stronger, and better organized with every election cycle. With such strength comes a responsibility to exercise it wisely and effectively.

CHAPTER TWO

Green Tactics and Strategy

"Strategic Voting" Is Strategic Suicide

By Howie Hawkins
Synthesis/Regeneration 32, *Fall 2003*

When Granny D used her speaking time at the Code Pink antiwar demonstration in Washington, D.C., in early March to tell the Greens "not to divide us" by running a Green presidential candidate, she was herself being divisive. Her demand was divisive within the peace movement, which needs to unite on antiwar demands and not exclude anyone based on their electoral approach. Her political tactic mirrors that of Bush when he says if you are not with the U.S. war on terror, you are with the terrorists. There are always more than two choices in any political question.

Granny D is not alone in making this demand on the Greens. Ronnie Dugger, Michael Moore, Carl Davidson, Daniel Ellsberg, and Noam Chomsky are among the other notable progressives who are telling progressives to support the Democratic nominee in order to beat Bush. Fortunately, few Greens are willing to rely on the Soft-Right Democrats to defend us from the Hard-Right Republicans. Unfortunately, too many Greens are accepting the sneaky version of this demand: strategic voting.

Various proposals have circulated under various names (safe states, strategic voting, tactical voting, three-dimensional, etc.), but they all boil down to the Green ticket either cutting a deal with the Democrats and exiting the campaign late, or not competing for votes with the Democratic candidate in the "battleground" swing states where the polls show the race between the Democratic and Republican tickets to be close and the electoral votes of those states up for grabs. Strategic voting proposals let the Greens run where they won't affect the outcome, but not where they might.

The minute the Greens stop campaigning where they might affect the outcome is the minute no one takes the Greens seriously. The minute the Greens start backhandedly supporting Democrats with a cute "strategic voting" scheme is the minute the public stops taking Greens seriously. This will be because the Greens have stopped taking themselves seriously. It is the minute that the corporate Democrats feel free to completely ignore their own Kucinich/Sharpton wing and take votes to their left for granted. It is the minute the whole dynamic of the election shifts to the right, with the Green Party looking like it isn't really serious about wanting governmental power to make changes.

The best way to fight the right is with a good offense around an independent campaign for a real alternative. The Democratic leadership is so complicit in Bush's tax cuts, corporate pandering, war powers, war budgets, and repressive legislation that it is hard to argue they are the lesser evil. It's more like the slicker evil of a Clinton versus the cruder evil of a Bush Jr.

Where's the Difference?

Neoconservative militarism and neoliberal economics are not Bush's exclusive preserve. The Democratic leadership and majority of congressional Democrats are every bit as committed to them as they are to pleasing their financial sponsors in the corporate oligarchy who want these policies.

Neoliberalism includes cuts in social spending, hikes in regressive taxes, cuts in progressive taxes, privatization, deregulation, corporate-managed trade, union busting, and corporate welfare. In a nutshell, it means the stick of austerity for workers, on the theory it will makes us work harder and raise productivity, and the carrot of welfare for the corporate rich, on the theory they will invest and the benefits of increased jobs and tax revenues will trickle down to the rest of us.

Neoliberal austerity is the post-Keynesian economic policy adopted by the corporate rulers as they ran into the internal limits to profits and growth under the Keynesian welfare/warfare state.

The new ruling-class consensus is the austerity/warfare state of neoliberal economics and neoconservative empire. That ruling-class consensus is the pro-war, pro-corporate bipartisan consensus. To be sure, the ruling class is divided about Bush, with some worried about the economic irrationality of the latest tax cuts, the instability his cowboy style of imperialism is stirring up in the Middle East and Europe, and the domestic instability his pandering to Christian fundamentalists may stir up at home. The worried wing of the ruling class will give strong backing to a Democrat like Dean, Kerry, Gephardt, or Lieberman who will be more sophisticated in administering militaristic neoliberalism. That is their fight, not ours.

A Democrat might beat Bush, but no Democrat is going to beat Bushism, which is to say the corporate oligarchy's bipartisan consensus. If a Democrat wins the presidency in 2004, there will be no change in the basic U.S. geopolitical strategy of military basing and control of oil in the Middle East and Central Asia to keep Western Europe, Russia, China, and Japan from becoming potential rivals to U.S. hegemony. Nor will there be any change in the basic neoliberal policy of motivating workers to work harder by imposing hardship and motivating the rich to invest with corporate welfare incentives.

If the Greens don't run a strong campaign seeking every vote they can get in every state, there will be no electoral opposition to the bipartisan consensus of the U.S. as global occupation force and no electoral alternative to the neoliberal policies of economic stimulus by heightening inequalities.

Keeping Our Eyes on the Prize

Who wins the presidential election matters little because most of the power structure is not up for election. There is no election for corporations' private economic power and ability to effectively veto reforms they don't like by divesting, not for the repressive apparatus of the national security state, not for the regulatory bureaucracy that is captured by the corporations they are supposed to regulate. Whoever wins must govern within that power structure.

What matters is whether there is a movement that is organizing people to solve their own problems. That was Nader's central theme in 2000 and, I hope, the point of the Green Party. That theme is far more radical than the policy positions Nader advocated because to solve their problems people need real democratic power, and that is a threat to the whole system.

The Democrats mobilize people to win elections, not implement platforms. I would hope that the Greens are about advancing their program. There will be no hearing for that program, and no vehicle for people to organize around it, if the Greens do not run a strong campaign in 2004 against *both* corporate parties. Without that Green campaign, the election will be about who is stronger on "defense" and who can best restore corporate profitability (read: squeeze workers even harder) to end the economy's stagnation. There will be no opposition to militaristic neoliberalism and the Green Party will have rendered itself irrelevant.

The Green Party's political independence is not only about policy planks in the platform, but even more fundamentally about political class independence from the corporate ruling class. It is about the Green Party as an *institution* independent of corporate money as opposed to the Democratic Party as an *institution* dependent on corporate money and, when governing, dependent on corporate investment.

The big corporations have an effective veto on reforms because they can threaten a capital strike. The Democrats will never challenge that corporate blackmail and thus can never carry through a progressive program. Political independence is an issue of the parties' class and institutional bases, not just the characteristics of individual candidates.

Were the Greens to give backhanded support to the Democrats in a strategic-voting scheme, they would be entering into a de facto coalition with the corporate rulers as subordinate partners. The Greens would be dependent on what the Democratic candidates said and did and thus surrender the Greens' political independence, their power and their voice, and their very identity as a political force that believes a different world is possible.

Nothing would be more dispiriting and demoralizing for Greens and progressives generally than a defensive, self-defeating campaign to elect another pro-war, pro-corporate Democrat as the lesser evil to the Republican version. On the other hand, an all-out Green campaign for every vote possible in every state could be the inspiration and rallying point for a movement for the Green alternative.

These Green alternatives will not be heard without an all-out Green campaign. That a Green campaign might "spoil" the Democrats' chances is exactly what compels attention to the Green alternative. Greens should embrace that attention, not try to finesse it away with a strategic voting scheme that erases the reason why the Greens would get attention.

Spoiling the Democrats is not our goal. Our goal is to advance our program. We do not have to win the office to win the debate by defining what the issues are. If we can define the debate, we set the agenda for the future and lay the basis for the democratic structural changes in society needed to replace the corporate oligarchy's bipartisan consensus around neoliberal austerity and neoconservative empire with the Green alternative.

Debating the Election: The Democrats Don't Deserve Our Support

By Sharon Smith
Socialist Worker, *September 19, 2003*

After the 2000 election, Green Party presidential candidate Ralph Nader was roundly denounced by Democrats as a "spoiler" who helped George Bush defeat Al Gore (ignoring the U.S. Supreme Court's decisive role during the Florida debacle in stealing the election for Bush). As the 2004 election approaches, the vast majority of the left—including many who campaigned for Nader in 2000—has made defeating Bush (by implication, with a Democrat) its number-one priority.

The Green Party itself is considering a "safe states" strategy—campaigning for a Green candidate only in states where Democrats or Republicans hold an uncontested majority, effectively an endorsement of the Democrats. As left-wing journalist Norman Solomon wrote recently, "The Bush team has neared some elements of fascism," while *Z Magazine*'s Michael Albert argued, "However bad his replacement may turn out, replacing Bush will improve the subsequent mood of the world and its prospects for survival."

These are widely accepted justifications for rallying behind the Democrats as "the lesser of two evils." By this "lesser evil" logic, many progressives now attracted to Howard Dean and Dennis Kucinich because of their opposition to the Iraq war will ultimately end up supporting a mainstream Democrat who seeks to win swing votes from the Republicans. Dean himself—who boasts, "I was a triangulator before Clinton was a triangulator"—might well fit the bill.

Out of sheer hatred for Bush, progressives can agree that the war party in power should be brought down. But the Democratic Party is a war party in waiting.

"Lesser evil" support for the Democrats has been repeated by sections of the left every four years since the Great Depression. But far from broadening the scope of left-wing politics, it has stunted the development of a radical social movement in the U.S. For this reason, it is necessary to view the role of "lesser evil" politics historically.

The term "fascist" has also been applied to conservative Republicans Barry Goldwater in 1964, Richard Nixon in the 1970s, as well as Ronald Reagan and George Bush Sr. in the 1980s, to express the urgency of voting Democrat on Election Day. To be sure, this Bush administration, dominated by neoconservatives, models itself on Reagan's.

And there are differences between the Democratic and Republican parties on issues such as abortion rights. But the two parties, each funded and controlled by corporate donors, agree on fundamental aims, if not on the strategies to achieve them.

Both are pro-capitalist and pro-imperialist—dedicated to furthering the interests of the U.S. ruling class at home and expanding U.S. power globally. Bloody wars and political repression are unique neither to this Bush administration, nor to Republicans.

Democrat Harry Truman's first presidential act was to order two atomic bombs dropped on the Japanese cities of Hiroshima and Nagasaki. Lyndon Johnson, the Democratic Party's "peace candidate" in 1964, had by 1965 massively escalated the Vietnam War—a war that killed 1.3 million Vietnamese and 58,000 U.S. soldiers.

Nor is Bush's USA PATRIOT Act the first time that the party in power has used large-scale repression at home. Democrat

Woodrow Wilson signed the Espionage Act of 1917, banning protest against U.S. participation in the First World War, and his administration detained and deported thousands of immigrants. In 1942, Democrat Franklin Delano Roosevelt forcibly "relocated" the entire Japanese-American population on the West Coast into concentration camps for the rest of the Second World War. The Democratic Party's reputation as a liberal alternative to the Republicans is greatly exaggerated—mainly by its liberal supporters. One need look no further back than the Clinton administration.

As a candidate in 1992, Clinton promised to "put people first," but instead of advancing liberal principles, Clinton stole the Republican's agenda on key issues. The hallmark of Clinton's presidency was ending "welfare as we know it" in 1996—dismantling sixty-one-year-old New Deal legislation obliging the government to provide income support to the poor.

Clinton also helped to pave the way for Bush's USA PATRIOT Act when he signed the 1996 Anti-Terrorism and Effective Death Penalty Act. Also in 1996, Clinton signed the Defense of Marriage Act banning gay marriage, and under his tenure the U.S. prison population nearly doubled in size.

There is no reason to assume, as many do, that a Gore presidency would have avoided war after September 11. Clinton oversaw UN-sponsored sanctions against Iraq that led to the deaths of more than one million Iraqis, and U.S. warplanes dropped bombs on Iraq almost daily during his time in office. And Clinton signed the Iraq Liberation Act in 1998, calling for the U.S. "to seek to remove the regime headed by Saddam Hussein." Clinton's secretary of state, Madeleine Albright, admits in a recent *Foreign Affairs* article, "I personally felt [Bush's new Iraq] war was justified on the basis of Saddam's decade-long refusal to comply with UN Security Council resolutions on weapons of mass destruction."

There is another reason why supporting the Democrats as a "lesser evil" is a mistake. For nearly a century, this logic has blocked the possibility for building an alternative to the left of the Democrats. Every four years, leftists must betray their principles simply to keep a Republican out of office.

In 1964, antiwar activists adopted the slogan "Half the way with LBJ," only to see Johnson escalate the Vietnam War. In the

1990s, liberals scurried to provide cover for Clinton's welfare repeal. As former Health and Human Services official Peter Edelman noted, "So many of those who would have shouted from the rooftops if a Republican president had done this were boxed in by their desire to see the president reelected."

Largely because the left and the labor movement have remained tied to the coattails of the Democratic Party since the 1930s, the U.S. remains the only advanced industrial society without a labor or social democratic party funded by unions instead of big business. If the left is to move forward, its collective memory must stretch further back than the last Republican administration—and it must set its sights much higher than promoting the current crop of Democratic Party contenders.

As social activist Howard Zinn argued in the pages of this newspaper, "[T]he really critical thing isn't who is sitting in the White House but who is sitting in—in the streets, in the cafeterias, in the halls of government, in the factories. Who is protesting, who is occupying offices and demonstrating—those are the things that determine what happens."

The course of the struggle, not the outcome of the 2004 elections, will shape the future of the left—and experience has shown that endorsing the Democratic Party pulls the left into its fold, not the other way around.

Debating the Election: We Have a Responsibility to Work to Defeat Bush

By Norman Solomon
Socialist Worker, September 19, 2003

Activists have plenty of good reasons to challenge the liberal Democratic Party operatives who focus on election strategy while routinely betraying progressive ideals. Unfortunately, the national Green Party now shows appreciable signs of the flip side—focusing on admirable ideals without plausible strategy.

It's impossible to know whether the vote margin between Bush and his Democratic challenger will be narrow or wide in November 2004. I've never heard a credible argument that a Nader campaign might help to defeat Bush next year. A Nader campaign might have no significant effect on Bush's chances—or it could turn out to help Bush win. With so much at stake, do we really want to roll the dice this way?

We're told that another Nader campaign will help to build the Green Party. But Nader's prospects of coming near his nationwide 2000 vote total of 2.8 million are very slim; much more probable is that a 2004 campaign would win far fewer votes—hardly an indicator of, or contributor to, a growing national party.

Some activists contend that the Greens will maintain leverage over the Democratic Party by conveying a firm intention to run a presidential candidate. I think that's basically an illusion. The prospect of a Green presidential campaign is having very little effect on the Democratic nomination contest, and there's no reason to expect that to change. The Democrats are almost certain to nominate a "moderate" corporate flack.

Howard Dean should be included in that category. Let's take Dean at his word: "I was a triangulator before Clinton was a triangulator. In my soul, I'm a moderate." If Dean becomes the Democratic presidential candidate next year, at that point there would be many good reasons to see him as a practical tool for defeating Bush. But in the meantime, progressive energies and support should go elsewhere.

There has been a disturbing tendency among some Greens to conflate the Democratic and Republican parties. Yes, the agendas of the two major parties overlap. But they also diverge. And in some important respects, any of the Democratic presidential contenders would be clearly better than Bush (with the exception of Joseph Lieberman, whose nomination appears to be quite unlikely). For the left to be "above the fray" would be a big mistake. It should be a matter of great concern—not indifference or mild interest—as to whether the Bush gang returns to power for four more years.

I'm not suggesting that progressives mute their voices about issues. The imperative remains to keep speaking out and organizing. As Martin Luther King Jr. said on April 30, 1967: "When machines and computers, profit motives and property rights are considered more important than people, the giant triplets of racism, militarism and economic exploitation are incapable of being conquered." The left should continue to denounce all destructive policies and proposals, whether being promoted by Republicans or Democrats.

At the same time, we should not gloss over the reality that the Bush team has neared some elements of fascism in its day-to-day operations—and forces inside the Bush administration would be well positioned to move it even farther to the right after 2004. We don't want to find out how fascistic a second term of George W. Bush's presidency could become. The current dire circumstances should bring us up short and cause us to reevaluate approaches to '04. The left has a responsibility to contribute toward a broad coalition to defeat Bush next year.

No doubt, too many Democratic Party officials have been arrogant toward Green Party supporters. "Democrats have to face reality and understand that if they move too far to the right, millions of voters will defect or vote for third-party candidates," Tom Hayden pointed out in a recent article on *Alternet*. "Democrats have to swallow hard and accept the right of the Green Party and Ralph Nader to exist and compete." At the same time, Hayden added cogently, "Nader and the Greens need a reality check. The notion that the two major parties are somehow identical may be a rationale for building a third party, but it insults the intelligence of millions of Blacks, Latinos, women, gays, environmentalists and trade unionists who can't afford the indulgence of Republican rule."

The presidency of George W. Bush is not a garden-variety Republican administration. By unleashing its policies in this country and elsewhere in the world, the Bush gang has greatly raised the stakes of the next election.

In an August essay, Michael Albert of *Z Magazine* wrote: "One post-election result we want is Bush retired. However bad his replacement may turn out, replacing Bush will improve the subsequent mood of the world and its prospects of survival. Bush represents not the whole ruling class and political elite, but a pretty small sector of it. That sector, however, is trying to reorder events so that the world is run as a U.S. empire, and so that social programs and relations that have been won over the past century in the U.S. are rolled back as well. What these parallel international and domestic aims have in common is to further enrich and empower the already super-rich and super-powerful."

Looking past the election, Albert is also on target: "We want to have whatever administration is in power after Election Day saddled by a fired-up movement of opposition that is not content with merely slowing Armageddon, but that instead seeks innovative and aggressive social gains. We want a post-election movement to have more awareness, more hope, more infrastructure and better organization by virtue of the approach it takes to the election process."

I'm a green. But these days, in the battle for the presidency, I'm not a Green. Here in the United States, the Green Party is dealing with an electoral structure that's very different from the parliamentary systems that have provided fertile ground for Green parties in Europe. We're up against the winner-take-all U.S. electoral system. Yes, there are efforts to implement "instant runoff voting," but those efforts will not transform the electoral landscape in this decade. And we should focus on this decade precisely because it will lead the way to the next ones.

By now, it's an open secret that Ralph Nader is almost certain to run for president again next year. Nader has been a brilliant and inspirational progressive for several decades. I supported his presidential campaigns in 1996 and 2000. I won't in 2004. The reasons are not about the past, but about the future.

Statement on Green Strategy 2004 and Call for Dialogue and Action
By Eighteen Green Party activists
Circulated online, December 14, 2003

As we move closer to 2004, Greens are debating strategy. Both from within and outside of the Green Party, there is enormous pressure on us. Greens and non-Greens alike are strongly opposed to the policies of the Bush administration. But Greens do not agree whether defeating George Bush, or at least not assisting in his re-election, should be a factor in our strategy.

The signers of this letter definitely agree that the Green Party needs to develop a strategy for next year's presidential campaign.

We have different ideas at this point on what particular strategy is best, though we are in full agreement that any strategy which is likely to assist in the reelection of George Bush should be avoided.

We are not signing this letter in support of the Democratic Party, or of any of its candidates, though some individual signers may be supporting one of those candidates. We are not signing this letter because we regret past Green election efforts.

We are signing this letter for several important reasons.

First, the Bush administration has demonstrated a determined will and ability to manipulate the people of this country following the tragic events of September 11, 2001. They have done this to a degree worse than other political parties could have done. They have seriously undermined the democratic foundations of our country, done immense harm to the ecosystem, and alienated scores of nations, big and small, who were once our friends.

Second, the beliefs and opinions of many people and organizations who share our views and struggles for justice and the environment are important to us. They have pleaded that we take the defeat of Bush into serious consideration. We cannot totally turn our backs on their opinions solely because they have not chosen to be active in the Green Party or join our electoral campaigns.

Third, the corrupted election system in the United States creates a dynamic that harms our interest in the short and long term. It permitted the corporate-party candidate with fewer votes in 2000 to take over the White House. While all Greens hold sacred the right to participate in the democratic process—what is left of it in the United States—the signers of this letter believe that we neither can nor should ignore the gross faults in the system which assist the greater evil in elections. The harm that can come both to this country and to the Green Party by ignoring the corrupted system that is used to count votes cannot be ignored.

Lastly, the continued growth and strength of the Green Party depends upon how we address this issue. Contrary to what some claim, we believe that to ignore the vast numbers of progressives, many of whom are independent of any political party, bodes poorly for the future vitality of the Green Party. There are no easy choices for the Green Party in 2004, and the growth of any political party requires that it listen to its natural constituencies, including those who have not yet fully joined.

The use of the term "lesser evil" or "greater evil" in describing major-party candidates is instructive. The great majority of the members of the Democratic Party power structure have repeatedly demonstrated that they are not prepared, willing, or able to offer solutions to most of the problems the United States faces. But that party is, nonetheless, and in general, the lesser of evils. Looking at the greater of evils which we also face, we do not believe we can ignore this difference. While it is small enough to demand the presence of an alternative political party, it is not small enough to completely ignore. The history of the failures and harmful actions of many Democrats are not so relevant to voters in 2004—the choices we face in this election are.

As already noted, we do not all favor a single strategy, and some of us strongly disagree with each other's strategy at this point. The strategies we severally favor range from not running at all, to running in ways that will focus our campaign energies in certain states, to calls to possibly drop out of the race near Election Day if it is very close.

But we all agree that the Green Party should not ignore the damage to the country and to the Green Party that could result by ignoring the reality around us and pretending that there is no difference or that the difference is insignificant. The forthcoming issue of *Green Horizon Quarterly* features four articles that detail different strategies.

We call for:

1. Candidates seeking the Green Party presidential nomination to describe the strategy they would follow.

2. The Green Party to debate all strategies with respect, and for the national Green Party to take a stance on its preferred strategy. All state parties are encouraged to hold special meetings to discuss and democratically decide, using instant runoff voting, which strategy they prefer, followed by a similar decision process from the national party's Coordinating Committee. We are a grassroots party and must make decisions of our grassroots known and not leave a void for our candidates to fill.

3. All Greens to declare their solidarity with our brothers and sisters in progressive organizations across the country in

calling for the defeat of the illegitimate Bush administration, while at the same time demanding that the electoral system be reformed to include instant runoff voting, fair ballot access, and public financing.

Agreed to, in alphabetical order: Medea Benjamin, California; Dee Berry, Missouri; Jenefer Ellingston, Washington, D.C.; Tom Fusco, Maine; Holly Hart, Iowa; Ted Glick, New Jersey; Pat LaMarche, Maine; Rick Lass, New Mexico; Linda Martin, California; Dean Myerson, Washington, D.C.; John Rensenbrink, Maine; Anita Rios, Ohio; Steve Schmidt, Florida; Tom Sevigny, Connecticut; Charlene Spretnak, California; Ron Stanchfield, New York; Penny Teal, Connecticut; Rhoda Vanderhart, Kansas.

Run, Ralph, Run, But as a Green

An open letter to Ralph Nader, initiated by Greens for Nader (Mark Dunlea, Howie Hawkins, and Walt Contreras Sheasby) December 10, 2003

We, the undersigned, are writing to urge Ralph Nader and the Green Party to work together to run a strong, united presidential campaign in 2004.

On Election Day 2004, America needs a progressive alternative to the pro-corporate, pro-military, anti-environment agenda offered by the two major parties. Of the various progressive candidates presently considering running, Ralph Nader is by far the strongest. It is important that the Greens and Nader run together.

A strong Green presidential campaign is needed to energize and mobilize progressive voters in America, to give an electoral voice to those who promote peace, democracy, and social and economic justice. Without such a campaign, the political debate and the Democratic Party will continue to move to the right.

Among the reasons for a Nader Green presidential campaign:

- Nader is the most prominent progressive spokesperson in America, long recognized as the most trusted person in the country.

- The similarities between the two major parties are much greater than the differences.

- The Republicans stole the 2000 presidential election, and the Democrats didn't challenge the theft. The Republicans are planning to do it again.

- The world is threatened by America's drive for corporate globalization and an American military/economic empire. Both major parties embrace this goal.

- Nader and the Greens are both stronger if they work together. It would be a disaster for both and for the progressive movement if the two divide.

- If the Democrats win, as they should based on the polls, corporate interests will still be in power, not progressives. Our issues will only succeed if there is a strong independent progressive movement willing to challenge a Democratic administration, not apologize for their shortcomings.

"Anybody But Bush" Is Not a Progressive Solution

The Democrats and their allies are urging the Greens to be silent, to sit on the sidelines while the Democrats fight the Republicans for control of the patronage that comes with control of the national government. Without a strong progressive electoral alternative, the Democrats have moved relentlessly to the right in a futile effort to win elections by offering similar policies as the Republicans but with a friendlier face.

Some self-declared progressives are running scared, demanding that the Greens not run a candidate, or that the Greens backhandedly support the Democrat by not campaigning in the swing states. To be sure, Bush is scary, particularly since September 11. Invasions launched against Afghanistan and Iraq; pre-emptive wars against "America's enemies"; a policy of an American global empire; a curtailment of civil liberties in America; more tax cuts and corporate welfare for the rich. However, the Democrats in Congress supported these steps.

We cannot rely on the Slick Soft-Right Democrats to fight the Crude Hard-Right Republicans. The Democrats haven't done it during the first three years of the Bush administration. There is no good reason to start relying on them now. The best defense against the Hard Right is not defensive support for a Softer Right, but a strong offensive around a real campaign for a progressive alternative.

The argument that it is the wrong time for a progressive third party has been raised in virtually every election cycle over the last thirty years, that it is more important to defeat Nixon, to defeat Reagan, to defeat Bush I and II than it is to build a party that reflects our principles. Yet no matter how many times they have pleaded with progressive third-party forces to "wait till next time," these voices have never said it is time to run, that it is time to admit that the Democratic Party will not support a progressive agenda.

There are differences between the policies of the Democratic and Republican parties. Just as there are differences between GM and Ford, General Electric and Westinghouse, the American and National League in baseball. But the similarity between the two parties is much greater than the differences. Both parties increasingly are financed by many of the same corporate and special interests and act accordingly after the election, rewarding their supporters. The Democratic track record on issues they cite to attract progressive voters— the environment, women's rights, labor, the federal bench—is much worse than their rhetoric at campaign time.

The list of the failures of the Democratic Party at the national, state, and local levels is dismal, and is far too long to be chronicled here. Their recent shortcomings include welfare, criminal justice, universal health care, campaign finance reform, global warming, childhood poverty, the ERA, hunger, homelessness, pesticides, genetic engineering, progressive taxes, corporate welfare, nuclear power, the Middle East, nuclear weapons, the military budget, child care, consumer rights, banking, insurance, the war on drugs, foreign policy, corporate crime, etc.

The Democratic Party seldom if ever takes principled stands. Instead, Democrats make decisions based on how it will help them with voters and reward their campaign contributors. At best, the Democratic Party believes for some strange reason that most voters are more conservative than they are, and pander to "them" by moving to the right, while telling progressives not to worry, it will work out in the end, just vote them into power. It didn't work with Clinton in 1992; why would anyone expect it will work with Dean in 2004?

The major-party candidates will of course offer sound bites and photo opportunities on some of these issues. After all, the first Bush president used polluted Boston Harbor as an effective environmental photo op against Dukakis. Their positions will just lack substance, fail to educate, fail to advance a true progressive agenda both during the election and afterward.

The Democrats will not offer an alternative to the failed economic system that has greatly increased the wealth for a few, while making many poorer, with the middle class barely keeping pace over the last decade. For a long time the Democrats have been a right-of-center party. The likely nominee of the Democratic Party, Howard Dean, fits the mold of Bill Clinton and Al Gore. The few progressive presidential candidates within the Democratic Party pull a few percentage points and are treated as fringe players, largely ignored by the media and the party leadership. Their role is not to make the Democratic Party more progressive but to try to pull progressives into the voting booth for the Democrats. These candidates will have been sent back to the sideline by springtime.

The Democratic Party Is Not a Peace Party

The drive for war by the Bush administration since September 11 is frightening. If ever we needed the Democrats to act like a true opposition party, it was in the days after September 11. Instead they hopped on the bandwagon to bomb Afghanistan, curtail civil liberties, invade Iraq, lock up immigrants, and increase corporate welfare to "restart the economy."

The bipartisan approach to U.S. military interventions under both Democratic and Republican presidents since 1950 has resulted in the killing of an estimated eight million individuals. It has resulted in a military-industrial complex that has continued to grow in power and tax expenditures, despite the warnings of Republican Dwight Eisenhower when he left the Oval Office. Under both parties the torturers were trained, the CIA plotted, the weapons became more deadly, democratic governments were overthrown, American imperialism expanded.

One can argue that, apart from the atomic bomb, some of the nastiest military operations, especially the overthrow of progressive foreign governments, came during the Republican administrations. Yet the planning and implementation of many of the military ad-

ventures stretched over both Republican and Democratic administrations. Some of the biggest misadventures, such as Vietnam, the
Bay of Pigs, and the Balkan War, came primarily with the Democrats at the helm. Democrats were in charge of the invasion of the
Dominican Republic in 1965; shooting peace demonstrators in
Panama in 1966; supporting death squads in El Salvador and Hon-
duras in the late 1970s; supporting the mujahideen in Afghanistan
in the late 1970s; killing five hundred thousand Iraqi civilians in
the 1990s; bombing Sudan and Afghanistan in 1998. And the
Democratic members of Congress have usually overwhelmingly supported the many military adventures of the Republicans when they
controlled the White House, including the invasions of Afghanistan
and Iraq.

The Democratic Party has long joined with the Republicans and
supported the one-sided American position in the ongoing conflict
between Israel and Palestine, often isolating the U.S. from every
other country in the world in votes in the United Nations. Even after
the collapse of the Soviet Union, the Clinton administration refused
to seek any cuts in the military budget and continued to support the
development of new nuclear weapons.

Ralph Nader and the Greens Need Each Other

There is no more progressive candidate than Ralph Nader to communicate the Green's agenda to both progressives and the larger
population. He has a strong track record of over thirty years of activism, with an incredible number of groups and issues he has
helped launched. He has a strong staff team that has coordinated
and can coordinate a national presidential campaign. He demonstrated his ability four years ago to raise a significant amount of
funds and to generate thousands of volunteers. While there are
some issues that we wish he would speak out on more, he is still
good on those issues and getting better.

The 2004 presidential election will be a challenging one for
Greens, Nader, and progressives. Some feel that the best the Greens
can hope to do is to survive. We need to run our strongest candidate. Without a doubt that is Nader.

Yes, there needs to be better coordination with the Green Party
and the Greens should ask to sit down and negotiate this with

them. That also means that the Greens take on larger responsibilities for the national campaign than four years ago.

The Greens are a stronger entity than they were four years ago. They have obtained official ballot status in more states and have run stronger and winning campaigns throughout the country. Electoral successes in places like Maine, California, and elsewhere have generated more national attention. The national Coordinated Campaign Committee (CCC) has made some significant progress in strengthening our national political operations. While the party needs to get stronger, and its internal process can be difficult, the party is an asset that Nader strongly needs.

It would be a major historical mistake for the Greens and Nader to run independently of one another, hurting both in the short and long term. The Green Party is now part of Nader's legacy; anything he does to harm the Greens harms himself. The Greens and Nader need to build unity among progressives; if they can't build unity among themselves, the 2004 presidential election will likely be a disaster for both.

Bush Stole the 2000 Election— and Is Ready to Do It Again

While Democratic partisans argue that Nader cost Gore the election, this is untrue for a variety of reasons, as most campaign experts know.

One, most progressives know that the election was stolen by Bush. Gore won the nationwide popular vote; he also won the Florida and electoral college vote. The U.S. Supreme Court gave away the election. The Democratic Party and the Gore campaign did little to prevent the theft of the election, starting with their failure to aggressively challenge the illegal disenfranchisement of African-American voters in Florida or even to demand that every vote be counted.

Nor have the Democrats made it a major priority to demand election reform since the election, starting with the failure to adopt fairer electoral systems such as preferential voting, or to address the problems with the electoral college. The proposals that have been adopted through the federal Help America Vote Act (HAVA) have increased the likelihood that the election will be stolen again through manipulation of computerized voting results and disenfranchisement of many new voters through improper enforcement of ID requirements, but the national Democratic Party has been largely silent on these issues.

Second, the Nader and Green electoral efforts in 2000 helped the Democrats more than it hurt them. Polls show that more than a million people voted just because Nader was on the ballot. Many of these voters also cast votes for Democratic candidates for other offices, and helped provide the margin of victory in at least two U.S. Senate races, allowing the Democrats to reclaim control of the U.S. Senate. Without Nader on the ballot in 2002, the Democrats promptly lost control. In addition, whenever Gore responded to the Nader candidacy by articulating a more progressive, grassroots agenda, his standing in the polls went up. Whenever he tried to sound more like a Republican to attract the center-right votes, his standing went down.

For the record, polls showed that if Nader had not been in the race, of the three million Americans who cast votes for him, 25 percent would have voted for Bush, 38 percent for Gore, and 37 percent would not have voted. The net gain from Nader voters for Gore would have been 13 percent (38 percent minus 25 percent), not 100 percent. However, the Democrats have decided to throw away this 13 percent net gain by failing to embrace preferential or IRV voting.

What Strategy to Follow in the 2004 Presidential Election

There is no agreement yet on the best strategy for the 2004 presidential election—just as there wasn't agreement on the best strategy for 2000.

In the closing weeks of the campaign, Nader focused on states where the election was close, apparently in the hope that the additional media coverage would generate more national votes. Many Greens would have preferred to concentrate on the states where the election was a runaway, like New York, where voters were "free" to vote for whomever they wanted. The end result was that Nader and the party fell several million votes short of the 5 percent national vote total needed for major-party status.

A similar debate, at least partially if not largely in response to the "spoiler" argument, is taking place in 2004. Various versions of a "safe-states" strategy are being promoted, where the Greens and Nader consciously avoid pulling votes in toss-up states. Others object to such a strategy for ideological and party-building reasons (e.g., maintaining ballot lines). It also seems that it would be difficult to get agreement on what the "safe states" are.

This discussion is important but will likely be difficult to come to agreement on, especially as the election unfolds. The dynamics of the "Anybody But Bush" argument will also change once the Democratic nominee is selected, and his specific policies come into focus. Right now, too many "liberals" are projecting their own positions on the Democratic Party; that mistake will become clearer as we get closer to the election, and the center-right positions of the candidate are more highlighted.

Run, Ralph, run—as a Green.

Letter to the Steering Committee and the Presidential Exploratory Committee of the Green Party
By Ralph Nader
December 22, 2003

I am writing to withdraw my name from consideration as a potential nominee for the Green Party presidential ticket in 2004.

I write this with regret because of my support for your platform and civic activities, because of our shared political history, and because of the numerous efforts I have made, over the years since 1996, to help grassroots Greens build the party. Since running as your nominee in 2000 through all fifty states—from the disenfranchised Anacostia in Washington, D.C., to corporate-dominated Alaska, from downtown Hartford to the pilot industrial hemp field of Hawaii (not to mention those states where we had to help build the party from scratch)—I have met with Greens from around the country and the world, scheduled and completed more than forty-five fund-raisers in some thirty states, assisted in starting the Campus Greens, and supported more than a few state and local Green candidates. I remain a registered Independent. But my efforts to build the Green Party and my public contributions on issues of importance to Greens can be compared favorably with those who wear their Green Party registrations as some badge or bona fides.

More recently, as part of my exploratory effort, I have met or spoken with Greens from all over the country in extensive conversations, heard from even more through sign-on letters, Kucinich supporters, Greens for Dean, state and local Green groups, newspaper and magazine accounts, including the *Green Pages* and *Green Horizon*, etc., all of which illustrate how the reaction to George W. Bush has fractured—more than galvanized—the Greens as a party. Most individuals have the best intentions, and there are people who have now dedicated years to help building the Greens. However, many of the communications I have received express volumes about the maturity of the Greens as a political party.

Although its growth has been slower than many of us would like, the Green Party at least remains poised to respond to the voters' desire for a third party. The failure of the two major parties both to engage a hundred million nonvoters and to provide existing voters with choices over a broad range of important issues has been a continual reality for Greens. With this in mind, uncertainty expressed by the party's leadership regarding the conditions under which the party may or may not field presidential and vice-presidential candidates in 2004 can only be interpreted as a confused retreat.

Specifically, the Steering Committee has declared in reference to whether "the Green Party will (or won't) run a high- (or low-) profile candidate for President in 2004, and that the candidate will (or won't) drop out in their [*sic*] run for the presidency before election day, possibly making some kind of accommodation (or not) with the Democrats and their candidate" that:

> The truth is, no one person or group of persons, inside or outside of the Green Party, will make those types of critical decisions in the Green Party. The strategy the Green Party pursues will be arrived at through a comprehensive process that is beginning now and will go on in every state Green Party, either through conventions or primaries. The conventions and primaries will in turn select delegates from every state Green Party who will come together at our National Convention in the summer of 2004 to make a final, collective decision as

to whether the Green Party will run a presidential candidate, and, if so, who that person will be.*

The occasion for this letter is not simply that there are robust contending views about whether to have a presidential candidate and under which strategies and conditions, but that—should I decide to run—it is not feasible within the difficult parameters of state and federal election laws to wait and see what the Green Party will do in June 2004. Indeed, the framework and schedule you have chosen for making a decision seems itself tilted against anyone contemplating a serious run as your nominee. Many grassroots Greens who have views contrary to this procedure are not, nor are they going to be, in control of how this decision is going to be made or unmade. It has already been made.

I cannot, nor could any serious potential candidate, embark on a committed campaign for president as a Green Party nominee when the party will not even be certain whether or how it wishes to run a candidate until June 2004. Nor would it be tolerable (not to mention counterproductive for ballot lines, local candidates, party growth, and vote totals) for the party to impose on its nominee varying geographical limits to campaigning. Nor, under such ambiguous conditions, could a committed candidate run the risk that individual state parties would prevent the national nominee access to their ballot lines for whatever conceived motives, with little penalty for nonacquiescence to the convention decision. The deadlines for obtaining ballot access in many states come due prior to or around your convention's decision. Were I to become a candidate, I would not want to launch a campaign with such an uncertain compass regarding what should be a bedrock, genetic determination to run presidential and vice-presidential candidates all out—which is what, after all, national political parties—as opposed to movements—do.

As you know, I have scrupulously refrained from interfering in any internal Green Party matters. For purposes of encouraging more

---

* Green Party of the United States mailing signed by members of the Steering Committee, June 5, 2003. See also, as just two of many additional recent examples, December 16, 2003, GPUS Proposal to Create a Presidential Support Committee, "whether we will have a Presidential candidate is not 100 percent settled"; October 28, 2003, National Press Release, "The decision about whom, how, and whether to run in the 2004 national election will be made democratically by all the accredited state Green parties at the Milwaukee convention."

intensive and resourceful initiatives, I have commented on the need to expand the number of state Green offices through more assiduous fund-raising and on the importance of running more candidates. The Green Party has endless opportunities to field candidates, especially among the 2.5 million elective offices at the state and local levels, many of which offer no opposition to the incumbents by the other major party. Given the absence of decision that has been effectively formalized into an unchanging, misguided national procedure on the presidential front, I submit that 2004 might be the year that the Green Party makes a deeper commitment to building the party through state and local candidacies. I and many Greens concur that this is the party's clearest present strength and will be the source of its important talent in the future. During the 2001, 2002, and 2003 elections, Greens won approximately 25 percent of the local offices they contested.

Accordingly, for the reasons described above, I am withdrawing my name from consideration and wish the party and its local community adherents the best in their future endeavors. I still believe that Americans deserve more political parties and better choices than the rhetoric and offerings of the two major parties. I believe in giving people real power to achieve solutions to the problems we have today and in the long-term potential for a reorganized Green Party. In the event that I should still decide to become a presidential candidate, any collaborative efforts that are possible, especially at the state and local level, would be welcome.

Sincerely,
Ralph Nader

Letter to Ralph Nader Urging Reconsideration of Withdrawal

By the Green Party Steering Committee
December 24, 2003

Dear Mr. Nader,

In response to your letter of December 22, we regret your decision not to place your name on the ballot in the Green Party primaries. We believe that the pairing of your legacy with the Green Party was a powerful combination. We are sorry that you have chosen to discontinue this relationship for the purposes of the 2004 presidential race.

We truly appreciate your past and promised future support of Green candidates for elected office. We are convinced that your presence on the campaign trail was a great aid to many of the over one thousand Greens who have run for public office since your own campaign in 2000. We know that your Green presidential bids in 1996 and 2000 led to the formation of dozens of new state parties and hundreds of new Green locals. Your efforts, combined with those of hundreds of thousands of people across the nation, have produced for the first time in seventy-seven years a national progressive party with proven staying power: the Green Party of the United States.

In this light, we sincerely urge you to reconsider your decision.

We also wish to express our confusion at your suggestion that the Green Party is not preparing to field a presidential ticket in 2004. As you know, our 2003 National Meeting in Washington, D.C., produced "a clear mandate" for the Greens to run a presidential ticket in 2004 (http://www.gp.org/press/pr_07_21_03b.html).

Additionally, as you know, the national party has established four well-staffed and funded committees hard at work on preparations for the 2004 presidential race: these are the Ballot Access Working Group, the Coordinated Campaign Committee, the Annual National Meeting Committee, and the new Presidential Campaign Support Committee, which subsumes our old Presidential Exploratory Committee within it. The letter you refer to, as we have told you, was a fund-raising letter written by a former staff person, not a statement of Steering Committee opinion or party policy; after that letter went out, the Steering Committee reassigned responsibility for writing our fund-raising appeals to one of our number.

Six candidates are currently participating in the Green Party presidential primaries: Peter Camejo (California), David Cobb (California), Paul Glover (New York), Kent Mesplay (California), Carol Miller (New Mexico), and Lorna Salzman (New York). The eventual Green Party nominee will be whichever candidate wins the allegiance of the members of the state party affiliates of the Green Party of the United States and, thus, the votes of their delegates to the 2004 Green Presidential Nominating Convention in Milwaukee, June 23–28. The date and location of the convention were chosen by the Coordinating Committee of the Green Party of the United States (http://www.gp.org/press/pr_06_20_03.html). The Steering Committee does not have the power to select the nominee, to choose the dates or site of the convention, or to decide how the candidate will be chosen. These decisions are made democratically by the elected delegates of our affiliated state parties.

We remain committed to the proposition that America needs not just an opposition candidate, but an opposition party. Your commitment and support of the Green Party for the past seven years has brought us and our country closer to a true democracy. We are grateful for your contributions and look forward to more great work together in the future.

Endorsment, Not Nomination

Letter to the Green Party Steering Committee
By Ralph Nader
March 24, 2004

Dear Friends,
As you may have seen from media appearances and public remarks, our independent campaign is advancing a people's agenda of social and economic justice, protection of the environment, and ending the militarization and corporatization of our country and its policies at home and abroad.

Thus far, the campaign has drawn people from across the political spectrum. We have received calls from many Green Party members who want to work with Nader for President 2004. Some Greens are also urging a draft-Nader movement. Some state parties have asked whether I would accept a ballot line in their state. We have also received support from some Reform and Libertarian Party members, Independents, first-time voters and disaffected members of the two major parties.

What is developing is a true independent coalition of voters who oppose the direction in which our country is being taken. There are people in all parties and no party who want to unite to take a strong stand against the corporatist two-party duopoly that is taking the United States downward and taking apart our domestic economy. These are people who are saying enough is enough! They want a government that is truly of, by, and for the people.

After my letter in December to the Steering Committee, I have been asked by individuals and representatives of state parties as well as the Steering Committee to respond to a number of inquiries. First, I will not intrude on the party's presidential selection process. As you know, I am running as an Independent and am not seeking nor accepting the Green Party nomination. If you do not choose a presidential candidate in Milwaukee, I would welcome your endorsement and have said the same to other third parties as well. And if individuals want to work with our campaign as part of the broad independent coalition that is developing, we would be grateful.

Should the national Green Party decide to endorse my candidacy and have its members focus their efforts on state and local races, then state Green Party ballot lines and the participation of Greens in a variety of ways would be mutually helpful. However, having spent years helping to build the Green Party, I do not want to be put in a position of responding to individual state parties and thereby dividing the national party because of state ballot requirements. So the rest is up to your decision. With a big task ahead of us we are challenging an entrenched corporate political system that will not relinquish any of its power without a mobilized opposition. We need to work synergistically. As Frederick Douglas said, "power concedes nothing without a demand."

No matter what the national party decides at its convention, I intend to use the platform of my candidacy to advance many Green values and issues and will also encourage serious state and local Green Party candidates across the country.

Together, in many ways, we can expand the challenge to the corporate governments and their political party proxies.

Sincerely,

Ralph Nader

Greens Should Endorse Nader

By *Greens for Nader*
April 15, 2004

The 2004 Nader for President campaign is developing as a broad coalition drawing support from across the political spectrum. In a March 24 letter to the Steering Committee of the Green Party of the United States, Ralph Nader wrote that he would welcome Green Party participation in the coalition and endorsement of the campaign: "Should the national Green Party decide to endorse my candidacy and have its members focus their efforts on state and local races, then state Green Party ballot lines and the participation of Greens in a variety of ways would be mutually helpful."

The signers of this statement agree with the above and are advocates of sustaining the effective, long-standing alliance between Ralph Nader and the Green Party. Nader's letter expresses a similar sentiment: "I intend to use the platform of my candidacy to advance many Green values and issues and will also encourage serious state and local Green Party candidates across the country. Together, in many ways, we can expand the challenge to the corporate governments and their political party proxies.... We need to work synergistically."

Nader's willingness to champion the cause of the Green Party by running as our presidential candidate in 1996 and 2000, at a time when we were just beginning to get organized, enormously helped our growth. The 2000 campaign established the Green Party in many states as the leading alternative party in the minds of voters and the press.

This year the Nader campaign has the potential to unite those who want take a strong stand against the cash-register/big-money politics that are undermining public life in the United States. It would be a lost opportunity if the Greens were to ignore the national coalition forming around his campaign or to be viewed as running against Nader.

He will be the only high-profile candidate advocating

- an end to the U.S. occupation of Iraq and large cuts in the military budget;

- single-payer health insurance;
- a living wage and labor rights reform;
- repeal of NAFTA and GATT/WTO;
- creation of jobs through rebuilding of public infrastructure;
- tax system reform (ecological and progressive taxation);
- open debates and full public financing of elections;
- instant runoff voting and proportional representation;
- replacing nuclear power and foreign fossil fuel dependence with domestic renewable energy sources.

A Green Party candidate would also speak out on these issues, but as Greens approach our Milwaukee convention we find that there is not unity within the party for a candidate who could mount a serious challenge in the presidential arena. It will be the Nader campaign playing that role this year. If the Green Party is not a participant in the campaign coalition, the electorate will find it hard to understand why not. On the other hand, if Greens are its most prominent activists, many of those drawn to alternative politics through the campaign will find an organizational home in the Green Party.

Ralph Nader, uniquely, has the ability to shake the foundations of the two-party system. Having been our standard-bearer in 1996 and 2000, he is identified with the Greens in the public's mind. The appearance of Nader's name on as many state Green Party ballot lines as possible would be mutually beneficial. Therefore, the undersigned advocate that the Greens make a decision in Milwaukee to endorse the Nader campaign. This—along with focusing on state and local races—is our best option for unifying and growing the Green Party in 2004.

The following Green Party 2004 national candidates have indicated agreement with the above statement:

Sheila Bilyeu, Washington, D.C.

Peter Camejo, California

Carol Miller, New Mexico

Lorna Salzman, New York

An Open Letter to Ralph Nader

By the Editors of The Nation
February 16, 2004

Dear Ralph,

According to the latest news reports, you've pushed up your self-imposed deadline for announcing your decision about an independent 2004 presidential campaign from the end of January to mid-February. We're glad to hear that, because maybe it means you're still not sure about the best path to follow. For the good of the country, the many causes you've championed, and for your own good name—don't run for president this year.

Ralph, you've been part of the *Nation* family for a long time, from the day in 1959 we published one of your first articles, the exposé of "The Safe Car You Can't Buy." Since then, you've been a consistent advocate for active citizenship, investigative scholarship, and environmental stewardship. It wasn't hype when we called you Public Citizen Number One.

We know you've never been one to back down from a fight. When people tell you you can't do something, if you think it's the right thing to do, you do it anyway. That stubborn devotion to principle is one of your greatest strengths. It inspired a generation of Nader's Raiders in the 1960s and 1970s, it helped produce notable victories like the creation of the Environmental Protection Agency and the Occupational Safety & Health Administration, and it inspired a new generation of young people who flocked to your "super rallies" in 2000. The issues you raise on your Web site, NaderExplore04.org—full public financing of elections, new tools to help citizens band together, ending poverty, universal health care, a living wage, a crackdown on corporate crime—are vital to the long-term health of our country. When those issues are given scant attention by major-party candidates and ignored or trivialized by the sham joint-candidate appearances known as presidential debates, we join in your outrage.

But when devotion to principle collides with electoral politics, hard truths must be faced. Ralph, this is the wrong year for you to run: 2004 is not 2000. George W. Bush has led us into an illegal preemptive war, and his defeat is critical. Moreover, the odds of this becoming a race between Bush and Bush Lite are almost nil. For a variety of reasons—opposition to the war, Bush's assault on the Constitution, his crony capitalism, frustration with the over-cautious and indentured approach of inside-the-Beltway Democrats—there is a level of passionate volunteerism at the grassroots of the Democratic Party not seen since 1968.

The context for an independent presidential bid is completely altered from 2000, when there was a real base for a protest candidate. The overwhelming mass of voters with progressive values—who are essential to all efforts to build a force that can change the direction of the country—have only one focus this year: to beat Bush. Any candidacy seen as distracting from that goal will be ex-coriated by the entire spectrum of potentially progressive voters. If you run, you will separate yourself, probably irrevocably, from any ongoing relationship with this energized mass of activists. Look around: Almost no one, including former strong supporters, is call-ing for you to run, compared with past years when many veteran organizers urged you on.

If you run, your efforts to raise neglected issues will hit a deaf-ening headwind. The media will frame you as The Spoiler. It's also safe to predict that you will get far fewer votes than the 2.8 million you garnered in 2000, and not only because your rejection of the Green Party raises expensive new hurdles to getting your name on state ballots. A recent online survey by the progressive news site *AlterNet.org* found that only one in nine respondents said they'd vote for you if you run this year, a 60 percent drop-off from the number who said they voted for you in 2000. If you run and get a million votes or fewer, the media will say it means your issues were not im-portant. This can only hurt those causes, not to mention the tangi-ble costs another run may impose on the many public-interest groups tied to you.

You have said your candidacy could actually help Democrats by raising issues against Bush that a Democratic candidate would avoid and by boosting turnout for good candidates for the House and Senate, where the slender bulwarks against Bushism must be reinforced. But these arguments do not compel a candidacy by you. As a public citizen fighting for open debates and rallying voters to support progressive Democrats for Congress, or good Independents or Greens for that matter, you can have a far more productive impact than as a candidate dealing with recriminations about being a spoiler or, worse, an egotist. And the very progressives distressed by the prospect of your candidacy would contribute eagerly to have that voice amplified.

And if you think that this year you can help the anti-Bush cause by running and peeling off disgruntled Republicans, McCainiacs, Perotistas, and the like while not disrupting the Democratic charge, please be honest with yourself. Once upon a time, maybe as late as 1992, when you dallied with a "none of the above" campaign and got 2 percent of the vote in New Hampshire from write-ins in both the Democratic and Republican primaries, your appeal stretched across the political spectrum. No longer, alas. Your nephew, Tarek Milleron, wrote recently that if you run in 2004 it will be "the year of the Elks clubs, the garden clubs, meetings with former Enron employees, the veterans groups, Wal-Mart employees," not progressive super rallies. But how many Elks club presidents are inviting you to speak? How many veterans groups? Such relationships take time to build and can't be conjured out of thin air in the midst of a presidential campaign.

You once told us you play chess at many levels at once. For all we know, you're thinking of running hard and then, if the race is close, throwing your support to the Democrat in the final days. While such a tactic might make for a satisfying conclusion to an otherwise futile quest, we don't think it justifies the risks, antagonism, confusion, and contortions that such a run would entail.

Ralph, please think of the long term. Don't run.

Sincerely,

The Editors

Whither *The Nation*? An Open Letter
By Ralph Nader
February 19, 2004

As I reread slowly your open letter, which kindly started and closed with your demand "Don't run," memories of past *Nation* maga-

zine writing, going back to the days of Carey McWilliams and earlier, came to mind. I share them with you.

Long ago the *The Nation* stood steadfastly for more voices and
choices inside the electoral arenas, which today are more dominated than ever by the two-party duopoly trending toward one-
party districts:

"Don't run."

The Nation's pages embrace large areas of agreement with the
undersigned on policy matters and political reforms, especially the
abusive power of Big Business over elections, the government, and
the economy:

"Don't run."

The Nation has been sharply critical of the Democratic Party's
stagnation, the corporatist Democratic Leadership Council and its
domination by Big Money. This is the same party that has just
ganged up on its insurgents and reasserted its established forces:

"Don't run."

The Nation has urgently reported on a tawdry electoral
system—ridden with fraud and manipulation—that discourages
earnest people from running clean campaigns about authentic ne-
cessities of the American people and the rest of the world:

"Don't run."

The Nation first informed me as a young man about the deliberate barriers—statutory, monetary, media, and others—to third
parties and independent candidates for a chance to compete, bring
out more votes, and generate more civic and political energies. This
led me to write my first article on these exclusions against smaller
candidacies in the late 1950s:

"Don't run."

The Nation has often encouraged the longer-run effect of small
candidacies (civil rights, economic populism, women's suffrage,
labor and farmer parties), which have pushed the agendas of the
major parties and sown the seeds for future adoption:

"Don't run."

The Nation has dutifully recorded the hapless state of the Democratic Party, which for the past ten years has registered more and
more losses at the federal, state, and local levels. The party even
managed to "lose" the presidency in 2000, which it actually won,
even with all other "what ifs" considered, both before (Katherine

Harris's voter purge), during (the deceptive ballots), and afterward (recount blunders by the party):
"Don't run."

The Nation has editorialized about the spineless Democrats who could have stopped the two giant tax cuts for the wealthy, the unconstitutional war resolution, the Patriot(less) Act, and John Ashcroft's nomination (to mention a few surrenders). Yet you have not pointed to any external ways to stiffen the resolve or jolt the passivity of Jefferson's party, which lately has become very good at electing very bad Republicans all by itself:
"Don't run."

The Nation believes this cycle is different and that the Democrats have aroused themselves. This view is not the reality we experience regularly in Washington. Witness the latest collapse of the party's opposition to the subsidy-ridden, wrongheaded energy and Medicare drug-benefit legislation—two core party issues:
"Don't run."

The Nation's venerable reputation has been anything but conceding the practical politics of servility, which brings us worse servility and weaker democracy every four years:
"Don't run."

The Nation has intensely disliked being held hostage to antiquated electoral rules, from the electoral college to the winner-take-all system that discounts tens of millions of votes. Such a stand would seem to call for candidates on the inside to highlight and help build the public constituency for change over time:
"Don't run."

It doesn't seem that *The Nation* would disagree with the conclusions of George Scialabba, who wrote last year in the *Boston Review*, "Two-party dominance allows disproportionate influence to swing voters, single-issue constituencies, and campaign contributors; it promotes negative, contentless campaigns; it rewards grossly inequitable redistricting schemes, and it penalizes those who disagree with both parties but fear to 'waste' their votes (which is why Nader probably lost many more voters to Gore than Gore lost to Nader)":
"Don't run."

The Nation's open letter does not go far enough in predicting where my votes would come from, beyond correctly inferring that there would be few liberal Democratic supporters. The out-of-power party always returns to the fold, while the in-power party sees its edges looking for alternatives. Much more than New Hampshire in 2000, where I received more Republican than Democratic votes, any candidacy would be directed toward Independents, Greens, third-party supporters, true progressives, and conservative and liberal Republicans, who are becoming furious with George W. Bush's policies, such as massive deficits, publicized corporate crimes, subsidies, pornography, civil liberties encroachments, sovereignty-suppressing trade agreements, and outsourcing. And, of course, any candidacy would seek to do what we all must strive for—getting out more nonvoters, who are now almost the majority of eligible voters:

"Don't run."

The Nation wants badly to defeat the selected president Bush but thinks there is only one pathway to doing so. This approach excludes a second front of voters against the regime, which could raise fresh subjects, motivating language, and the vulnerabilities of corporate scandals and blocked reforms that the Democrats are too cautious, too indentured to their paymasters to launch—but are free to adopt if they see these succeed:

"Don't run."

The Nation has rarely been a hostage to prevailing dogma and electoral straitjackets. Its pages have articulated many "minorities of one" over its wondrous tenure and has watched many of its viewpoints today become the commonplace of tomorrow.

I have not known *The Nation* to so walk away from those engaging in a difficult struggle it champions on the merits, in a climate of conventional groupthink—much less with a precipitous prognosis of a distant outcome governed by a multitude of variables. Discussions and critiques from a distance, after all, are a dime a dozen in an election year. O apotheosis of the exercise of dissent inside and outside the electoral commons since 1865:

"Don't walk."

Ralph Nader

2004 and the Left
By *Ted Glick*
Published on www.dissidentvoice.org, March 30, 2004

Two thousand and four is turning out to be an important political year in many ways. For those on the political left, the independent, non-Green Ralph Nader presidential campaign is bringing to the fore a number of important strategic and tactical issues, among them: an assessment of the danger—or not—of a second Bush administration; what our attitude should be toward progressives in the Democratic Party; the political and organizational nature of the kind of "third party" needed; and with whom in the process of party-building we should be willing to make alliances.

Democrats as Greater Evil?

I have been surprised over the past couple of days to read and hear committed leftists arguing that a Kerry administration would be "the greater evil," as one person put it in an e-mail, compared to Bush. Two days ago in New York City, Peter Camejo said, [and I am] quoting directly, "Kerry will be able to do what Bush wants to do better."

I find this point of view puzzling and troubling. I appreciate where it is coming from. I have certainly felt and thought from time to time that, as the saying goes, it is better to have the wolf out in the open (the Republicans) than in sheep's clothing (the Democrats), with the apparent sheep doing the dirty work cloaked by a veneer of progressivism. But an objective comparison of what the Bushites have done compared to what was done by the Republican-lite Clinton administration can only lead to one conclusion: a second Bush-Cheney-Rumsfeld-Ashcroft-Delay-Wolfowitz-etc. administration, emboldened by a successful reelection campaign victory, will be worse, in many cases much worse, on the vast majority of issues.

Indeed, Ralph Nader, the candidate of many of those on the left who say there is virtually no distinction between the two corporate-dominated parties, has said over and over again that his primary reason for running is to "retire Bush," to "open a second front" of the anti-Bush campaign. Although his tactics in doing so are extremely problematic (see below), the fact that he has been so consistent on this point has apparently not influenced many of his supporters on the left who see virtually no difference between the Democrats and the Republicans. It is a strange thing to observe.

Democrats Far from Monolithic

I think we need to open up a national discussion about the nature of the Democratic Party and, indeed, what is happening within it as far as an upsurge among progressive Democrats angry at its leadership's collaboration with Republicans. One example is what happened in October of 2002 when, because of the massive grass-roots pressure of the peace movement, 156 members of Congress voted against giving Bush the authority to go to war against Iraq. One was an independent, six were Republicans, and one hundred and forty-nine were Democrats.

Another example is the fact that, of the fifty-five or so members of the Congressional Progressive Caucus (some of whom are solidly progressive, others not so much), not a single one is a Republican.

And of course there is the phenomenon of the Howard Dean movement and the reality that the political tone of the Democratic Party debates in the last half of 2003 and early 2004 were much more progressive than we saw in 1999–2000.

A progressive political party that does not take these realities into account in determining strategy or, worse, that acts and speaks as if these facts are not facts, will be a political party that is marginal and of little effect.

My twenty-nine years of involvement in organizations committed to the building of an alternative to the Democrats and Republicans have convinced me that there are three mutually reinforcing, overall tasks which we must be about if we are to ever get to the point of having a progressive party which can actually challenge for power:

1. We must run candidates on "third-party" lines and build independent organizations engaged in grassroots organizing around the issues affecting working people. We need candidates willing to

stand up and be crystal clear about their allegiance to the interests of the people and our seriously endangered ecosystem and not the corporate-dominated parties, able to demonstrate that there is a base of voting support for independent candidacies. As much as possible there should be connections between the electoral and the nonelectoral activity.

2. We must be about the process of changing the electoral rules of the game. We must move from winner-take-all to the use of instant runoff voting and, longer-term, proportional representation. We need public financing of elections. These are the two electoral reforms that can do the most to open up the political system to those who have been historically disenfranchised.

3. At the same time, we must pay careful attention to the struggle within the Democratic Party between its progressive and Democratic Leadership Council wings. We need to maintain our connections with those with whom we share generally similar positions on the issues (as in the Kucinich and Sharpton campaigns). Over time, if we do our first two tasks well, there will be an increasing number of Democrats who become former Democrats as they come over to our side. At some point we can expect a major rupture between the progressive and DLC wings and the possibility of a massive new independent force emerging if we keep building political pressure from the outside, demanding that the Democrats take progressive positions, which in many cases they will either not do or do to a minimal extent.

The United States of America is not Western Europe, Latin America, South Africa, New Zealand, or any of the many countries in the world which use some form of proportional representation. We have an anachronistic, nineteenth-century, winner-take-all electoral system which makes our electoral tasks much, much more difficult. That reality must be taken into account as we work to change it. Ideological or tactical rigidity ensures, absolutely guarantees, that we will never get out of this electoral straitjacket.

Political and Organizational Principles

There are certain principles, however, that must undergird our efforts. Politically, our independent political movement and its organizational expressions must be against racism, sexism, homophobia, and ageism. We must oppose corporate globalization and imperialism, which widen the gulf between the super-rich tiny minority and the vast world majority. We must oppose militarism and wars of occupation for national or corporate domination. We must support various efforts to democratize our political and economic system, including the strengthening of the right of workers to organize. We must call for a crash program to move immediately from the use of fossil fuels to clean energy sources. We must build our movement and its organizations in a fully democratic way.

One would think that these would not be controversial points among progressives. Most are not. But the sad fact is that, based upon the platform put forward on his Web site (www.votenader. com), Ralph Nader's campaign is seriously deficient when it comes to issues of racism and sexism.

As of Monday, March 29, over a month after Nader announced his plans to run as an Independent, his "Ralph Nader Stands with the People" Web site section takes no positions on a number of basic issues of importance to communities of color and women. Among them:

Police brutality. Affirmative action. Reparations. Immigration and immigrant rights. Reproductive rights. Violence against women. Racial profiling of African Americans and Latinos. Land loss by Black farmers. Native American treaty rights and issues.

Sprinkled throughout this platform are references to race/culture and gender issues in the context of the overall progressive populist character of the platform. Nader, to his credit, does specifically refer, in the context of his opposition to the Patriot Act, to "Americans of Arab descent and Muslim-Americans feeling the brunt of these dragnet, arbitrary practices." He calls the death penalty "racially and class unfair." He spells out the higher rates of unemployment for African Americans and Latinos. He uses the words "environmental racism" in the context of his environmental plank. He calls for "equal pay for women, childcare." But that's about it.

During Nader's 2000 presidential campaign he was much better on issues of specific concern to people of color and women. One of the major reasons for this was that, during and after his 1996 effort, he was criticized both from within and outside the Greens for his refusal to address any issue other those which were about corporate power, by and large. It appears that, regrettably, Ralph did not internalize those criticisms and that the much better politics of 2000 had more to do with the platform and input of the Green Party on whose line he was running.

Organizationally, the Nader presidential campaign has been set up as a completely top-down operation controlled by one man, rather than emerging as a result of the Green Party's internally democratic political process.

Questionable Alliances

Nader says that the reason he had to go independent and not participate in the Green Party's internal process was because the Green National Convention is happening too late. But the fact is that Nader was consulted before that date was set: he was given three possible dates it could happen, and he chose the latest dates, the ones on which it is happening, the same last weekend in June as the 2000 Green Party National Convention in Denver, Colorado, where Nader was nominated!

I have come to the conclusion that, most likely, the major reasons for Nader's decision not to run as a Green were political concerns about the Greens' holistically progressive set of positions and organizational concerns that he would have to "share power" with others he would not personally choose for his presidential campaign organization.

Instead, Ralph has brought into his campaign people like Pat Choate, key Pat Buchanan backer in 2000, Russell Verney, key organizational operative for Ross Perot, and members of the completely opportunistic and divisive Fred Newman/Lenora Fulani/New Alliance Party/Committee for a Unified Independent Party group.

Strategically, he has prioritized outreach to alienated Republicans, conservative independents, and the Reform Party constituency as his contribution to getting Bush out of office. Perhaps this helps to explain his serious weaknesses on issues of racism and sexism.

So far the evidence of every poll that I have seen is that Nader is wrong when he says that he will be attracting more Republican than Democratic votes. The latest one, as this is being written, is a

Zogby poll from a week ago which shows Kerry ahead of Bush in a two-person race, 48–46, but tied when Nader is included, 46–46–3. Even if Nader turns out to be right on this question, what is he building for the long haul, other than a personal following? The Green Party and independent progressives should not be aligning themselves within a political-party-like campaign with people and political forces like Choate, Verney, and Newman. Such an alliance, if it happened, would be a classic example of an unstable and seriously problematic tactical alliance that will go nowhere afterward. On issues like electoral reform, fine, but these are not the political forces we should be aligning with as we work toward a strong and principled independent political party. Our focus should be on outreach to and the building of working relationships with activists in communities of color, the women's movement, working-class-based community organizations, groups like the Labor Party, lesbian, gay, bisexual, and transgendered people—in other words, with constituencies which are generally progressive.

No-Name Candidacies

So what do I think we should do in 2004?

I have been publicly writing and saying for a year and a half that the Green Party should run a presidential candidate in 2004. I was open to Nader being such a candidate until I heard him speak in mid-December and began to realize that this was a different person than the one I actively supported in 2000. I did what I could to urge Cynthia McKinney to run, but she ultimately decided not to.

So since the beginning of the year I have been supporting former Green Party national counsel David Cobb (www.votecobb.org).

I support David because he has put building the Green Party, the consistently progressive Green Party, as his top agenda item if he is chosen as the GP presidential candidate. He has also prioritized running his campaign in a way which contributes to getting Bush out of office. He openly supports what he calls a "strategic states" campaign, a much preferable option to working with ex–Reform Party types, and prioritizing outreach to Republicans and conservative independents.

Some call David a "no-name" candidate. I suppose he is, compared to Nader's name recognition, ability to get national press, and ability to raise money. If those are the primary considerations, then David is not your candidate.

I know something about "no-name" candidacies. I was one in 2002 when I ran as the Green Party of New Jersey's candidate for U.S. Senate against corrupt Bob Torricelli and multimillionaire Doug Forrester. I was virtually unknown by the New Jersey electorate, other than among some progressives. I had lived in New Jersey less than four years when I made the decision to run. And yet, by mid-September, I was at 3 percent in a Zogby poll, and an internal, low-budget poll we did had me at 7–8 percent. We were excited and hopeful about the possibilities for a strong showing in November. My campaign manager thought 5–10 percent was a realistic possibility, and I agreed.

Then Torricelli dropped out in late September and the Democrats brought in relative "white knight" Frank Lautenberg, a popular, former three-term U.S. senator, to replace him. My poll numbers went down to 1 percent, and I ended up with 1.2 percent, 25,000 votes.

But then came 2003, and the defection because of my campaign, as he explained it, of Democratic State Assemblyman Matt Ahearn to the Green Party. Over the course of 2003, as the state coordinator, I worked with Matt and others in the Green Party of New Jersey leadership organizing workshops and providing support to prospective candidates, and we ended up with forty-nine Green Party candidates. Thirty-nine were candidates for State Assembly and Senate, a huge increase over the last state election, and the average percentage of the vote was twice as high as the last comparable election. Many of our municipal candidates got double-digit percentages, some in the mid-thirties.

So my "no-name" candidacy seems to have had a very positive impact in building the Green Party of New Jersey.

It's time for the Green Party to move beyond its Ralph Nader phase. Ralph has done much over the past seven years to help us get to this point, but a positive has turned into a likely negative. There are over two hundred Green Party members elected to local office throughout the country. Nader had little to do with the vast majority of those victories. He has made his decision that he is taking another road in 2004. Let's forge our own, one true to our political principles and commitment to democracy.

Endorse Nader

By Howie Hawkins
Green Horizon Quarterly, *Summer 2004*

The Bush–Kerry presidential race in 2004 is looking more and more like the Nixon–Humphrey race in 1968. The U.S. has launched an aggressive war in a far-away country. Domestic dissent from the war is growing rapidly. And both major party candidates support the war.

But there is one major difference in 2004. The U.S. has an anti-war party—the Green Party—with enough of a voter base and the ballot lines to have a real impact on the election.

However, with radical conservatives in the White House, the Green Party is under enormous pressure from the social movements they hope to represent politically and from the liberal intelligentsia and the corporate media to support the Democratic presidential candidate. In response, various proposals have been put forth by Greens for a "safe-," "smart-," or "strategic-" states campaign in which the Greens would not campaign in the so-called "battleground" or "swing" states where they might "spoil" Kerry's chances. Two principal reasons are put forth for a safe-states strategy.

Anybody But Bush

One reason is the Anybody-But-Bush argument: removing Bush from the White House trumps all other progressive objectives in this election. This argument crashes on the fact that John Kerry has supported the principal elements of Bush's agenda, including the overt and covert wars for regime change in Afghanistan, Iraq, Syria, Haiti, and Venezuela; the repressive Patriot Act; the "fast-track" bills of 2001 and 2002 authorizing Bush to expand NAFTA/WTO-type trade agreements without congressional review; and the No Child Left Behind bill creating federal mandates for high-stakes testing in public education.

Moreover, for more than two decades the Democratic Party, including John Kerry, has been busy working hand in hand with the Republicans to dismantle the New Deal/Great Society legacy that was the Democrats' only claim to progressive politics. Both major parties share a bipartisan consensus around neoconservative militarism and neoliberal state management of the capitalist economy. Despite its rhetoric of limited government, neoliberal policies of regressive taxes, social spending cuts, deregulation, privatization, corporate-managed trade, and corporate welfare boil down to state-guaranteed welfare for the rich and state-enforced free-market austerity for working people. And neoliberalism depends on the neoconservatives' militaristic means of enforcing its economic policies. As *New York Times* columnist Thomas Friedman, a pro-Democratic proponent of neoliberalism, put it in his "Manifesto for a Fast World" (*New York Times Magazine*, March 28, 1999): "[T]he hidden hand of the market will never work without a hidden fist.... The hidden fist that keeps the world safe for Silicon Valley's technologies is called the United States Army, Navy, and Marine Corps."

If the Democrats have not resisted Bush and the bipartisan consensus around militaristic neoliberalism during the Bush Jr. administration and for more than two decades before, there is no reason to start counting on the Democrats to resist now.

Anti-Green Backlash

Many safe-states advocates concede that Anybody But Bush is a weak argument. They put forth a second argument for a safe-states campaign: the Greens cannot afford to alienate the social movements in which Anybody-But-Bush sentiment is strong. They argue that the Greens must adopt a safe-states strategy to deflect the liberal backlash against the Greens that blames Nader and the Greens for supposedly enabling Bush to beat Gore in 2000.

The role of the Greens is not to reflect reality, but to change reality. Even if the social movements upon which the Greens hope to base their political fortunes are supporting the Democrats, that doesn't mean the Greens should, too. That is how the populist, socialist, farmer-labor, and progressive parties disappeared—they followed the union leadership into the Democratic Party. That is how the votes of the progressive social movements since the 1960s stopped making political gains—their leaders were co-opted into the Democratic Party, which takes their movements' votes for granted.

But in fact reality is more favorable to the Greens than the anti-

Green backlashers would have us believe. The backlash is not strong in the grassroots of the social movements. From my experiences in door-to-door canvassing and petitioning and in social-movement meetings, as well as observing national opinion polling about whether Nader is to blame for Bush and whether he should run in 2004, it is clear that the backlash against Nader and the Greens is not deep or wide. With the corporate media repeating their anti-Green, anti-Nader drumbeat ad nauseam, the backlash is coming mainly from the "liberal intelligentsia," as Nader refers to them.

I prefer to call them the "professional liberals." They are the paid officers and staff of the unions, community organizations, environmental groups, women's groups, civil rights groups, and liberal think tanks. Their social networks and career interests tie them to Democratic administrations. Their professional peers are Democrats. Their grants and jobs in Democratic administrations are at stake. They are naturally going to be the most vocal in the counter-attack against the Greens and will be the last progressives to break with the Democratic Party. The Greens should stop worrying about what the professional liberals think and focus on taking their message to the rank and file of the unions, the environmental groups, people-of-color communities, and so on, because the Democrats are taking their votes for granted.

A Green safe-states strategy would only encourage the anti-Green backlash. It will show its proponents that they can intimidate the Greens out of competing in elections where the Green candidate might hurt the Democratic candidate. An all-out Green presidential campaign, on the other hand, would demonstrate the clear choice between the Green platform of peace, justice, democracy, and ecology and the militaristic neoliberalism of both corporate-sponsored parties. An all-out Green campaign could win over many in the rank and file of the social movements from underneath the professional liberals in their formal leadership, and should create a crisis of conscience among those in leadership who still have any real commitment to progressive principles.

Nominate Cobb or Endorse Nader?

The presidential options for the Greens in 2004 have now distilled down to two: nominate David Cobb or endorse Ralph Nader's independent candidacy.

These options revolve around three issues: impact, election strategy, and party-building.

The U.S. presidential election is now a three-way race between Bush, Kerry, and Nader. Nader is in the middle of this race because the polls show that, at the least, he has enough to "spoil" the election for Kerry. That fact alone makes Nader's candidacy a topic of debate in the media and on the street.

There is no evidence that a Green Cobb candidacy will have any impact on the national election, particularly if Cobb does not run all-out in battleground as well as "safe" states. The implicit message will be that the Greens really want Kerry to win. The minute the Greens take that position is the minute the media and the general public will stop paying attention to the Greens in the presidential election. We will be irrelevant to the outcome.

If the Greens want to have an impact on this election, endorsing Nader's independent candidacy is the only option we have.

Could Nader Win?

Furthermore, Nader's impact could be far greater than that of a potential spoiler for Kerry. The 2000 National Election Survey data show that only 9 percent of voters who preferred Nader actually voted for him. Fifty percent of Nader supporters didn't vote at all. Twenty-six percent of Nader supporters voted for Gore as the lesser evil to Bush. And 19 percent of Nader supporters voted for Bush as the lesser evil to Gore.

If all the voters who preferred Nader had voted for him in 2000, he would have won the election, receiving 54 million votes to Bush's 43 million and Gore's 38 million (if we add the Nader supporters who voted for their lesser evil to Nader's total and subtract them from Bush and Gore's totals). (These numbers are derived from Harvard political scientist Barry Burden's 2001 study of the National Election Survey data: "Minor Parties in the 2000 Presidential Election," see http://psweb.sbs.ohio-state.edu/faculty/hweisberg/conference/burdosu.pdf.)

In 2004, with antiwar sentiment rising and Nader the only antiwar candidate, Nader could well rise into serious contention. It would be a tragedy if the Greens were on the sidelines in such a race supporting another candidate. But whether or not that scenario unfolds, the role of the Green Party should be mobilizing that latent majority who prefer Nader/Green policies, not running an unknown candidate because we fear spoiling the election for Kerry and the Democrats who oppose almost everything the Greens stand for. A strong vote for Nader will be a victory because it will help set the national political agenda just as Perot's 19 percent showing in 1992 compelled both major parties to rush to balance the federal budget.

David Cobb has run a good, energetic primary campaign, with visits to a majority of the states, a great Web site, and lots of local media coverage. He has listened to Greens and adapted his message accordingly, now emphasizing the party-building role his campaign could play over his original safe-states strategy, which itself has been nuanced to accommodate the needs of each state, for example, agreeing to run hard in the battleground state of Iowa because the Green ballot line there depends on the presidential election result.

Party Building and Unity

But Cobb's party-building argument is weak. Greens can run candidates for local, state, and congressional offices all over the country to recruit new people into the party, get our issues into the media and public debate, and achieve other party-building goals. Indeed, these locally based races will be able to accomplish these objectives better because such candidates may well be a factor in these elections while Cobb will be marginal to the Bush–Kerry–Nader race.

If the Greens endorse Nader and are the most visible force in the Nader campaigns of each state and community, Nader supporters can easily be recruited to the Green Party to continue these politics after the election. The Nader campaign will be a far bigger magnet for new people than a Cobb campaign simply because it will affect the outcome of the national election and receive corresponding massive media attention.

Whatever the Greens decide at their convention in Milwaukee, it is important that all sides maintain organizational unity and cooperation despite differences on the nomination question. The Greens have come too far over the last twenty years to split over one nomination in one election.

Letter to *The Nation*
By Peter Miguel Camejo
June 17, 2004

The Nation has taken the lead in liberal Democratic Party circles in opposing Ralph Nader's independent candidacy and the Greens' running a presidential slate. It seems that *The Nation*'s candidate is John Kerry and it hopes to help him win by silencing anyone who truly opposes Bush's policies. It urges a vote for Kerry, who voted for the Patriot Act, for "unequivocal support" of the Iraq war, who opposes the World Court, opposes the Kyoto Protocol, and so on.

The editors want to help Kerry win by preventing any candidate from running who is for peace and democracy. So those who disagree with *The Nation* have no choice, no one to vote for. This reflects tremendous arrogance toward American voters because it is essentially the voters whose rights they would deny. They want to force these voters to vote against what they believe. To justify this policy, the editors hide behind the undemocratic, winner-take-all, no-runoff electoral laws. And these undemocratic electoral policies are fully supported by their candidate and party, Kerry and the Democrats (see www.avocadoeducationproject.org).

The Nation has joined the chorus of those blaming Nader for Bush's selection. Seven million Democrats voted for Bush in 2000, more than two hundred thousand in Florida alone. We are still looking for one Green who voted for Bush. The Democratic Party's campaign's blaming Nader for Bush is a transparent attempt to teach our citizens who question the two-party system that they must not dare challenge these two corporate parties. "It's either the Democrats or you get a Republican," they are told. "Learn to submit to the rule of money. If you challenge them it only gets worse. Remain silent and accept whatever the Democrats give you!"

The Nation's hostility toward the Green Party is reflected in its coverage, for example, of the gubernatorial recall election in California. For the first time, a party to the left of the Democrats, the Green Party, was included in nationally televised debates. In the eight months of the recall election, *The Nation* avoided any mention of the Green Party or its candidate, myself. All the major papers across the country and every mainstream TV station reported on all six "major" candidates. But like Stalin's servile editors, *The Nation* carefully edited out the Green candidate from its cover story ("California Chaos," September 1–8, 2003), which showed pictures of all the major candidates minus the Green.

When historians look back, they will marvel at how presenting candidates who will fight for democracy and peace in the 2004 elections was opposed by so many who claimed to support those goals. Just as today we look back in disgust when, 130 years ago, *The Nation*, in a different context, opposed rights fo African Americans, whom it called "the least civilized race in the world."

It's Not Easy Being Green
The Nation *Editors reply to Peter Miguel Camejo*
June 17, 2004

Peter Camejo has many strong opinions—for which we admire him—a few of which are even correct. Others are not. It is misleading to describe our coverage of the Green Party as scanty or hostile or to say we support the major-party duopoly. A glance at our archives reveals extensive reporting on Greens, including this mention of Camejo, from Marc Cooper ("California's Gray Politics," August 19–26, 2002): "With the two major-party candidates inspiring little excitement or loyalty, the November election ought to be fertile territory for third-party movements like the California Green Party. But while recent statewide polls show a surge of support for third-party contenders, Green gubernatorial candidate Peter Camejo, a Marxist-Leninist turned socially responsible investment banker, has yet to emerge from anonymity; his support is estimated at no more than 4 or 5 percent."

We're sorry Camejo found us insufficiently enthusiastic about his candidacy during the recall fight. We tended to focus on which candidate would capture the governor's office in Sacramento rather than on the fortunes of a minor party. Camejo himself embraced that sensible logic in the campaign, when he said he would "not condemn those voters who feel forced to vote for a Democrat like Cruz Bustamante."

On presidential politics we disagree. We believe the number-one priority this November is to defeat George W. Bush. To that end, we have criticized Ralph Nader's decision to run. We have not, as Camejo charges, editorialized against the Greens' running a presidential slate, especially if the party is wise enough to choose a candidate and strategy that avoid tipping the race to Bush in battleground states. Judging from the delegate count as the Greens convene their National Convention in Wisconsin, it seems that the bulk of Camejo's party may agree.

Do we think winner-take-all systems are the best choice? No, and over the years we have run several articles and editorials supporting instant-runoff voting and other forms of proportional representation. Unfortunately, this November we have to deal with the voting system in place. In the end, the voters will of course make up their own minds, and despite Camejo's overheated imagination, no *Nation* editors will be standing at voting booths preventing them from choosing whom they wish. Also, The Nation has not in its editorials blamed Nader for 2000.

As for our California-recall cover: Camejo's thunderous invocation of Stalinist airbrushing strikes us as overwrought, but we are sorry he feels slighted by not being included on it. Our satiric movie-poster graphic, which—along with candidates Larry Flynt, Gary Coleman, and "the Terminator"—featured the headline "California Chaos: A Political Epic With a Cast of Thousands," may have been in questionable taste, but it was scarcely a thought crime.

The Editors

CHAPTER THREE

The Milwaukee Convention

Green Party Unity

By Peter Miguel Camejo
Circulated online, June 14, 2004

As we enter the last two weeks before our National Convention the Green Party is clearly divided. No single position regarding how we should participate in the 2004 presidential elections has a consensus.

The current political climate has forced us to deepen our discussion around issues such as lesser-evil voting and long-term strategies for building the Green Party. We are facing unprecedented, relentless attacks from the Democrats (and some ex-Nader supporters) accusing the Green Party and Nader of having "elected" Bush in 2000.

The fear that the Green Party might be perceived as reelecting Bush in 2004 led a group of eighteen Green activists to sign a statement saying that voting for a Democrat (i.e., the lesser of two evils) in some states is the best strategy for building the Green Party this year. The signers of this statement included well-known Greens such as Medea Benjamin, Dean Myerson, John Rensenbrink, Anita Rios, Steve Schmidt, Ted Glick, and many others. Their presentation is clear and to the point.

In response to their position, other Greens presented an analysis in the Avocado Declaration stating that lesser-evil voting is misguided and will block the development of the Green Party. The Avocado Declaration was also signed by a large number of Greens, including well-known activists such as Mayor Jason West, Donna Warren, Matt Ahearn, Howie Hawkins, Marybeth Wuerthner,

Linda Schade, Forrest Hill, Jo Chamberlain, and Steve Welzer. Some Greens worked in the Democratic Party primary campaigns of Dennis Kucinich and Howard Dean. Some are calling for voting for Kerry, and some favor our party not running or endorsing any candidate.

Greens Are Deeply Divided

We are approaching the National Convention unusually divided. I believe, however, that there is a way for us to reach a substantial consensus and come out of the convention united.

I am calling for the national nominating convention to endorse both Cobb and Nader equally—and to allow each state to decide whether to put David Cobb, Ralph Nader, or "no candidate" on their ballot line.

Such an agreement will result in four candidates—two presidential and two vice presidential—campaigning for peace, the rule of law, abolishing the USA PATRIOT Act, defending our liberties, supporting fair taxes, promoting free elections (IRV and PR), fighting for alternative energy, raising the minimum wage, protecting human rights and those of immigrants, and defending our planet. Instead of Greens walking out of the convention divided and fighting each other behind different candidates, we could adopt a win-win solution, allowing us to close ranks to oppose the two parties of money and defend the Green Party.

This proposal—parity support for Cobb and Nader—would allow each state to nominate whichever candidate they feel would be most advantageous to have on their ballot ("Free States"). The national Green Party would agree to do whatever it could to ensure that the relevant state authority recognized that candidate as the standard-bearer of the Green Party in that state.

By uniting behind a dual-endorsement agreement, we will come out of the convention with a strategy that the overwhelming majority of Greens can support. We will move forward to build the party together, accepting that we have differences and that these differences are normal in a democratic organization. The key is how we handle these differences to best protect and build our party.

Show Respect for Each Other

After the 2004 elections we must continue in a unified way to build our party on the local and state levels as we continue our discussions, debates, and forums on the best way to deal with the complexity of our undemocratic electoral system.

I dream of all the Greens who entered the presidential primary standing together at our convention saying "this, too, will pass—we are united behind the Green Party, and someday we will overcome and have free elections in America!"

In proposing this unity concept, let me say we should all congratulate David Cobb for the exceptional personal effort he has made to fight for the nomination; and also show respect for all the other candidates who entered the race: Lorna Salzman, Kent Mesplay, Paul Glover, Carol Miller, and others whose names are not yet listed on the Green Party of the United States (GPUS) Web site.

But we should also stand behind Ralph Nader, who has been the target of unfounded, relentless, and vicious attacks for having been our nominee in 2000. Nader is above 5 percent in many polls and has been as high as 12 percent among younger voters. His instrumental work in helping to create a new organization to fight for open debates, the Citizens' Debate Commission, has been an important contribution to the future of our party and democracy in America.

It is of historical importance that we assist, rather than block, Nader's chances of entering the presidential debates. After I was allowed to participate in the debates during the California recall election, the Green Party gained new respect among a wide range of voters. Similarly, the door may be opening for Nader to enter the presidential debates this election. Such an event would be unprecedented, exposing millions of Americans to a truly progressive viewpoint.

I call on the pro-Nader delegates to help enable David Cobb to run for president. He will be the first registered Green in the history of the United States to run for president. Let him go forward defending the Ten Key Values and our party. Let us help him, not oppose him or the Greens who have rallied around his campaign.

I also call on the Cobb delegates to respect the Greens who support Nader's independent campaign and help us to move that campaign forward as a voice for peace and justice and Green values—as an example of our willingness, in a nonsectarian manner, to join with other forces in the struggle for democracy and open elections.

Let us unite behind an agreement to endorse both Cobb and Nader. Such a conclusion to our convention, although unusual, is by far the best way to build the party, heal the wounds of our division, and unify our members. In the same spirit, we should also accept that some Greens will openly support Kerry. Let all Greens be free to continue our debate on these issues, but let us act in a manner that supports unity, while allowing all voices to be heard—consistent with our decentralized, grassroots party.

When the Green Party in California became divided over the recall of Governor Gray Davis last year, we reacted in a similar manner. We agreed that all Greens should act according to their conscience, but also agreed we should present our party's views in the recall election. Many Greens across the nation hardly knew how divided we were. Instead of fighting each other, we closed ranks, worked together to build the party, and continued to debate our political differences.

We need to act similarly in regard to the presidential election this year. The mass media and the Democrats are anxiously waiting to see us fighting each other. They want headlines like: "Nader Defeats Cobb" or "Nader Defeated." Instead, let's give them a big surprise: Cobb wins, Nader wins, Greens unite and launch a campaign for democracy, peace, and social justice in their battle to save our planet. There are no losers, only winners, among all of us who support the Ten Key Values!

A Few Thoughts for the Green Party

By Ralph Nader
Presentation at Green Party National Committee Meeting,
June 25, 2004

Dear Members of the Green Party,
Since 1996 we have carried the banner for free elections, clean elections, and the Ten Key Values for creating a just nation and world, all over our beloved country. But the corporate supremacists and

their two-party monopoly have sent the American people their own message—exclusivity, rigged elections, bought politicians, no political choices, increased concentration of power and wealth, hostility against workers, consumers, small taxpayers, the environment, community values, and a sane foreign policy. In fact—the Republican and Democratic parties have left *most voters* with only one incumbent party through redistricting and carving up the country into *one-party domination*. This is not even a semblance of democracy.

We have to break up this political plutocracy of the corporate government by *combining* our efforts to strengthen our opposition rather than *subtract from them*. There are too many good people in our country who know how to build the good society, who have real solutions—technical, social, and economic—to our problems, yet who have no political voice. *We strive to be their voice.* Our voice and your voice must find unity this weekend to extend our mutual call for action throughout our land.

In this spirit, I had the privilege of selecting Peter Miguel Camejo as my vice president. He brings so much to our candidacy—knowledge, experience, commitment, precision, civic courage, and over forty years of struggle for justice. He brings *bilingual eloquence* that for the first time will enable us to communicate Green values to thirty-nine million Latinos on a ticket already polling at 6–7 percent nationwide, and 12 percent among voters in their teens and twenties. He has run twice on the Green ballot for governor of California, distinguishing himself in the recall debates last year before a worldwide television audience.

As you know, what is already in place for our candidacy is important for local, state, and national Green Party efforts this year. You can make a decision tomorrow that would amplify your resources, visibility, and lasting ballot presence, and impact races at the state and local level, where building the Green Party is so critical. With the Republicans and Democrats supporting the war, the Patriot Act, and endless military and corporate welfare budgets, there is less and less left over for the people, their children, and their future, especially the tens of millions of poor people. And this corporate political duopoly is making American people pay for their own oppression, their own deprivation, their own disrespect. *Enough of the politics of fear.* It is time to shift the power. It is time for the solution revolution. It is time to choose between fear and fortitude.

On the exercise of free accessible elections at all levels, we are working to bring together third parties and independents.

I find Peter Camejo's Unity Resolution [see preceding chapter] as being in the interests of state Green parties, and as the best way to keep the Green Party together and advance common pursuits of justice. This resolution will make it possible for the Nader/Camejo campaign to support candidates, help preserve your ballot lines, and expand the resources of the Green Party. I have had some experience since 2001 in participating at forty-three fund-raisers and other activities for Greens in thirty-one states and the disenfranchised District of Columbia. I felt that this effort was both my duty and pleasure.

Many of you have urged my attendance. In my letters to Greens a few months ago I indicated that the Greens should make their decision by themselves, absorbing all well-intentioned advice, *on the merits*. There is no role for any dramatic arrivals from this quarter. If you decide on nominations, you will achieve different results than if you decide on endorsements. Some want you to lie low this election and not receive many national votes in the close states. This is a peculiar way to expand your party and establishes a poor precedent that the Democrats will seek to exploit. In any event, it is your decision as delegates to make a deliberative choice. *May your conscience be your guide.*

Thank you for reading these words. Best wishes for your convention,

Ralph Nader

P.S. I am on my way to our Oregon convention this Saturday, but will try to call your gathering this evening in the spirit of further solidarity.

The Green Party's Step Backward

By Alan Maass
Socialist Worker, *July 2, 2004*

The Green Party rejected the independent campaign of Ralph Nader at its convention last weekend. Instead, the Greens nominated a little-known attorney and activist from California, David

Cobb, as their presidential candidate.

Cobb won the party's presidential nomination by a narrow majority of the nearly eight hundred delegates voting at the convention, heading off a further vote that could have led to an endorsement of Nader's independent campaign. Nader and his vice presidential running mate, Peter Camejo—a Green Party veteran who ran twice for governor of California, winning more votes in these elections than any Green candidate in the U.S. other than Nader—had asked for an endorsement of their independent presidential campaign, rather than the party's nomination.

As close as the outcome was, the contrast between Cobb and Nader/Camejo—and what these campaigns mean for the future of the Green Party—was stark.

The most important issue is that Cobb and his supporters represent a so-called "safe states" strategy. The idea is that the Green Party presidential candidate should help defeat George Bush in the November election by not running an all-out campaign in "battleground states" where the Greens could do well enough to tip the balance to Bush—as Nader is accused of doing in the 2000 election.

An online columnist for a newspaper in nearby Racine, Wisconsin, summed up the implications when he suggested that Kerry supporters should "put on a Cobb button" to show Greens coming to the Milwaukee convention "where you stand." "If you want John Kerry to be president, you should hope David Cobb wins big in Milwaukee," wrote the columnist.

Medea Benjamin, a leader of Global Exchange and the Green Party's U.S. Senate candidate in California in 2000, says explicitly that Greens are justified in supporting a vote for Kerry, even though he is opposed to most everything on the Green Party agenda. "In the swing states, where this election's going to be determined, [Greens should] recognize that we owe it to the global community to get rid of George Bush," Benjamin says. "And if people in those swing states support that strategy of getting rid of George Bush, then voting for Kerry might be the strategic vote for them."

Supporters of Nader and Camejo at the convention rejected this argument. "We're the Green Party," Gloria Mattera, cochair of the New York State Green Party, told a Nader/Camejo rally. "It's not our job to elect a pro-war Democrat into the White House."

As Jason West, the Green Party mayor of New Paltz, New York, who came to national prominence by defying state law to marry gay and lesbian couples, put it: "I've been asking Democrats all over the country how the world would be a better place under President Kerry than President Bush, and no one's been able to give me a good answer. The problem with the "safe states" strategy is it leaves unchallenged the illusion that John Kerry is a progressive who is going to do something very different from what Bush is doing now."

At a time when even mainstream commentators are recognizing that the differences between the Republican and the Democrat in the 2004 presidential election are tiny compared to the policies they share in common, Cobb's nomination represents a retreat by the Green Party from offering a clear and uncompromised left-wing alternative to two parties of the status quo.

Cobb himself left it to supporters like Benjamin and New Jersey Green Ted Glick to push the "safe states" strategy. In his convention speech on Saturday, for example, Cobb didn't even raise the issue of the Greens' attitude toward Kerry and the Democrats, though it was the decisive political question. Instead, his campaign made Nader the main issue—criticizing the party's 2000 presidential candidate for seeking only an endorsement and not the Green nomination.

This was a play for support among what Green Party national cochair Ben Manski estimated was "a majority of Greens [who] would prefer to see a Green presidential nominee, but running in all states unflinchingly."

It's understandable that Greens would want to have Nader as their party's candidate, rather than simply endorse his campaign. What was surprising, though, was the number who spoke about Nader with the kind of venom normally associated with the Democratic Party's anti-Nader attack dogs. Complaints about Nader— that he's aloof and egotistical, that he won't join the Green Party, that he has refused to fund-raise for the Greens—circulated throughout the convention.

Actually, Nader's 1996 and 2000 presidential campaigns are, by most accounts, primarily responsible for quadrupling the number of organized state Green parties and guaranteed ballot lines in the last eight years. Nader wasn't a Green Party member in either campaign, but he promoted the party at every appearance. And since the 2000 elections, Nader raised more money than any Green at the national, state, and local levels, according to his campaign's estimates.

It's impossible to square the image of Nader as an egoist who hasn't lifted a finger to "build the Green Party" with the man who campaigned in all fifty states as a Green in 2000 and won 2.7 million votes in the best showing for a left-wing presidential candidate in half a century.

But Cobb's vice presidential running mate, Pat LaMarche of Maine, doesn't seem to care. As she told the *Milwaukee Journal-Sentinel*: "[Nader] walked away and said afterward, 'Oh, by the way, if you want to throw flowers at me, go ahead.'"

The contempt for Nader contained in this comment is typical among a layer of Greens and dates back to the aftermath of the 2000 election, when—even as Nader was being savaged for "throwing" the election to George Bush—leading Greens privately and sometimes publicly vented their complaints. Early on, Cobb associated himself with the attacks on Nader and used it to lay the basis for his campaign for the nomination.

Last year, when Nader was making his decision about whether to run for president again, eighteen well-known Greens, among them Ted Glick, issued an open letter calling on Nader not to run. Now, many of these figures are outspokenly critical of Nader for seeking the endorsement of the Green Party, rather than the nomination. In other words, their gripe with Nader isn't his relationship to the Green Party, but the fact that he ran at all.

Ross Mirkarimi, a cofounder of the California state Green Party, says he fears that the rejection of Nader because he isn't a Green Party member "may have been two steps backward." Mirkarimi pointed to European countries where left parties typically come together in alliances and coalitions to run common electoral campaigns. "I was a little bit turned off by this purist, insular attitude from other Greens saying, 'No hand holding with somebody from another party, you have to be a Green,'" he said. "That to me was strategically short-sighted."

Donna Warren, a Green from Los Angeles and leader of the party's Black caucus, is blunt. "What I think took place is that some small-minded Greens failed to see the big picture," said Warren, who won hundreds of thousands of votes as the party's candidate for lieutenant governor of California in 2002. "When they got to the convention and they saw an opportunity for our voice to be heard over a national stage, they decided that they wanted to keep it within their own confines."

The Greens' venting about Nader is especially cruel coming as the Democratic Party has stepped up its attack. As the Green convention was getting under way, the Congressional Black Caucus lured Nader to a meeting where members tried to browbeat him into withdrawing from the race.

Every effort of Nader's to get on the ballot is being challenged with all the resources that the Democrats can bring to bear. In the run-up to a Nader rally in Oregon last weekend—where the campaign hoped to draw more than one thousand people to meet a requirement for getting ballot access—the Democrats even brought out Howard Dean to attack Nader.

Meanwhile, the Democrats have openly intervened within the Greens, sponsoring the formation of a "Greens for Kerry" organization. But the Democrats haven't needed to devote their own operatives. Left-wing writers—including former Nader supporters like columnist Norman Solomon—have devoted numerous articles to making the case against Nader, and for a vote for Kerry to defeat Bush.

Camejo believes the Democrats' attacks on Nader set the stage for Cobb's challenge within the Green Party. "What's behind all of this is that they have friends who say that they'll be angry if the Greens support Nader," he says. "It's the pressure from the Democrats. They don't want to defend Nader. They want to hide. That's their policy. We're going to be the exact opposite."

Cobb's campaign to win the Green Party nomination has been years in the making. He was able to take advantage of a delegate structure, based partly on the undemocratic electoral college, which gives disproportionate weight to small states with weak state parties.

Thus, Cobb won about five thousand votes in the California Green Party primary, for less than 12 percent of the total. Fewer people than that voted for him in all of the other state caucuses and primaries combined leading up to the convention. Yet Cobb came to Milwaukee with nearly one-third of delegates already committed to him. Camejo, who won thirty-three thousand votes in the California primary alone, had less than half the number of delegates that Cobb did.

Camejo says that he and Nader have support from a majority of Greens at the grassroots. But this wasn't organized into representation or support at the convention. So the Nader/Camejo forces were fighting an uphill battle from the start.

Camejo proposed a unity resolution that would have produced endorsements for both Nader/Camejo and the Cobb campaign, leaving it up to state parties to decide which campaign would get the Green ballot lines. But Cobb rejected the compromise.

At a meeting of supporters after the convention vote, Camejo said that one battle ahead was to "organize those Greens who agree with us to make sure our voice gets heard."

Ross Mirkarimi says that "what's really at play here for the Green Party's long-term survivability is what happens on the local level. For the Green Party, concentrating hard on local partisan and nonpartisan races is where our bread and butter is." Still, the prominence of Nader's 2000 campaign was an undeniable asset to the Greens in local and state races—and catapulted the party into the national political debate.

As for what happens next, don't expect to hear much about the Cobb campaign—whether you're in a "safe" state or not. As one Green put it, "This campaign is a zero. It doesn't matter whether he campaigns in a safe state or a battleground state, because no one's going to pay any attention."

The nomination of Cobb is a step backward, away from an uncompromising challenge to the two-party "duopoly" and away from the prominence that the Greens have achieved, thanks in good part to Nader's 2000 campaign.

For the Nader/Camejo campaign, losing the Green Party endorsement means further difficulties getting on the ballot. Campaign officials say they have the resources to qualify as an independent campaign in most of the twenty-two states and the District of Columbia where the Green Party could have helped with its endorsement. California will present the biggest obstacle in terms of the number of signatures that need to be gathered.

In 2000, the Nader presidential campaign that won 2.7 million votes was much more than a Green Party operation. It drew supporters and volunteers from a much wider milieu—activists from the global justice movement and other struggles, alongside people new to any political activity who questioned corporate domination of the Washington status quo.

This time—despite the abuse heaped on him by Democrats and the pull of the "Anybody But Bush" syndrome—Nader continues to score more than 5 percent support in opinion polls as an anti-war, anti-corporate, pro-worker candidate. "I think that what happened here was a setback," Donna Warren said after the convention vote, "but I don't think that it's going to stop this campaign. It can't stop this campaign."

Green and Growing: An Activist Report Back from the Green Party Convention
By Ted Glick
June 29, 2004

The Green Party of the United States took a huge step forward on Saturday, June 26, in Milwaukee, Wisconsin. And it wasn't because the assembled delegates nominated someone, David Cobb, for president.

It was because of *how* it was done.

Going into the convention there was deep concern on the part of many Greens around the country about what was going to happen. For a year or longer there has been a sometimes-bitter internal debate about what should be done as far as "the presidential question." The perceived threat of an emboldened, second Bush administration has led some to work for Dennis Kucinich. A small group is now working for Kerry, although it is a very small group. Some have said that they will be voting for Kerry and are urging others to do the same.

The three main positions going into Milwaukee were to neither nominate nor endorse anyone, to nominate former GPUS general counsel David Cobb, or to nominate no one and then endorse Ralph Nader. A variant of the pro-Nader position, one pushed by California Green Party leader Peter Camejo, called for no nomination and then an endorsement of both Cobb and Nader.

A nominated candidate would get the Green Party ballot line in twenty-two states and Washington, D.C. An endorsed candidate would get some measure of political support but not necessarily a state Green ballot line; it would be up to each individual state party to determine what it wanted to do. In some states a lack of a nomination would probably mean no candidate would be on the ballot because of state election law.

The political struggle over these positions was intense, and it went down to the wire.

Convention week was begun on Monday with a huge announcement by Nader that he was choosing Camejo to be his vice presidential candidate. Score one for the pro-Nader forces.

Two days later Medea Benjamin, like Camejo a California Green Party leader, issued a statement headlined, "Want to Get Rid of Bush and Grow the Greens? Support David Cobb." Touché.

As people gathered in Milwaukee for the official first day of the convention on Wednesday, the battle was joined. A primary "stage" for the ongoing debate was the lobby of the Hyatt Regency hotel, a union hotel where many delegates were staying and where many meetings and caucuses were held. Proponents of Nader/Camejo and Cobb, as well as those supporting other positions, set up their leafleting and lobbying teams and for three days mingled with each other and with other delegates trying to gather the necessary 50 percent plus one needed to win.

Significantly, there were no physical altercations or, as far as I am aware, even any nasty emotional outbursts between those on the respective sides, while there was a great deal of reasoned discussion, as well as robust, vigorous, and competitive debate.

This same process of debate and discussion went on at state caucuses, in the room full of literature tables, in the hallways, and throughout the convention.

A Close Race

Everyone knew that it was close. David Cobb went into the convention with about 33 percent of the delegates pledged to him. Those supporting Nader, as well as candidates Camejo, Lorna Salzman, Carol Miller, and Paul Glover, all of whom personally supported Nader, had about 28 percent of the delegates. Twenty-three percent of the delegates were officially uncommitted, 12 percent were for no nominee, and the remainder were for Kent Mesplay and other candidates.

Thursday evening was set up by the Green Party convention planners as the one time prior to Saturday's decision-making when all the candidates would meet in an open forum. For close to two hours Camejo, Cobb, Mesplay, and Salzman (Miller and Glover were not there) answered a series of questions put to them by the moderator in front of a room completely jammed with many hundreds of delegates, observers, and press.

Camejo and Cobb, as the two main protagonists, were both "on their game." Both came across as articulate and passionate in support of their positions. Toward the end of the forum/debate, things got heated as Camejo accused Cobb of being a supporter of John Kerry and Cobb countered by articulating what he has been calling a "smart growth" strategy which prioritizes building the Green Party while also running a campaign which helps to get Bush out of office.

One piece of hard news emerged at the debate when Cobb announced that his campaign had chosen Pat LaMarche, a 43-year-old single mother of two and radio personality from Maine, to be his vice presidential running mate. In 1998, running as the Maine Green Party's candidate for governor, she received 7 percent of the statewide vote, winning ballot status for the party.

Friday morning began with the Cobb campaign distributing a statement they called "The True Position of the Cobb/LaMarche Campaign on the Iraq War: End the Occupation, Bring the U.S. Troops Home Now." The statement quoted from press releases issued in April and May and posted on the www.votecobb.org Web site, while also criticizing Camejo for "misrepresent[ing] the position of the Cobb/LaMarche Campaign on the Iraq war" at the Thursday evening debate.

Throughout the day the pro-Nader people distributed a leaflet urging those who supported Nader/Camejo to vote a certain way on Saturday. In the first round, they said, vote as mandated by your state. In the second round, when almost all states released delegates to vote their conscience, vote for no nominee, the Nader forces urged. If a majority on the second round voted no nominee, this would then allow for a vote to endorse Nader/Camejo, or endorse both Cobb/LaMarche and Nader/Camejo, in the third round.

In late afternoon both campaigns put out another piece of literature. The Nader campaign distributed a letter from Ralph Nader in which he explained that he would not be coming to the convention but articulated the rationale for why the convention should endorse him. Nader spoke later that evening via telephone hookup to a pro-Nader rally of, according to reports, about 200 delegates and observers.

The Cobb campaign leaflet highlighted what it called an inconsistency between Ralph Nader's position of trying to influence Kerry/the Democrats and "retire Bush," and Camejo' s position, articulated Thursday evening, that "Greens should never, ever vote for a Democrat." The leaflet asked, "What is the Nader/Camejo strategy?"

Day of Decision

As people began arriving at the Midwest Airlines Convention Center Saturday morning the politicking continued. Cobb forces were buoyed by an unexpected endorsement in that morning's major Milwaukee daily newspaper, the *Journal Sentinel*. The headline read, "David Cobb for the Greens."

The day's historic events began with the adoption of a comprehensive and impressive, updated national Green Party platform that had been worked on for many months with much input prior to Milwaukee from Greens all over the country. Then we got down to the main event.

Matt Gonzalez had been decided upon as the election administrator by the GPUS's National Coordinating Committee. Gonzalez is the chair of the San Francisco Board of Supervisors and nearly won last year in a nationally publicized election for mayor of San Francisco.

In the first round there were no major surprises. David Cobb led with 308 votes, followed by Peter Camejo with 119, Ralph Nader with 117, no nominee with 109, Lorna Salzman with 40, Kent Mesplay with 24, and various other candidates with smaller numbers, including Joann Beeman, a "favorite daughter" and elected drain commissioner from Michigan.

Both sides were nervous as Gonzalez adjourned the session for lunch. Over lunch caucusing continued with appeals to hold firm by Camejo to both the California and New York delegations, two Nader/Camejo strongholds. Cobb campaign leaders felt hopeful but not certain that they could win on the second round. The outcome depended primarily on how the 109 first-round "no nominee" votes were cast on the second round.

Prior to Saturday both the Cobb and Nader campaigns had "worked" the "no nominee" delegates. The Cobb campaign argued that those who held that position—people who, in general, wanted the Green Party to focus its limited resources on local campaigns this year—should see a Cobb nomination as their second preference, that a Nader endorsement would be a worse alternative for those who wanted to build up Green Party strength via local campaigns given David Cobb's first priority of using his campaign to build the Green Party.

The convention readjourned about 2:30 p.m. to start the second round of voting. It was reported that there were four options for delegates. One option was David Cobb. Another was no nominee. The third was Kent Mesplay, and the fourth was Joann Beeman. There were no other options because, unlike the first round, the convention rules mandated that only no nominee and candidates who signed a statement affirming that they would accept a GP presidential nomination would be eligible to receive votes after the first round. Cobb, Mesplay, and Beeman were the only candidates who signed that statement.

It was obvious to everyone that the big question was whether or not David Cobb and Pat LaMarche would be able to gain the additional seventy-seven delegates needed to have 50 percent plus one. If they failed to do so, that would give a major boost to the Nader/Camejo side and continue the voting into future rounds.

The first three states, Alabama, Arizona, and Arkansas, reported no movement toward Cobb. But the fourth state, California, was a different story. Cobb gained twenty-two votes as compared to the first round, going from thirteen to thirty-five. The pro-Cobb delegates cheered.

As the reports continued, a clear trend began to emerge. Cobb was holding his own in every state, gaining one, two, or three up until Maine, home state of Pat LaMarche, which thrilled the pro-Cobb delegates by going from seven in the first round to eighteen in the second.

A few rounds later, Minnesota gave Cobb an additional ten delegates as compared to the first round, and as the reports continued the Cobb vote kept gaining ground. By the time it got to Virginia, he was right there with, unofficially, seventy-seven additional votes. When Virginia gave him six more votes that pretty much sealed it. All that was needed was for the same trend to continue, for Cobb to lose no ground in the remaining four states.

When Wisconsin went 33–1 for Cobb, a gain of eight votes, everyone knew it was over. All that remained was for Texas, which had passed when they were called earlier, to announce that thirty-four of their thirty-five votes were for Cobb. Texas is where David Cobb was born, lived, and did Green Party organizing until a year or so ago.

For many the celebration began, genuine joy over a hard-fought victory. Hugs and kisses and dancing in the aisles erupted until David burst onto the stage and introduced Pat LaMarche for her first speech to the assembled delegates. Following it, David came to the podium and spoke graciously about Ralph Nader and Peter Camejo as he called for a strong campaign by the Green Party, indicating his intention to go to Ohio, Pennsylvania, "and New York, if you want me," to help efforts in those states to get Cobb/LaMarche on the ballot.

For others, the feelings certainly ranged from mixed to deep disappointment. But as the session was adjourned by Matt Gonzalez, many of us left the convention center feeling extremely proud not just about the results but about the political maturity displayed by the convention as a whole in the way we had just dealt with a hugely difficult, months-long, often-painful issue.

Green and Growing

This was an amazing week, an emotional roller-coaster for those of us immersed in it. For large numbers of the delegates, it was a strengthening experience and not just because we successfully navigated the dangerous shoals of decision-making regarding the big presidential question. There were the many dedicated activists we met from all over the country who we know will keep building this important organization at the key, local, grassroots level for months and years to come. There were the local Green elected officials like Matt Gonzalez, Jason West, Joyce Chen, and Brenda Konkel and many others that we met and interacted with, as well as the candidates running for office all over the country. There were the valuable workshops and caucuses on a whole range of issues, the great street party Friday evening, the general spirit of unity and common purpose that pervaded the deliberations. The women's caucus, youth caucus, and Black caucus all took steps forward. International visitors and speakers reminded us that we are part of an international movement worldwide and that we have major responsibilities to the world's struggling peoples and threatened ecosystem.

The numbers show it: there is clear, persistent, quantitative growth on the part of the Green Party of the United States, now with affiliates in forty-four states, with 205 Greens in office and ballot-qualified in twenty-two states and D.C. But just as important, Milwaukee '04 demonstrated that there is also qualitative growth.

As David Cobb said in his inspiring speech Saturday night, the Green Party is chock-full of "ordinary people doing extraordinary things." In this time of great danger but also great possibilities, this is no small thing.

How the Greens Chose Kerry over Nader

By *Walt Contreras Sheasby*
Published on www.unrepentantnadervoter.com, July 19, 2004

The battleground at the Green Party National Convention on June 23–29 stretched from the West (Oregon, Nevada, New Mexico) to the Great Lakes (Minnesota and Wisconsin) and the corners of the Atlantic coast (Maine and Florida). Those are the seven Unsafe States with Green ballot lines, and denying those ballot lines to Ralph Nader was the mission accomplished at the convention in Minneapolis. David Cobb won the election with 408 of 770 ballots cast, based on the strength of his support in places like Montana, Nebraska, Wisconsin, South Carolina, North Carolina, Georgia,

Tennessee, and, of course, his native state of Texas.[1] The urban branches of the party were overcome largely by bending the rural twigs sprouting in Bush country.

From the Green Politics Network to the Cobb/LaMarche Debacle

The convention result was largely engineered by veterans of the Green Politics Network (GPN), which was founded in spring 1992 by John Rensenbrink, Dee Berry, and others opposed to the "Fundi radicalism" of the early Greens. There had been a national Green organization called the Greens/Green Party USA since 1991, growing out of the Committees of Correspondence formed in St. Paul in 1984. The GPN, however, shunned these radicals and hoped to link up electoral-oriented pragmatic reformers into a confederation based on state parties rather than membership locals.

In 1995–96 many of the radicals balked at a presidential campaign, while others worked on the search for a candidate. According to Patrick Mazza of the Oregon Pacific Party, "In states such as Ohio and Texas, G/GPUSA activists blocked efforts to put Nader on the ballot."

Immediately after the election on November 16–17, 1996, an invitation-only meeting of sixty-two Nader supporters was held at the Glen-Ora Farm in Middleburg, forty miles west of Washington, D.C. This historic farm had been surveyed by George Washington at age sixteen. It seems appropriate now that after gathering in a room where JFK used to hold meetings after his election in 1960, many attendees then are now supporting another JFK in 2004.

When Howie Hawkins, a leader of the Greens/Green Party USA and a New York Nader campaigner came to Glen-Ora, he was blocked from entering on the first day, and on the second day, as Mazza put it, "Hawkins was told in no uncertain terms the new organization is a fait accompli."

Rensenbrink announced that it "has been a long, arduous, often agonizing journey," but the Middleburg Meeting "heralds the emergence, at last, of a viable, vigorous, and facilitative Association of State Green Parties (ASGP)."

Nader told the sixty-two ASGP founders at Middleburg that "whoever's going to go for the Democratic nomination in 2000 has got to realize they are going to lose if they don't stop the drift into the corporate maul."[2] The cards were all on the table four years before Nader's second Green campaign, but as the election neared November 2000, the GPN veterans and some Nader novices began to urge their candidate to take a dive.

Nader had written the forward to Rensenbrink's *Against All Odds: The Green Transformation of American Politics* in 1999, and had told left Greens that the author was a sterling radical and to be trusted, but within a year Rensenbrink was openly venomous toward his former mutual admirer. Rensenbrink conceals his personal rancor in a jumble of indictments that are taken at face value by the liberal media and Green novices: "[Nader] doesn't want to be a Green, he runs with his coterie rather than party organizers, he doesn't involve local Green leaders and he doesn't get the racial issue. I fear if Nader runs, he'll drag down every other Green in this country."[3]

As the A.P. wire reported on June 23, 2004, "Delegate John Rensenbrink of Maine said he was a Nader adviser but had to break with the candidate over his insistence on running an aggressive campaign in swing states, believing it could lead to Bush's reelection. While no backer of John Kerry, Rensenbrink believes the Democrat is the lesser of two evils." Apparently even less of an evil than Nader himself.

Pot-Boiling the Twigs

Various anti-Nader, Anybody-But-Bush, and openly pro-Kerry Web sites and listservs all tried to influence gullible Greens before the convention. The GreensforKerry.com Web site (registered through Go-Daddy.com) was revealed as belonging to NextGeneration.org, a campaign consulting firm mostly for environmental causes but also working for Democratic politicians.[4]

A mass e-mail letter was sent to Greens by Jeff Bennett in San Francisco, who claimed to be a member since 1998, saying: "It is shocking to me that the Green Party would even consider endorsing Ralph Nader for president this year.... But now I see that the Green Party leaders might not be working for environmental protections and social justice at all. Maybe they just want to break the two-party system, even if they break the planet in the process." No one in the Greens in the Bay Area recalled ever seeing or hearing the name of the sender.

Not to be outdone by covert Democrats, seven Green Party politicians, headed by David Segal, a city councilor in Providence, Rhode Island, formed Greens for Impact (GFI) to "encourage voters in swing states to vote for John Kerry in the general election." Segal revealed that the real aim of the Rensenbrinkians was not independent political action but dependent political action, as with the German Greens: "Though small, the Green Party sometimes has enough sway to change the outcome of an election, but as a party that does not believe in fascism and extortion, our segment of the progressive movement must work together with the dominant left-of-center party, as our fellow Green Party members in Europe and many other nations have done."[5]

The most ambitious effort was funded by George Soros through the Democrats' 527 groups,[6] three of which combined to focus their anti-Nader TV advertising firepower on six states that were decided by two percentage points or less in 2000—Wisconsin, New Mexico, Florida, New Hampshire, Iowa, and Oregon. In addition the groups formed TheNaderFactor.com to also beam Internet pleas by repentant Greens and Naderites.[7]

The Real Strategy

To deny those six or more states to Nader, primary battles had to first be won in as many of the forty-five states with delegates as possible, even though only twenty-three states have a ballot line at the moment. In fact, some of the key skirmishes were in states that failed to get a Green line this year, such as Texas and Illinois. Other delegates were selected by relatively small Green formations in the South, stretching from Arkansas, Tennessee, and Georgia to North Carolina and Virginia, all states without a ballot primary which nevertheless chose and sent delegates to keep Nader off the ballot in other states.

Belinda Coppernoll, secretary of the Green Alliance, the left tendency in the Green Party, and a delegate from Ellensburg, Washington, summed up the process:

> The GPUS Coordinating Council (aka GPCC), which is the national leadership and governing group, is made up of two GPUS reps from

each state; was heavily dominated by pro-Cobb leaders who pushed the pro-Cobb agenda for the last year relentlessly. Several in the GPUS leadership were responsible for Nader not seeking the GP nomination last fall when he went out on his exploratory committee. These same aggressive anti-Nader Greens dominated the Steering Committee as well, and the Rules/Procedures, Convention committees. They used their internal power to get the nominee they had pre-selected (Cobb) and tried to use a variety of manipulative tactics and undemocratic processes in their quest to stop Nader/Camejo from winning the GP endorsement or even sharing it with David Cobb, so there would be two progressive choices on the ballot lines. Little was fair or balanced in the conduct of this nominating election process.[8]

The unlikely candidate who defeated Nader, forty-one-year-old David Cobb, said that he would campaign vigorously for all Green candidates in the forty states not considered critical to the outcome of the presidential race.[9] He will be the Green Party candidate on the ballot in all the states that supported Nader, including the biggest, California, as well as Nevada, Utah, Arizona, New Mexico, Kansas, Oklahoma, Mississippi, Florida, Michigan, Pennsylvania, New York, and Vermont. The spectacle of rural states blocking progressive states is an old one in America: it appears in the guise of the electoral college, which overrides any popular vote. The breakdown of the delegate allocation at the convention reveals exactly how that worked.[10]

Had the contest been decided by "one person equals one vote," the Nader/Camejo ticket easily would have been the overwhelming winner; among Greens, the polls show 70 percent support for Nader.[11] While California only had about one-seventh of the delegates at the convention, they represent over one-half of the registered Greens in the country. David Cobb, a Texan who moved to California, won only 5,000 votes, or 10 percent, in the California primary. As a stand-in for Ralph Nader, Peter Camejo won 76 percent, or 33,000 votes, in the California primary, but nationally he had less than half the number of delegates that Cobb claimed. This was on the basis, in many cases, of meetings of less than a hundred Greens in various states without a ballot primary. Those who could afford to go were given delegate status, regardless of whether they faithfully reflected the vote on the candidates.

Moreover, many of the delegates claiming to favor other candidates or to be uncommitted in order to be sent to the convention may have intended to vote for Cobb all along, as soon as they were released from their state mandates after the first round of voting. Some of the most prominent longtime allies of John Rensenbrink, like Tony Affigne from Rhode Island, arrived in Milwaukee as nominally undecided delegates. In several states a significant number of Nader/Camejo or Lorna Salzman votes in the first round turned to Cobb/LaMarche votes in the second round.

As Kevin McKeown, mayor of Santa Monica, California, explained: "In the first round on Saturday, our California delegates were bound to the statewide primary results from March. California cast thirteen votes for Cobb out of our 132 delegate seats, based on his 10 percent showing in the California primary."

"In the second round, it became apparent that Cobb had organized at the county level, particularly in the Bay Area, to get his delegates appointed. When they were released from the primary vote mandate of all California Greens, they switched to Cobb." This meant an extra twenty-six votes for Cobb. "The shift in the California vote alone was enough to put Cobb over the top. If California had again voted the primary outcome of 10 percent Cobb in round two, Cobb would not have had a majority."[12]

As one delegate, Ken Smith, reported: "The only other person waiting with me was sitting two chairs over to my right, and she was our Lorna Salzman team leader. I could swear she also had a Nader/Camejo poster, but in the second round it somehow transformed itself into a Cobb sign.

"The first person to arrive on the left of this so-called Lorna Salzman California delegation row ... was Medea Benjamin. Medea placed three Cobb posters on the chairs to my left, and a second woman with a Cobb sign then sat down on my right. Now why would I think that maybe there was some type of a pre-planned conspiracy?"

In the decisive second round, in which Nader/Camejo delegates and those of other candidates supporting that ticket were asked to vote for no nomination, the tally was Cobb, 408; No Nominee, 308; Mesplay, 43; Beeman, 8; abstain, 3.

John Rensenbrink's Maine delegation cast all but one vote for Cobb. In Missouri, a state which has long had a large left Green community in St. Louis that is not actively involved in the party, Dee Berry of Kansas City delivered all her state's votes to Cobb.

Blair Bobier of the Pacific Green Party in Oregon delivered virtually all his state's votes to Cobb. Texas alone cast 34–1 votes for Cobb on the basis of a meeting not much larger than the number of delegates. Georgia chose its delegates at a small meeting far removed from Atlanta during the heightened security of the G8 Summit when travel and lodging were difficult to arrange. As a result, the Georgia State Green Convention that sent twelve delegates to Milwaukee—eleven obligated to voting for Cobb—had a grand total of seventeen people in attendance.

In Wisconsin, Minnesota, and Montana the influence of the old New Party chapters that entered the Greens there was decisive.

The Anybody-But-Bush syndrome prevailed at this convention, and John Rensenbrink was honored in the final moments with an orchestrated homage. The Greens will probably come to regret their rigging of the tally in order to stop Nader. The low vote in November for the Cobb/LaMarche ticket will disappoint and anger those Greens who have invested their hopes in the party. There will be a considerable price paid in ballot lines by the less-secure states who depend on a certain percentage of the vote to stay on the ballot.

On the other hand, it is clear that the Greens for Nader and the Green Alliance do not intend to leave the party or allow themselves to be pushed out by the Rensenbrink wing. To the would-be terminators, the left wing of the Greens promises, "We'll be back."

Suicide Right on the Stage:
The Demise of the Green Party

By Jeffrey St. Clair
Published on www.counterpunch.org, July 2, 2004

> "Ignorance of remote causes disposeth men to attribute
> all events to the causes immediate and instrumental:
> for these are all the causes they perceive."
> —Thomas Hobbes, *Leviathan* (1651)

So this is what alternative politics in America has degenerated to: Pat LaMarche, the newly minted vice-presidential candidate of the

Green Party, has announced that she might not even vote for herself in the fall elections. The Greens, always a skittish bunch, are so traumatized by the specter of Bush and Cheney that they've offered up their own party—born out of rage at decades of betrayal by Democrats from Carter to Clinton—as a kind of private contractor for the benefit of those very same Democratic Party power brokers.

Take a close look at what LaMarche, a not-ready-for-primetime radio "personality," had to say to say to her hometown newspaper in Maine only days after winning the nomination in Milwaukee.

"If the race is tight, I'll vote for Kerry," LaMarche said. "I love my country. But we should ask them that, because if Dick Cheney loved his country, he wouldn't be voting for himself."

This is the sound a political party makes as it commits suicide.

LaMarche's running mate, David Cobb, is no better. The obscure lawyer from Texas is a dull and spiritless candidate, handled by some truly unsavory advisers (more on them in future columns). In action, he functions as a kind of bland political zombie from a Roger Corman flick, lumbering across the progressive landscape from Oregon to Wisconsin and back again, to the tune of his liberal political masters. The tune? The familiar refrain of "Anybody But Bush."

Bland, yes, but it worked, thanks to the likes of Medea Benjamin and the pompous Ted Glick. At their recent convention in Milwaukee, the Green Party, heavily infiltrated by Democratic Party operatives, rejected the ticket of Ralph Nader and Peter Camejo in favor of the sour campaign of Cobb and LaMarche.

This won't harm Nader much. Indeed, it may liberate him. Free of the Green Party's encyclopedic platform, Nader can now distill the themes of his campaign to the most potent elements (war, jobs, corruption, and the environment) and, unburdened by the concern of party building, Nader can, if he chooses (and he should), focus his efforts only on the battleground states, where Kerry must either confront Nader's issues or lose the election. It's as simple as that.

The fatal damage in Milwaukee was done to the Green Party itself, where Cobb and his cohort sabotaged the aspirations of thousands of Greens who had labored for more than a decade to build their party into a national political force, capable of winning a few seats here and there and, even more importantly, defeating Democrats who behave like Republicans (cf. Al Gore). The fruits of all that intense grassroots organizing were destroyed in an instant. But behold: the rebuffed Nader continues to poll nearly 6 percent without the Green Party behind him. Yet, you can't discern Cobb's numbers with an electron microscope. Of course, the pungent irony is that's precisely the way Cobb and his backers want it. So, the Greens have succeeded in doing what seemed impossible only months ago: they've made the quixotic campaign of Dennis Kucinich, which still chugs along claiming micro-victory after micro-victory long after the close of the primaries (indeed there have been more victories after the polls closed than before), seem like a credible political endeavor. Of course, Cobb and Kucinich share the same objective function: to lure progressives away from Nader and back into the plantation house of the Democratic Party.

But at least Kucinich remained a Democrat. Cobb and LaMarche were supposedly leaders of a political party that formed not in opposition to Republicans, but from outrage at the rightward and irredeemable drift of the Democratic Party. Apparently, the Green Party has not only lost its mind, it's lost its entire central nervous system, including the spine—especially its spine. They've surrendered to the politics of fear. And once the white flag is raised there's little chance of recovering the ground you've given up.

Always nearly immobilized by an asphyxiating devotion to political correctness, the Green Party has now taken this obsession to its logical extreme by nominating a pair of political cretins at the top of its ticket. Under the false banner of the Cobb/LaMarche campaign, the Green Party is instructing its members to vote for its candidates only in states where their vote doesn't matter. This is the so-called safe-state strategy.

Safe? Safe for whom? Not for Afghan or Iraqi citizens. Not for U.S. troops. Not for the detainees at Gitmo, Bagram, or Abu Ghraib. Not for migrant farm laborers or steelworkers. Not for the welfare mother or the two million souls rotting in American prisons. Not for the spotted owl, the streams of Appalachia, or the rain forests of Alaska. Not for the residents of Cancer Alley or the peasants of Colombia or teenage girls slaving away in Nike's toxic Indonesia sneaker mills. Not for the Palestinians, the Lakota of Pine Ridge, or elementary school students from the hard streets of Oakland. Not for the hopeless denizens of death row or three-strikers in for life for a gram of crack or gays hoping to unite in marriage or even cancer patients seeking simple herbal relief from excruciating pain.

A crucial player in this unsavory affair was Medea Benjamin, the diva of Global Exchange. In rationalizing her decisive vote backing the Cobb/LaMarche ticket, Benjamin emitted this profundity: "John Kerry is not George Bush." Apparently, that tiny sliver of genetic variation is all it comes down to these days.

Yes, Medea, you're right. Kerry is simply Kerry, a bona fide war criminal, with a record of political infamy that is just as malodorous as that of George Bush—only it's longer. Over the past four years, Kerry has been complicit in the enactment of some of Bush's most disgusting policies. Indeed, these days Kerry offers himself up mainly as a more competent manager of the Bush agenda, a steadier hand on the helm of the Empire.

Kerry stands unapologetically for nearly every issue that caused the Greens to bolt the Democratic Party. He was present at the founding of the Democratic Leadership Council, the claque of neoliberals that seeks to purge the Democratic Party of every last vestige of progressivism and reshape it as a hawkish and pro-business party with a soft spot for abortion—essentially a stingier version of the Rockefeller Republicans.

Kerry enthusiastically backed both of Bush's wars and now, at the very moment Bush is signaling a desire to retreat, the senator is calling for twenty-five thousand new troops to be sent to Iraq, where under his plan the U.S. military will remain entrenched for at least the next four years.

Kerry supported the Patriot Act without reservation or even much contemplation. Lest you conclude that this was a momentary aberration sparked by the post–September 11 hysteria, consider the fact that Kerry also voted for the two Clinton-era predecessors to the Patriot Act, the 1994 Crime Bill and the 1996 Counter-Terrorism and Effective Death Penalty Act, which were just as bad if not worse.

Although he regularly hams it up in photo ops with the barons of big labor, Kerry voted for NAFTA, the WTO, and virtually every other job-slashing trade pact that has come before the Senate. Kerry, who has courted and won the endorsement of nearly every police association in the nation, regularly calls for putting another one hundred thousand cops on the streets and even tougher criminal sanctions against victimless crimes. He refused to reconsider his fervid support for the insane war on drug users, which has destroyed families and clogged our prisons with more than two million people, many of them young Black men, whom the draconian drug laws specifically target without mercy. Kerry backs the racist death penalty and mandatory minimum sentences.

A couple of weeks ago the Congressional Black Caucus jeered Ralph Nader when he spoke to them about his campaign, a bizarre reception for a man who has been a tireless advocate for civil rights and poor people. If this group of legislators actually cared about the welfare of their constituents, instead of merely their sinecure within the party, they would hire the twin dominatrixes of Abu Ghraib, Lynddie England and Sabrina Harman, to clip a dog leash on Kerry (who disgustingly said he'd like to become the second Black president) to interrogate him about his dreadful record on civil rights when he comes calling seeking their support. Of course, they won't. The Congressional Black Caucus is perhaps the only political conclave with clout as vaporous as the Greens.

Kerry, and his top adviser Rand Beers (a veteran of the Clinton and Bush National Security Council), crafted Plan Colombia, the brutal and toxic war on Andean peasants, waged for the benefit of oil companies under the phoney rubric of drug eradication. His scrawny energy plan, devoid of any real emphasis on conservation or solar power, calls for more offshore oil leasing, widespread natural gas drilling, transcontinental pipelines, and strip-mining for coal. His deficit-fixated economic policy, scripted by Wall Street bond tycoon Robert Rubin, is even more austere than Clinton's.

Like Joe Lieberman, Kerry markets himself as a cultural prude, regularly chiding teens about the kind of clothes they wear, the music they listen to, and the movies they watch. But even Lieberman didn't go so far as to support the censorious Communications Decency Act. Kerry did. Fortunately, even this Supreme Court had the sense to strike the law down, ruling that it trampled across the First Amendment.

All of this is standard fare for contemporary Democrats. But Kerry always goes the extra mile. The senator cast a crucial vote for Clinton's wretched bill to dismantle welfare for poor mothers and their children and, despite mounting evidence to the contrary, he continues to hail the mean-spirited measure as a tremendous success.

This is merely a précis of the grim résumé of the man the Green

Party now supports through the proxy candidacy of David Cobb. The message of the Cobb campaign is: a vote for Cobb is a vote for Kerry. Translation: a vote for Cobb is a vote for war, and everything that goes along with it.

It's also a vote for political self-annihilation. David Cobb is the Jim Jones of the Green Party. Form a line and pass the Kool-Aid.

Risk-free voting? I wouldn't bet your life on it.

Why I Changed My Voter Registration Today

By Norman Solomon
Published on www.commondreams.org, June 28, 2004

This morning I mailed a form changing my party registration from "decline to state" to the Green Party. It's a tiny individual step in response to a hugely important collective action—the party's decision at its National Convention to nominate David Cobb for president.

A majority of the delegates went for a candidate who relied on grassroots organizing and respectful debate. Cobb won the nomination after proving his capacity to engage in substantive dialogue with Green Party activists and other progressives. Without that capacity, he probably wouldn't have ended up taking his position in favor of a "safe states" approach to this year's presidential race.

How thoroughly Cobb and his running mate, Pat LaMarche, will implement such a strategy remains to be seen. Hopefully, history will record that in 2004 the Green ticket boosted the party's strength among progressives nationwide while making common cause with the wide array of movements determined to prevent a victory for the Bush-Cheney gang on Election Day.

As a practical matter, ending the George W. Bush presidency on November 2 will require sufficient votes for John Kerry in most of the twenty or so swing states: Oregon and Washington; Nevada, Arizona, New Mexico, and Colorado; Iowa, Illinois, Wisconsin, Minnesota, Michigan, Missouri, Ohio, Pennsylvania, and Delaware; New Hampshire and Maine; West Virginia, Arkansas, and Louisiana; and, of course, Florida.

(Since I live in California, where Kerry is running twelve to fifteen points ahead of Bush, I'm safely voting for Cobb. But if I lived in one of the twenty closely fought swing states, I'd vote for Kerry.)

With the swing states all too close for comfort, activists should be emphatic that the Green Party's presidential campaign this year ought to concentrate its efforts on "safe states"—where the Bush–Kerry race isn't close.

The Green Party should not be at cross purposes with the progressive movements struggling to end the Bush presidency. People in those movements will long remember, for good or ill, how the Green Party conducts itself between now and the day that seals the fate of the Bush White House.

One of the potential key benefits of Cobb's nomination is that he seems genuinely interested in hearing—and being responsive to—grassroots activists. This is a refreshing and vital departure for a Green Party presidential nominee. So, more than ever, it's time for activists to speak up.

If strategic thinking prevails, the possibility exists that the Green Party in 2004 will strengthen itself from the bottom up while also providing tangible solidarity in the national effort to defeat Bush. If the Green Party proves equal to this momentous task, it could open up new possibilities for the years and decades ahead.

A Reply to Norman Solomon and Medea Benjamin: Believing in a Green Resistance
By Todd Chretien
Published on www.counterpunch.org, July 26, 2004

> These are the times that try men's souls. The summer soldier and the sunshine patriot will, in this crisis, shrink from the service of their country; but he that stands it now, deserves the love and thanks of man and woman. Tyranny, like hell, is not easily conquered; yet we have this consolation with us, that the harder the conflict, the more glorious the triumph. What we obtain too cheap, we esteem too lightly: it is dearness only that gives everything its value.
>
> —Thomas Paine, *The Crisis*, 1776

The great immigrant revolutionary, abolitionist, and supporter of women's rights Thomas Paine made the point in 1776 that in order to win any meaningful battle, it is necessary not only to fight when it is easy. It is necessary to fight, and in fact, it is especially important to fight, when all "pragmatic" opinion counsels compromise, retreat, and surrender. Had Washington's army sued for peace in 1776 at Valley Forge, then the world's first representative democracy would never have been born.

Visionary abolitionist Frederick Douglass advised John Brown to abort his ill-fated raid on Harpers Ferry not because he opposed the rebellion, but because he believed it could not succeed in its tactics. However, when John Brown was executed by the slave power, Douglass lauded him as the "man who started the war that ended slavery."

In 1937, Congress of Industrial Organizations union leader John Lewis dared the government to break the auto sit-down strikes and "shoot him first." The auto bosses and Roosevelt backed down, and we can thank the Flint rebels for the remnants of unions we still have today.

Rosa Parks refused to give up her bus seat to a white man, touching off a direct-action movement that bucked those who advised to let the apartheid courts work with "all deliberate speed." The racist backlash was intense and led to the deaths, beatings, and jailings of thousands of young Black and white freedom fighters. But Jim Crow died as well.

Any serious consideration of American history shows that Thomas Paine was right. Independence, abolition, unions, civil rights, suffrage, abortion, Stonewall. All great rebellions and reforms came into being because the minority who advocated "unreasonable" demands refused to disorganize their forces under the pressure of majority opinion. Instead, they held to their principles, gathered their forces, weathered the storm, and showed friend and foe alike that "truth and not lies are the motor force of history."

Today, we are at an historical crossroads. Bush has set the world on fire. He has invaded Iraq, Afghanistan, and Haiti; cheered on the Israeli war against the Palestinians; shredded our civil liberties with the Patriot Act; and wants to codify his version of the Old Testament into a constitutional ban on gay marriage. He wants to outlaw abortion and doesn't believe in global warming.

No doubt, he is a danger to the planet.

However, rather than opposing this madness, John Kerry has helped Bush light the matches. He voted for the invasions and wants to send more troops. He promises more, more, more of the same for Sharon's dirty war, and adds that we should get tough with Venezuela. He voted for the Patriot Act and vows to intensify the "war on terror" if elected. There are, of course, some differences. Kerry does not want to write his anti–gay marriage bigotry into the form of an amendment. He believes in global warming but thinks any radical action to reverse it will hurt American corporate power. He says he will appoint pro-abortion federal judges, but will follow Clinton's policy of slowly outlawing abortion to the young and the poor.

Unfortunately, many "sunshine patriots" are demanding that the antiwar movement that put over a million people in the streets in the spring of 2003 now line up behind a pro-war candidate. This is especially wrongheaded timing because the majority of the country is turning against the war and occupation. Medea Benjamin, Peter Coyote, Daniel Ellsberg, Tom Hayden, Barbara Ehrenreich, Norman Solomon, and many other liberal and progressive leaders tell us that a Kerry regime "would be less dangerous" than Bush. This may or may not be true. Remember, it was LBJ who escalated the war in Vietnam, not Nixon. But, even *if* Kerry is "less dangerous," he will be *more* capable of wreaking havoc on Iraq, Palestine, Venezuela, abortion, gay rights, civil rights, and unions *if* we sacrifice our political movement to getting behind him.

Tragically, rather than building on the great start we made in 2000 when Ralph Nader won 2.7 million votes for peace and justice, many of the very same people who helped that effort are trying to wreck it this time around. Rather than encouraging the Green Party and all antiwar organizations, unions, and civil rights groups to unite for a progressive campaign aiming to get millions of votes, they are condoning, if not actually leading, a campaign to vilify as "Republican dupes" those movement organizers and ordinary people who believe Ralph Nader and Peter Camejo are right to fight for the chance to carry our mobilization for peace and justice into the ballot box.

In Los Angeles in 2000, Democratic Party leaders stood on the balcony of the Staples Center and watched the LAPD teargas thousands of protesters. It seems to me that if we can't build a movement that learns not to vote for a party that directs police assaults on us, we don't have much hope of ever building a political challenge to corporate America. No doubt, the debate over presidential tactics will sharply separate many of us who have worked closely together in the past and will again in the future. While all of us who want a better world should argue respectfully, debate we must because the stakes are too high to hold our tongues.

Norman Solomon wrote last month that he was registering Green precisely because its National Convention nominated a candidate who promised not to challenge the two-party system where it counts. He joins the chorus of liberal voices who warn us that "this is not the year." But he is wrong. As Paine, Douglass, Parks, Lewis, Malcolm, Mario, Gurley-Flynn, and countless others understood, any movement that ever aims to win must learn to stand up for itself precisely when it is darkest. That's the only way the millions of people who hate the system that oppresses them can ever gain confidence in us to join us and transform our movement from a minority affair of protest into a majority tide of power. For whatever my effort is worth, I am registering Green this year because most of the people I know in the Green Party refused, and are refusing, to submit to the duopoly blackmail. Ralph Nader and Peter Camejo can't change the system by themselves, but every vote they receive will show the world that there are millions here in the United States who intend to conquer the hell of corporate power and the tyranny it rains down on the planet.

Hang on Citizen Paine, we're coming.

Growing the Green Party
By David Cobb
In These Times, *July 16, 2004*

Here's a story that you won't see in the corporate media: The Green Party is growing—getting bigger, stronger, and better-organized in every election cycle. Even after the infamous 2000 presidential election, when the media and Democrats blamed us for Bush's selection and ignored the blatantly illegal and biased behavior of Jeb Bush, Katherine Harris, and a Republican Supreme Court majority, our numbers have grown.

In 1996, the Green Party was organized in ten states, guaranteed a ballot line in just five, and had elected forty officeholders. Today, we have parties organized in forty-four states, twenty-three with guaranteed ballot access, and hundreds of Greens elected to public office, including the mayors of Santa Monica, California, and New Paltz, New York, and the president of the San Francisco Board of Supervisors. And, for the first time in our party's history, we have two registered Greens as our presidential and vice presidential candidates, myself and Patricia LaMarche, respectively.

The goals of the Cobb/LaMarche campaign are to present a genuine, progressive alternative, grow the Green Party, and have this year's election culminate with the removal of the White House's illegitimate occupant.

We are speaking truth to power in this campaign. We are the only party calling for decisive action on catastrophic global climate change and our addiction to fossil fuels, a living wage, universal health care under a national insurance plan, real steps toward racial equality, an end to the so-called USA PATRIOT Act, and the removal of U.S. troops from Iraq.

We are also confronting the "spoiler" issue head-on. When this question is raised, it provides us with an opportunity to talk about reforming a flawed electoral system. There isn't a spoiler problem. The problem is an antiquated, antidemocratic electoral system that forces people to vote for a candidate they really don't support in order to keep an even worse candidate out of office. We deserve a more democratic and more efficient electoral system, representing the diversity of people and opinions in our country.

Instant runoff voting (IRV) is one solution. IRV allows people to rank candidates in order of preference so that if your first-choice candidate doesn't win enough votes to make it into a runoff, your second-choice vote is automatically considered. IRV is used to elect officeholders in Australia, Ireland, and London, and is soon to be implemented in San Francisco. (Learn more about IRV, proportional representation, and other reforms to ensure fair elections on the Web site for the Center for Voting & Democracy at http://www.fairvote.org.)

Third parties have played a critical role throughout American history. In their heyday, third parties elected mayors, governors, and members of Congress. In fact, the entire social fabric of our society was woven from ideas that originated within third parties: the abolition of slavery, women's right to vote, Social Security, the 40-hour workweek and the direct election of U.S. senators, to name just a few.

What we are trying to accomplish through our work with the Green Party is greater than any one campaign or any one election. We are in this for the long haul. One of the key steps to growing our party and eliminating a dangerous global threat is ensuring the removal of George W. Bush from office. Bush is a huge problem. But he is not the problem. The problem is a corporate-military-industrial-prison-judicial system that is destroying the planet. We need to address the larger problem, but we also need to remove the most immediate threat to global peace—and that means getting Bush out of office.

I am in no way suggesting that anyone vote for John Kerry. Kerry is a corporatist and a militarist who supported the invasions of Iraq and Afghanistan, as well as the passage of the Patriot Act. He also opposes real universal health care and a living wage. However, although the differences between Bush and Kerry may be incremental, they are not inconsequential.

In forty or so states the electoral college votes have, for all intents and purposes, already been cast. For example, Massachusetts, California, and New York will go to the Democrats; Utah, Wyoming, and Texas to the Republicans. In these states, where our message is "Don't waste your vote," a vote for the Green Party is a powerful tool. In the battleground states that will decide the election, we understand if you won't vote for our ticket this time. That's okay. A vote is a powerful and personal decision. You can register Green and support us in every other way possible, especially with votes for state and local Green candidates and contributions of your time and money.

With the strategy we have articulated, we will grow the Green Party, provide voters with a genuine alternative, and make the world a safer and saner place to live.

Rigged Convention, Divided Party: How David Cobb Became the Green Nominee Even Though He Only Got 12 Percent of the Votes

By Carol Miller and Forrest Hill
Published on www.counterpunch.org, August 7, 2004

How did David Cobb become the Green Party presidential nominee against the overwhelming majority of the Green Party?

The answer is quite simple. The Green Party followed a policy that is fundamentally undemocratic and allowed the will of its members to be manipulated.

Primaries: The Will of the Voter

In five states, registered Green Party members, who are the rank and file of the party, had the opportunity to vote in a presidential primary. These five primaries represent the majority of registered Greens in the country.

The five primaries took place in California, Massachusetts, New Mexico, Washington, D.C., and Rhode Island. The total number of votes cast for a presidential candidate as recorded by *Ballot Access News* was 45,733.

The results from these primaries for the leading three candidates are as follows:

Camejo	33,255	72.7 percent
Cobb	5,569	12.2 percent
Salzman	4,953	10.8 percent
Others	1,956	4.2 percent

In the three largest states, California, Massachusetts, and New Mexico, David Cobb was defeated. In California he was beaten six to one by Camejo, and Lorna Salzman almost tied him for second place. In Massachusetts he was beaten by Lorna Salzman and in New Mexico by Carol Miller. Both Lorna Salzman and Carol Miller endorsed the Nader/Camejo campaign.

In D.C., Cobb received 37 percent of all votes cast. The total number of votes cast in the Washington, D.C., primary, including write-in votes, was 374. Cobb faced only one local opponent, yet received only 138 votes!

In Rhode Island, the one state in which Cobb actually won more than 50 percent of the vote, only eighty-nine votes were cast. The primary ballot included only Kent Mesplay and Cobb. It did not even include New York's presidential nominee, Lorna Salzman. The vote was seventy-one for Cobb and eighteen for Mesplay.

Overall, the total primary vote for candidates who support Nader/Camejo was over 83 percent compared to Cobb's 12.2 percent. Where Greens actually were able to vote, Cobb was roundly defeated.

Nominating Meetings: The Will of the Few and Selected

In all other states Green Party delegates were chosen at nominating meetings. These meetings varied in size but were overall quite small. The national Green Party Web site never reported the number of votes cast at any of the state nominating meetings. This cover-up, whether intentional or not, hid from Greens the small number of voters that were determining how large numbers of delegates were proportioned between the candidates.

Nor did the Web site explain the delegate formula or justify the size of each state's delegation so that Greens could follow the process. In fact the formula completely ignores the number of Greens registered in each state as a determinant for the number of delegates. Most Greens assumed that delegates were proportioned according to a one person, one vote system as any democratic organization would normally assume.

Only the Cobb campaign organized a turnout of their supporters for these nominating meetings. This enabled Cobb to appear to have a higher percentage of support than he would gain if local Greens had an easier way of expressing their views, such as a primary.

In caucuses where the turnout was relatively large, Cobb often did poorly. But in some cases Cobb supporters were able to get around their low vote count by packing the delegation selection. For example, in Maine, where Nader's name was on the ballot,

Nader defeated Cobb 52–42 (the remaining sixty-five votes went to thirteen other candidates). These votes represent 33 percent for Nader and 26 percent for Cobb. Yet during the vote at the convention in Milwaukee, eighteen out of nineteen Maine delegates voted for Cobb and one voted for Nader, or 95 percent for Cobb and 5 percent for Nader.

Democratic Violation of "One Person, One Vote"

Even this one-sided, basically one-candidate campaign could never have led to a Cobb victory at the convention without the help of a second undemocratic factor. The Green Party does not use a one person, one vote system but instead has an electoral college system that punishes states like California for its success in recruiting tens of thousands of Greens, while rewarding states that have only a small membership. Unlike the national electoral college, the Green Party's weighted voting gives some states hundreds of times more votes per Green member then other states.

For example, in Iowa there is officially no Green Party. The state liquidated it after they failed to reach the 2 percent threshold for their gubernatorial candidate in 2002. However, Iowa had nine delegates to the Green Party convention. There are ninety people registered as Greens in Iowa and over 150,000 registered Greens in California. Thus, in Iowa for every ten registered Green Party members there was one delegate to the nominating convention. If the party were to weigh all its members equally, then California would have received over 16,500 delegates instead of 132. The ninety Greens in Iowa had as much power in the party as 11,363 members in California.

Imagine a party in which candidate A gets 11,300 votes and candidate B gets 90 votes, and candidate B is declared the winner. Unfortunately, that party's name was the Green Party at the Milwaukee convention.

It is disturbing that while the Green Party platform opposes the electoral college and favors "one person, one vote," it does not practice what it preaches. Without the undemocratic voting process implemented by the national coordinating committee, Cobb had no chance of winning after the primary vote in California and the heavy opposition to his candidacy in other major states like New York and New Jersey.

Denying Candidates the Right to Appoint Their Delegates

But even taking into account this undemocratic ratio of representation that worked mightily for Cobb, he was still unable to win outright. He just didn't have enough delegates. To win the nomination, his supporters were allowed to alter the decisions of the small state meetings and primaries. This last nondemocratic step was achieved because Green Party rules do not allow a candidate chosen by its rank and file to appoint their delegates like all other parties have in American history. The only requirement for becoming a delegate is simply having the ability to attend the convention. Thus, whichever candidate can get their supporters to the convention can end up winning regardless of the votes of the primaries or caucuses, as in Maine.

In this manner Cobb was able to take delegate votes from other candidates. This was achieved simply by having his supporters show up and cast their votes for him after the first round of voting. Examples where this practice was highly evident include Maine, Missouri, California, and Texas.

In Maryland, two Cobb delegates attempted to become a Nader delegate and a Carol Miller delegate prior to the convention. They were only stopped because a Nader supporter prevented them from doing so by making it publicly clear that they were in fact Cobb supporters.

In California Cobb supporters were able to turn his 12 percent support in the primaries into a delegate vote of 26 percent by packing the delegation. Specifically, twenty-two votes shifted to Cobb during the second round of voting. These votes are equal to the margin by which Cobb won the election.

In effect the Green Party picks its presidential candidate not based on the will of its members but by discriminating against Greens in some states, and in the end, by allowing anyone to become a delegate who can show up at the convention. Cobb's support at most reflects but a small percentage of Greens. The overwhelming majority of the rank-and-file members opposed his candidacy.

Fighting Back

Cobb's amazing rise from 12 percent in the primaries against 83 percent for pro-Nader candidates to a majority at the convention was due to a well-organized campaign to turn a minority view in the Green Party into what appeared as a majority decision at the convention.

Behind the Cobb phenomenon is a very real political difference in the Green Party. As many articles have pointed out, the party is divided between those who want to oppose the two parties of money and those who support voting for the lesser of two evils to help prevent a Republican victory. Cobb represents a political capitulation away from our independence from the two corporate-controlled parties.

The nomination of Cobb is a step backward, away from an uncompromising challenge to the two-party "duopoly" and away from the prominence that the Greens have achieved, thanks in good part to Nader's 2000 campaign. It is time we take back the Green Party from those who want to capitulate to the Democratic Party!

A Response to Miller and Hill
By Dean Myerson
August 11, 2004

Carol Miller and Forrest Hill have distributed an attack article that spreads lies about the Green Party's convention in Milwaukee and the broader nomination process, in order to provide cover for seeking the Green Party of California's ballot line for the Nader/Camejo campaign, now that their ballot drive has failed. I am normally one who is opposed to responding to these attacks as we have a campaign to run. But this article has spread wide and now threatens to dismember the Green Party, a cost that Peter Camejo and some Nader supporters are apparently willing to pay in order to get ballot lines.

I personally call on Ralph Nader to disavow this article and any attempts to get Green Party ballot lines that are based on it. His surrogates are using the same tactics against the Green Party that the Democratic Party is using against him. He is staying above the fray, just as John Kerry is, regarding attacks on him.

Please read carefully, and as always, beware those who claim mandates unproven by any vote. Miller and Hill are quoted in straight text. I respond in italics.

Primaries—The Will of the Voter

In five states, registered Green Party members, who are the rank and file of the party, had the opportunity to vote in a presidential primary. These five primaries represent the majority of registered Greens in the country.

Voters cannot legally register as Greens or the state will not divulge that count in 27 states. These Greens are disenfranchised if Green registration is the criterion. Such a disenfranchising also overrepresents those who would get to vote if registration was the sole criterion. Also, some states prioritize registration because it impacts the ability to run candidates. California prioritizes registration because they can keep a ballot line by doing so, another reason California would be overrepresented if only party registration is used.

The five primaries took place in California, Massachusetts, New Mexico, Washington, D.C., and Rhode Island. The total number of votes cast for a presidential candidate as recorded by *Ballot Access News* was 45,733.

The results from these primaries for the leading three candidates are as follows:

Camejo	33,255	72.7 percent
Cobb	5,569	12.2 percent
Salzman	4,953	10.8 percent
Others	1,956	4.2 percent

Ralph Nader was not listed as a candidate on any of these ballots. Peter Camejo was listed as a candidate for the Green presidential ballot. None were listed as independent candidates. It is a basic matter that we cannot assume anything of voter intent except what was on the ballot. Greens in some of these states who voted for Camejo have specifically complained that they did not vote for

Nader and do not want their vote interpreted this way. Furthermore, if California Greens were in the same position as Greens in most of the country, in that they were being asked to vote for independent candidates who would not commit to use their ballot line, even those who now support Nader/Camejo might think differently. For Nader/Camejo to commit to run on a Green line only in California (and maybe a few other states) is fundamentally divisive for the Green Party. All of our state parties want a candidate for their Green ballot line. California Greens need to recognize what it is Nader/Camejo were asking of Greens elsewhere in the country at the convention: that they give up their right to have a presidential candidate so that California could have its preferred choice. Either that, or have a "no decision" convention that would undermine the purpose of having a national party.

In the three largest states, California, Massachusetts, and New Mexico David Cobb was defeated. In California he was beaten six to one by Camejo, and Lorna Salzman almost tied him for second place. In Massachusetts he was beaten by Lorna Salzman and in New Mexico by Carol Miller. Both Lorna Salzman and Carol Miller endorsed the Nader/Camejo campaign.

And none of these people ended up seeking the Green nomination. Thus, those delegates should be freed to vote their conscience, unless the Green Party prefers to let a few individuals tell delegates how to vote, independent of the will of voters.

In D.C., Cobb received 37 percent of all votes cast. The total number of votes cast in the Washington, D.C., primary, including write-in votes, was 374. Cobb faced only one local opponent, yet received only 138 votes!

In the Rhode Island primary, the one state in which Cobb actually won more than 50 percent of the vote, only eighty-nine votes were cast. The primary ballot included only Kent Mesplay and Cobb. It did not even include New York's presidential nominee, Lorna Salzman. The vote was seventy-one for Cobb and eighteen for Mesplay.

Overall, the total primary vote for candidates who support Nader/Camejo was over 83 percent compared to Cobb's 12.2 percent. Where Greens actually were able to vote, Cobb was roundly defeated.

Again, votes were cast for candidates who support Nader, votes were not cast for Nader, nor were they cast for an independent candidate. The votes for candidates who were a stand-in for Nader are not valid as votes for Nader. We cannot manipulate the intention of voters. We can only go by what was written on the ballot.

Readers might do well to talk to some Greens in Rhode Island, where support for Nader used to be strong. When he refused to commit to use their ballot line, his support decreased.

Nominating Meetings: The Will of the Few and Selected

In all other states Green Party delegates were chosen at nominating meetings. These meetings varied in size but were overall quite small. The national Green Party Web site never reported the number of votes cast at any of the state nominating meetings. This cover-up, whether intentional or not, hid from Greens the small number of voters that were determining how large numbers of delegates were proportioned between the candidates.

They were smaller but they were informed as to what the candidates were actually running for. When people knew that Camejo and Salzman were not actually seeking the Green nomination, they did not vote for them in most states. What this result actually shows is that Greens wanted a Green candidate, and one for their own ballot lines.

Nor did the Web site explain the delegate formula or justify the size of each state's delegation so that Greens could follow the process. In fact the formula completely ignores the number of Greens registered in each state as a determinant for the number of delegates. Most Greens assumed that delegates were proportioned according to a one person, one vote system, as any democratic organization would normally assume.

The formula does not use registered Greens because by law registered Greens in twenty-seven states cannot be counted. It does use population, statewide Green candidate voting history, elected Green count, and the Green Party's Coordinating Committee voting strength as factors.

Only the Cobb campaign organized a turnout of their supporters for these nominating meetings. This enabled Cobb to appear to have a higher percentage of support than he would gain if local Greens had an easier way of expressing their views, such as a primary.

The Cobb campaign organized to ask for and win the nomination. Is there a problem with this? Why didn't the Nader/Camejo campaign do so? Did they think the Green Party owed them a nomination or endorsement, just as the Democratic Party thinks they own our votes?

In caucuses where the turnout was relatively large, Cobb often did poorly. But in some cases Cobb supporters were able to get around their low vote count by packing the delegation selection. For example, in Maine, where Nader's name was on the ballot, Nader defeated Cobb 52–42 (the remaining sixty-five votes went to thirteen other candidates). These votes represent 33 percent for Nader and 26 percent for Cobb. Yet during the vote at the convention in Milwaukee, eighteen out of nineteen Maine delegates voted for Cobb, and one voted for Nader, or 95 percent for Cobb and 5 percent for Nader.

Nader told some Maine Greens early on that he would run on the Green line in Maine, so they supported him. When it became clear that he would not do this, they changed their mind.

Democratic Violation of "One Person, One Vote"

Even this one-sided, basically one-candidate campaign could never have led to a Cobb victory at the convention without the help of a second undemocratic factor. The Green Party does not use a one person, one vote system but instead has an electoral college system that punishes states like California for its success in recruiting tens of thousands of Greens, while rewarding states that have only a small membership. Unlike the national electoral college, the Green Party's weighted voting gives some states hundreds of times more votes per Green member than other states.

As all national organizations do, the Green Party uses representative democracy at the national level. It always has. This has never been a problem before. The difference in ratio is because not all states have party registration as described above. It has always been acknowledged that states that have dues-paying members will have fewer than they do registered Greens. Some states have both, and the ratio is quite large between signed-up members and registrants. Different forms of membership in our state parties make national representation complex.

For example, in Iowa there is officially no Green Party. The state liquidated it after they failed to reach the 2 percent threshold for their gubernatorial candidate in 2002. However, Iowa had nine delegates to the Green Party Convention. There are ninety people registered as Greens in Iowa and over 150,000 registered Greens in California. Thus, for every ten registered Green Party members there was one delegate to the nominating convention. If the party were to weigh all its members equally, then California would have received over 16,500 delegates instead of 132. The ninety Greens in Iowa had as much power in the party as 11,363 members in California.

The Iowa Green Party has not been "liquidated"; it is a political organization under state law and has no registered Greens, because it is not allowed to by law. Iowa Greens contacted the Nader campaign months ago and asked if he would run on a Green line in Iowa, and he said he would decide after the convention. With this, many Iowa Greens supported David Cobb, who would commit to run on their line.

Imagine a party in which candidate A gets 11,300 votes and candidate B gets 90 votes, and candidate B is declared the winner. Unfortunately, that party's name was the Green Party at the Milwaukee convention.

It's good that you refer to candidate A getting 11,300 votes. Nader got no votes because he was not listed on any primary ballot by his choice. Therefore, we have no way of knowing how many Greens would support his independent campaign.

It is disturbing that while the Green Party platform opposes the electoral college and favors "one person, one vote," it does not practice what it preaches. Without the undemocratic voting process implemented by the national coordinating committee, Cobb had no chance of winning after the primary vote in California and the heavy opposition to his candidacy in other major states like New York and New Jersey.

The Green Party has always used representative democracy at the national level. The formula for representation in Milwaukee was approved in 2003 and there were no complaints that it was an "electoral college" then. This complaint only appeared after the Nader/Camejo campaign lost.

Denying Candidates the Right to Appoint Their Delegates

But even taking into account this undemocratic ratio of representation that worked mightily for Cobb, he was still unable to win outright. He just didn't have enough delegates. To win the nomination, his supporters were allowed to alter the decisions of the small state meetings and primaries. This last non-democratic step was achieved because Green Party rules do not allow a candidate chosen by its rank and file to appoint their delegates like all other parties have in American history. The only requirement for becoming a delegate is simply having the ability to attend the convention. Thus, whichever candidate can get their supporters to the convention can end up winning regardless of the votes of the primaries or caucuses, as in Maine.

Green state parties choose their own process for choosing delegates. This is not controlled by the national party. From those states that I saw, they attempted to choose delegates that support the named candidate. Did the Nader/Camejo campaign offer to pay the way for their own delegates? The reason why Nader/Camejo did not select their delegates is that they did not campaign for the nomination.

In this manner Cobb was able to take delegate votes from other candidates. This was achieved simply by having his supporters show up and cast their votes for him after the first round of voting. Examples where this practice was highly evident include Maine, Missouri, California, and Texas.

Or maybe they changed their mind? Voting by round assumes that votes will change from round to round. I have talked to some delegates who changed their mind to support David Cobb in the second round, and they all had specific reasons, generally dealing with how Camejo campaigned for the nomination. Some Nader supporters have confirmed that Camejo's very negative campaign against David Cobb hurt his cause and converted some Camejo supporters to Cobb supporters.

Furthermore, in an interview with FoxNews.com *that is still linked on Peter Camejo's Avocado Education Project Web site, he says that he wants Greens to make their own choice at the convention. He has been quoted as saying early on that his delegates should be considered uncommitted. Now he says it is betrayal for them to not vote for him. Why the change?*

In Maryland, two Cobb delegates attempted to become a Nader delegate and a Carol Miller delegate prior to the convention. They were only stopped because a Nader supporter prevented them from doing so by making it publicly clear that they were in fact Cobb supporters.

In California, Cobb supporters were able to turn his 12 percent support in the primaries into a delegate vote of 26 percent by packing the delegation. Specifically, twenty-two votes shifted to Cobb during the second round of voting. These votes are equal to the margin by which Cobb won the election.

As stated above, they did so because of how Camejo behaved. A speaker was permitted to personally attack Cobb at a Camejo rally. Camejo badgered delegates to vote the way he wanted them to, rather than respectfully convincing them. Many delegates have complained about this.

In effect the Green Party picks its presidential candidate not based on the will of its members but by discriminating against Greens in some states, and in the end, by allowing anyone to become a delegate who can show up at the convention. Cobb's support at most reflects but a small percentage of Greens. The overwhelming majority of the rank-and-file members oppose his candidacy.

By what vote was it determined that an overwhelming majority of the rank and file oppose the Cobb candidacy?

Fighting Back

Cobb's amazing rise from 12 percent in the primaries against 83 percent for pro-Nader candidates to a majority at the convention was due to a well-organized campaign to turn a minority view in the Green Party into what appeared as a majority decision at the convention.

It was due to a well-organized campaign, period. It was a campaign that visited Greens in forty states, a campaign that actually asked for the nomination, and a campaign that stayed positive. A campaign that built the Green Party, as many Greens have written to us to confirm. There was essentially no campaign for a Nader endorsement until one week before the convention.

Behind the Cobb phenomenon is a very real political difference in the Green Party. As many articles have pointed out, the party is divided between those who want to oppose the two parties of money and those who support voting for the lesser of two evils to help prevent a Republican victory. Cobb represents a political capitulation away from our independence from the two corporate-controlled parties.

What the political differences are has no impact on the process used at the convention. Nader has repeatedly said he wants to make the Democratic Party better, that he wants to beat Bush. Even that he wants to coordinate with Kerry to beat Bush. The latter is from a CNN transcript of a Nader interview with Wolf Blitzer. There is no capitulation.

The nomination of Cobb is a step backward, away from an uncompromising challenge to the two-party "duopoly" and away from the prominence that the Greens have achieved, thanks in good part to Nader's 2000 campaign. It is time we take back the Green Party from those who want to capitulate to the Democratic Party!

This article is a response to a weak ballot-access drive by

Nader. He now needs to undermine the Green Party convention in order to give cause to state parties to ignore the result of the convention. No formal complaints about the convention process have been filed with the national party.

Cut and Run: The Green Party 2004 Convention

By Peter Miguel Camejo
August 17, 2004

Just prior to the opening of the Green Party National Convention in June of 2004 David Cobb, the soon-to-be Green Party presidential candidate, stated on *Democracy Now!*, "you can't cut and run" in response to a question from Amy Goodman on why he calls for continued occupation of Iraq by the United States on his campaign Web site. Cobb repeated a phrase, "you can't cut and run," made famous by both Bush and Kerry, to justify continued U.S. occupation of Iraq.

How did it come to pass that the Green Party, pledged to support peace and to oppose the Democrats' and Republicans' occupation in Iraq, nominated a candidate who only days before the convention was defending the imperialist occupation of Iraq on national radio? Cobb's position stood against that of 99 percent—if not 100 percent—of Green Party members, not to mention the overwhelming majority of the people on our planet.

The Green Party 2004 convention itself was a turn away from its founding principles; it represented a move by forces within the Green Party to "cut and run" from its own platform under the attacks of the Democratic Party to silence the Green Party.

The Green Party was founded because the two major corporate-run parties do not represent the interests of humanity. Their policies continue to support an endless march away from democracy toward war, to promote oppression and global exploitation, and to destroy the ecological systems needed to sustain life. The Green Party's goal was to offer an alternative to the two major parties, and to do so it developed a set of Ten Key Values upon which the party platform was based.

In the 1990s, thousands joined the Green Party and a few Green candidates were elected to city councils and school boards. Then in 2000, Ralph Nader, a nationally known figure with great popularity, became the Green Party's presidential candidate. Millions voted for the Green Party and everything changed. Tens of thousands joined the party. The number of candidates elected to office began to rise sharply. Suddenly the Green Party went from a curiosity to a threat to the two-party system.

Democrats Attack

The Democrats launched an offensive against the Green Party and Ralph Nader, accusing them of being responsible for the victory of George Bush. Green Party members have reacted in many different ways to these attacks. Some think we should run candidates only in local races while supporting a "lesser evil" strategy of voting for Democratic nominees in state and national elections. Others have taken a stance that the attacks on the Green Party represent an attempt to silence us and curtail democracy, and that therefore we should fight back.

Of the two currents that have appeared in the Green Party as a result of these attacks, one offers capitulation and the other resistance as the solution. These two opposing views have divided the Green Party.

This rift has been widened by the intensity of the Democratic Party's attacks against Ralph Nader. These attacks reached a level never before seen in American history when Nader announced he was again running for president instead of capitulating, on a platform in harmony with the Green Party.

The Politics of Capitulation

David Cobb, a relatively unknown figure in the United States and also in the Green Party, began a campaign whose central purpose was to disassociate from Nader and try to dodge Democratic Party attacks by disappearing under the radar. His campaign strategy of encouraging Green Party members to vote for the Democrats in contested states is a not-so-subtle form of capitulation. He called this strategy the "safe state" strategy.

This position was backed by a group of eighteen Green Party members, including some longtime leaders, in a statement urging Greens to adopt a "lesser evil" voting strategy.

Cobb went further and suggested a "safe state" strategy would actually help build the Green Party. He concluded that by avoiding attacks from the Democrats, the Green Party could grow at the grassroots level. Cobb promised supporters he would use his campaign to disassociate Greens from Nader and help the Greens grow by focusing only on local campaigns. In the past year, he has traveled throughout the nation, giving press interviews attacking Nader and letting people know he wants Kerry to win. He made a point of going to small Green state organizations, assuring them that he was the only candidate really concerned about grassroots organizing.

Cobb developed the slogan "Green and Growing," using the empirical fact that the party was growing, to make his campaign appear pro-Green as opposed to simply anti-Nader. His analysis, however, completely turns reality upside-down. The party has grown precisely because it rejected his views and ran Nader for president in 2000, stood up to the Democrats' charge of spoilers, and has run aggressive campaigns for statewide offices, U.S. Senate, Congress, mayor, and other local offices.

The Green Party primaries revealed the overwhelming majority of Greens did not support Cobb. In those states where primaries were held, representing the majority of registered Greens, Cobb received only 12.2 percent of the vote, while candidates supporting Nader received over 80 percent of the votes cast by Green Party members.

Most Greens knew the party had grown like never before precisely because of Nader's national campaign. Nationally there was a great deal of suspicion to Cobb's "safe state" strategy so he began calling it different names, such as "smart states," "investing your vote," and "voting your conscience," but in every case it simply means voting for John Kerry.

As the Democrats intensified their attacks, many Greens became aware that building the Green Party was not so easy. The Democrats have an enormous influence on liberal intellectuals, who have joined in a massive campaign against Nader and the Green

Party. Something called "Green Democrats" began appearing on special Web sites as part of a campaign to silence the Greens. Cobb soon found a strong base of support for his campaign among the Kerry backers within the party. The Democratic Party media began to see him as an ally in their campaign against Nader and to domesticate the Green Party.

Cobb's running mate, Pat LaMarche, gave her own "cut-and-run" strategy in an article in *Green Horizon*, published just prior to the convention, in which she wrote, "Maybe the entire green movement can slip under the radar while folks monitor all this hullabaloo about the presidential race." In her first interview following the convention, LaMarche stated she would vote for the Democrat, Kerry, not Cobb, even though she was Cobb's vice presidential candidate. LaMarche later said she had been misquoted.

Alliance with the Democrats

Medea Benjamin, a Green Party member from California and a supporter of the "lesser evil" strategy, made an appeal for Greens to support Cobb and called for a coalition with the Democrats.

Greens are involved in coalitions with Democrats, and sometimes Republicans, on specific issues all the time. Occasionally a local Democratic Party group will endorse a march for gay marriage or for peace. In fact, Medea's work through Global Exchange, a nonprofit, is itself supported by a coalition of people with various political viewpoints; i.e., Greens, Democrats, and independents working together on specific issues related to fair trade. But elections and the question of who should govern are different than forming coalitions on issues.

Political parties have platforms and represent social layers. The Democrats represent corporate America. That is a fundamental reason why the Green Party exists. The one alliance we cannot make with the Democrats is on who should govern, because we believe that people, not money, should run the United States.

People who join the Democratic Party or who call for people to vote for it are crossing the line between people and money. That is why I call it capitulation to call for a vote for Kerry. Democrats often make it a general condition that for them to minimally support progressive causes, progressives must accept voting for the

Democratic Party. This often leads to organizations like trade unions and environmentalist groups becoming prisoners of the Democrats. They can protest their hearts out, but when the chips are down they have to vote for pro-corporate candidates like Kerry and Edwards, otherwise the Democrats will turn on them.

Why Not Join the Democrats?

David Cobb and Medea Benjamin do not agree with Dennis Kucinich's call that all Greens abandon their party and join the Democrats and work to reform it. Instead they want the Greens to become an ally to those working within the Democratic Party. They see the Green Party agreeing not to run against certain Democrats, endorsing other Democrats, and in some cases voting for Democrats such as Kerry and then in turn the Democrats will agree not to attack us. In that sense they see the Green Party as a pressure group on the Democrats, as part of the Democratic Party family and an ally to the more "progressive" Democrats.

That is why Cobb's victory at the Green Party convention was hailed by Democrats and supporters of Kerry generally from *The Nation* to the Milwaukee daily newspaper.

The problem with this "make peace with the Democrats" view is that to create systematic change, progressives have to break with the Democratic Party. That is becoming clear to millions of people. Twenty-five percent of the electorate is no longer registered Democrat or Republican. Tens of millions of people are leaving the two-party system. The youth are starting to break. In fact, one out of every eight youth, 12 percent, say they will vote for Nader.

The Green Party 2004 convention chose formally to turn their backs on the youth who are rebelling against the two parties of war and backing Nader. The Cobb/Benjamin supporters favor an alliance with the Democrats, not with the antiwar youth. The Green Party cannot be built under a strategy of coalition with the Democrats. We will not inspire young voters to join our party by calling for voters to support pro-war, pro-corporate candidates like Kerry.

The New Party tried to use the strategy of developing an alliance with the Democratic Party to build a third-party movement. They supported the Democrats and the Democrats let them exist. But members who wanted to support Democrats found it easier to simply join the Democratic Party, and those who wanted a third party went toward the Greens, so the New Party collapsed. A similar end awaits the Green Party if it continues to follow a "lesser evil" voting strategy.

The Green Resistance

The good news is that a majority of active Green Party members do not agree with David Cobb. The broader membership voted massively against him in the primaries.

Cobb's victory at the convention itself is an issue the Green Party will have to struggle with. It highlights the fact that the Green Party does not follow its own views on democracy. The Green Party theoretically stands for "one person, one vote," yet in its internal decision-making process at the convention it opposed one person, one vote. The Green Party opposes the electoral college, yet imposed an extreme electoral college system in determining how delegates were chosen.

At the 2004 convention, the Green Party allowed whoever could make it to the convention to be seated as a delegate. Many of them voted for a presidential candidate without any respect for the wishes of the rank and file expressed in the primaries and state conventions. Such methods allow a candidate to pack meetings and conventions to turn a minority into a majority, as occurred at the 2004 convention.

Avocados

In response to the capitulationism wing of the Green Party, another wing, called the "avocados," has arisen who support the Avocado Declaration and oppose supporting Kerry.

This wing of the party was inspired, not turned off, by Ralph Nader's courage not to bend to the relentless attacks by Democrats against the Green Party. Instead of "cut and run" under the radar, Nader chose to stand against the war, and the Patriot Act and defend working people throughout the United States as visibly as possible.

The polls show eight to ten million people backing Nader. The majority of active Green Party members side with Nader, refuse to turn their back on the ten million people backing Nader, and are working to help Nader's campaign. This includes some of the best-known Greens, such as Matt Gonzalez, president of the Board of Supervisors in San Francisco, and Jason West, the mayor of New Paltz, New York.

Party Unity

The avocados offered a unity proposal at the convention so that both points of view within the party could coexist and debate over the different approaches could continue. The lesser-evil current, the supporters of Cobb, would not agree to the unity proposal because their agenda was to deal Nader a blow. To them, a dual endorsement for Nader and Cobb was still an endorsement of Nader. The Cobb supporters showed no remorse that they were winning the convention against the will of the majority of Greens. Quite the contrary, they were overjoyed at their success in working the undemocratic system within the Green Party to overcome the majority view and achieve a minority victory for Cobb.

The Democrats immediately congratulated them for their efforts. The convention adjourned, and Cobb supporters like Medea Benjamin went off to campaign for Kerry. LaMarche went off to assure the Democrats she would vote for Kerry, and Cobb went off to try and strengthen the pro–Democratic Party wing of the party. The Greens resisting the Democrats went off to campaign for Nader, starting with a rally of one thousand supporters in San Francisco that was hosted by Matt Gonzalez, to affirm their commitment to the Nader/Camejo campaign for peace and social justice.

Organizational Issues

There were several important issues regarding democracy at the convention. One issue was a loyalty oath. It turns out the Green Party proposed delegates had to sign a loyalty oath that they would not oppose whoever got the party nomination. The idea that Greens should ever sign loyalty oaths on issues of one's political views is alien to the very idea of the Green Party. Pressure from various states forced the oath to be dropped.

An effort not to allow some of the presidential candidates to address the conference was overcome by opposition from delegates. The Cobb supporters tried to oppose allowing some candidates to speak, especially the two women candidates, Lorna Salzman and Carol Miller, both Nader supporters. When faced with strong opposition, Cobb himself proposed that the solution was to have no candidate speak at the convention!

The rules at the convention allowed a candidate that did not have a majority to win the nomination. This was also supported by Cobb backers. But under pressure from Matt Gonzalez, Cobb backed off and said he would not accept the nomination without a majority of delegates. It is amazing that the Green Party, which opposes allowing any candidate to win without a majority and supports IRV elections, considered allowing their nominee for president to be picked without a majority of the voting delegates.

There are many other issues that need to be dealt with to turn the Green Party into a democratic organization that respects the votes of its rank and file and does not allow a minority to overrule the majority, as happened in 2004. The Green Party will either become an internally democratic organization, develop a clear separation from the Democratic Party, or it will decline. For the Green Party to continue to grow it must actually be Green, independent and democratic.

The victory of a minority faction that supports capitulating to the Democrats in the 2004 elections is a major threat to the future of the Green Party. The next few years will undoubtedly be a period of internal struggle for democracy and to defend the original purpose and platform of the party.

CHAPTER FOUR

Independence versus Anybody But Bush

Why Vote for Ralph Nader?

By Matt Gonzalez

San Francisco Examiner, *July 14, 2004*

These days it's popular, particularly in progressive circles, to attack presidential candidate Ralph Nader and his running mate, Peter Camejo.

Votes for Nader would likely otherwise go to Sen. John Kerry, and so the fear is that President Bush will be reelected—a possibility that naturally engenders strong feelings. But why is the right solution to attack Nader, who genuinely holds views different from those of Kerry and Bush? After all, Nader and Camejo are simply running for public office in a democracy.

The problem isn't that Nader and Camejo represent a duplicative platform, or fail to address issues being ignored by the two major parties—it's simply that their running cannot be accommodated within our two-party system. So the answer, for many, is that they shouldn't run. But why make the solution an undemocratic one? Why not insist that the system be changed?

Do you really think it's an accident that the Democrats can't come up with a solution to the spoiler problem? Ask yourself, have they spent four years trying to reform the electoral college? Or calling for majority elections so that we don't get a repeat of Florida—an election decided by a plurality victory? Why blame Nader?

One need only look at the two major candidates for president to see how much of a failure our political system is. On virtually every issue of significance, the candidates appear to be in agreement. For instance, they both supported the war in Iraq (although Kerry believes Bush is mishandling matters and would like twenty thousand more troops in the region), and both supported the Patriot Act (arguably the worst attack on civil liberties this country has seen in the last half-century). Both opposed the Kyoto Accords, which would have begun to address global warming, and both supported the World Trade Organization agreements, which subjugate our national and local interests to international commercial ones. Neither supports gay marriage, and even concerning the abortion question, Kerry says he'll appoint anti-abortion judges to the federal courts (but he says he'll make sure they don't want to repeal *Roe v. Wade*).

So, who is kidding whom? The progressives who are self-righteous in their condemnation of Nader, or those who believe the Democrats are not an opposition party?

Continuing to excuse the Democrats for not addressing the spoiler problem only ensures that the problem will not get fixed. Excusing Kerry from making concessions in this regard before you vote for him likewise ensures that the problem will not get fixed. Participating in attacks on Nader for running only props up an undemocratic system that must be reformed.

The stakes are not one presidential race, but rather whether a diversity of ideas will ever reach Congress. Without this reform there will only ever be one congressperson with the courage to oppose the war in Afghanistan. There will only be one senator to vote against the Patriot Act. This state of affairs is so bleak that pretending there is an opposition party in our two-party system can only charitably be called foolish. I hate to say it, but it's true.

Those who continue to say that Nader ruined the 2000 election ignore that over 7 million Democrats voted for Bush—250,000 of them in Florida. They ignore that sixty-six hundred votes in Palm Beach were spoiled by a butterfly ballot designed by a Democrat. Instead, they attack Nader, who has dedicated his entire adult life to fighting for consumer and civil rights. He has been a stalwart against growing corporate power. His running mate, Peter Camejo, has written on post–Civil War Reconstruction and has been a pioneer on socially responsible investing. The Nader/Camejo ticket offers voters something very different.

Attack them all you want, but years from now Nader and Camejo's effort will be remembered with Upton Sinclair's "End Poverty in California" campaign for governor of California and with the presidential efforts of Norman Thomas, Henry Wallace, Eugene Debs, and Bob LaFollette. They will be remembered as men who fought to make this a better democracy.

A Letter to the Black Caucus from a Black Woman Living in South Central
By Donna J. Warren
San Francisco Bay View, July 14, 2004

> "We respect your right to run, Mr. Nader. Withdraw."
> —Elijah Cummings, chair of the Congressional Black Caucus of the United States House of Representatives

To Rep. Cummings and members of the Black Caucus,
You demanded independent candidates Ralph Nader and Peter Camejo withdraw from the presidential race in favor of NAFTA-approving, Iraq-invading, Afghanistan-bombing, Sudanese-pharmaceutical-plant-bombing, right-wing-Israeli-prime-minister-and-convicted-murderer-Ariel-Sharon-supporting, impeachment-of-George-W.-Bush-for-the-forced-removal-of-democratically-elected-President-Jean -Bertrand -Aristide-refusing, and mandatory-minimum-sentencing-supporting John Kerry.

Kerry's contempt for human rights, international law, arms control, and the United Nations is unforgivable.

"Anybody But Bush" was your cry when Nader and Camejo visited your offices in late June. But let's be honest—when Bush delivered lie after lie after lie during his State of the Union addresses, it was the Democrats who stood and clapped. The Democrats made the monster George Bush!

You don't challenge the Democrats and Republicans in their abdication of our communities, but you challenge Nader and Camejo for fighting for our communities. During your meeting, you condemned Nader for choosing Camejo, who speaks Spanish fluently, because you fear Malcolm X's friend will take away your brown votes!

Peter Camejo changed the minds and hearts of Californians to oppose California's horrendous Three Strikes law during his campaign for governor. Three Strikes imprisons African Americans twelve to one for every white person for the same nonviolent crime. What have you done for us?

Does it matter to you that your constituents are hurt by redlining, lead-based paint poisoning, predatory lending, payday loan rackets, and dirty meat? It matters to Ralph Nader.

Does it matter to you that student Nader challenged Harvard University when they published the lie that Blacks are inferior to whites? It matters to me.

Does it matter to you that only Nader campaigned in Ward 8 of the District of Columbia, exposing that sixty-five thousand people live without a single supermarket, yet the District of Columbia has had Black mayors and a Black city council for the last thirty-five years? It matters to your constituents.

What are you afraid of? That Nader and Camejo may "mess up your little party" because they advocate for Black Americans and you don't.

"Anybody But Bush" is your mantra. But even if Bush self-destructs, how can you support John Kerry without demanding a mandate? Corporate interests pull the Democrats twenty-four hours a day. Without a mandate to pull John Kerry in a progressive direction, there's no way you can demand equity.

You told Ralph Nader you wanted him out of the race so Bush can't appoint another right-winger to the Supreme Court, but let's look at the record.

- Kerry promises to appoint anti-abortion judges while professing to protect a woman's right to choose.

- The Senate Democrats confirmed right-wing Supreme Court Judge Antonin Scalia ninety-eight to zero. Not one Democratic senator, including Gore, opposed Scalia.

The Democrats could have blocked right-wing Supreme Court Judge Clarence Thomas's confirmation—they were in control of the Senate—but eleven Democrats moved across the line to confirm Thomas fifty-two to forty-eight while Senate majority leader George Mitchell sat in his office twirling his thumbs.

You don't stop anything that hurts us!

- You could have filibustered the tax cut for the wealthy, but you didn't.

- You could have demanded gas-efficient car engines, but instead you sanctioned the SUV and gave the auto companies an eight-year holiday without requiring better gas efficiency.

- You could have opposed genetically engineering foods, the petroleum industry, and the WTO, but you didn't.

- You could have opposed the federal crime bill which imprisons drug addicts for the drugs our government allowed to flow into the inner cities, but you didn't.

- You could have opposed the "leave-no-child-behind-high-stake-multiple-testing fraud," but instead you chose to sacrifice our children.

- You could have said "no" to the Patriot Act, but you didn't.

You don't represent me!

In 2000, Congressman Julian Dixon sold me out like a $2 whore when, as ranking member of the House Judiciary Committee, he announced the CIA was not complicit in the destruction of the inner cities by crack cocaine. I'm tired of being sold out like a $2 whore by Black people living the good life as my representative in our nation's capital.

Thomas Paine said in the 1700s: "If there must be trouble, let it be in my day, that my child may have peace." Ralph Nader and Peter Camejo are voices taking on the trouble of our day so that we and future generations may have peace.

Get off your knees and demand the Democrats stop sabotaging the Nader-Camejo Campaign. Demand Ralph Nader and Peter Camejo be included in the debates. Don't go down like a punk. Remember the ancestors and stand tall!

Sincerely,

Donna J. Warren, a constituent

From "Maverick" to Attack Dog: Howard Dean's Gay Bashing of Ralph Nader

By Sherry Wolf
Published on www.counterpunch.org, July 10, 2004

Howard Dean gay bashed Ralph Nader on live radio before millions of listeners on NPR and no one chimed in to stop him. How could the Vermont also-ran, shilling for the anti-gay marriage John Kerry, slander the only presidential candidate who is for gay marriage by claiming over and over that Nader had accepted support from anti-gay Republicans?

Nader has not only come out for same-sex marriage—a basic civil right—but he is for ending legal discrimination against gays and lesbians that allows employers to fire someone for their sexual orientation in thirty-six states. Kerry and Dean oppose same-sex marriage, and both have repeatedly argued to leave it to the states to decide—reminiscent of the Dixiecrats of old who argued to leave desegregation to the enlightened minds of the Mississippi and Alabama legislators. As a result, segregation remained the de facto law of the land for a century after the Civil War.

Though Dean is often trumpeted as a great advocate of gay and lesbian rights because Vermont was the first state to offer civil unions while he was governor, the reality behind that partial victory exposes Dean's own opportunistic nod to the homophobes. When the Vermont Supreme Court unanimously ruled that gay couples were due the same legal rights of marriage as heterosexuals and ordered the legislature to pass a law to that effect in 1999, Dean made it clear that he would not sign gay marriage into law and pushed instead for civil unions.

Civil unions do not carry with them any of the 1,049 federal rights and benefits of marriage. When Dean did sign civil unions into law, he did so "in the closet," without the usual cameras flashing and notables in attendance. At the time of signing, according to the *Chicago Sun-Times*, Dean "was going around the state telling folks he was only doing it because the Vermont Supreme Court made him."

Kerry voted against Clinton's Defense of Marriage Act

(DOMA) in 1996—though 118 Democrats voted for it—but since then he has come out strongly against same-sex marriage and has repeatedly condemned the Massachusetts legislature for granting marriages to gay and lesbian couples.

Though the Democrats theoretically support the Employment Non-Discrimination Act (ENDA) that would eliminate the right of employers to fire someone for their sexual orientation, they have allowed it to languish on paper for a decade without ever hitting the floor of Congress. According to the *Washington Post*, Bill Clinton held a closed-door meeting in 1997 with advocates of ENDA—which has been chiseled away at to include notable exemptions for small businesses, the armed forces, and religious organizations. Clinton's "support"for gay civil rights was so half-hearted that he refused to use his influence to even get a vote on ENDA onto the House floor.

The Dean-Nader debate was aired on the very day when Republicans in the Senate were pushing to write discrimination against gays and lesbians into the Constitution via the Federal Marriage Amendment.

While Dean worked himself into a lather trying to slam Nader and prove his party's credentials as fighters for equal rights, neither Senators Kerry nor Edwards made an issue of this first attempt since slavery to include a denial of rights in the Constitution.

Those concerned with gay issues should remember the lessons from the Clinton years when deciding whom to vote for in November. Clinton's own Presidential AIDS Panel criticized his administration for failing to show a "coherent plan of action" against AIDS in 1998, despite the abundance of evidence indicating the effectiveness of preventive efforts, including needle exchanges. Though Clinton's "don't ask, don't tell" policy led to witch-hunts of gays in the military, gay press such as *The Advocate*, Lambda Legal Defense, and most AIDS activists in ACT-UP insisted that gay rights supporters vote for a second Clinton term in 1996 and not mobilize protests that might embarrass Clinton.

The only real substance to Howard Dean's charges against Nader was in his attack on the endorsement Nader has received from the right-wing Reform Party. And while I find this party of Neanderthal blowhards to be repugnant in its anti-immigrant and homophobic views—they are not the views of Ralph Nader!

Nader's clumsy handling so far of the Reform Party's endorsement should be challenged by his supporters, but taking heat from the likes of Democrats who have helped shape anti-gay policies such as "don't ask, don't tell" and DOMA is simply nauseating.

In the late 1980s and early 1990s, protests against gay bashing and for AIDS drugs and gay rights exploded onto the streets of dozens of cities in response to the reactionary policies of the Reagan and Bush I administrations. These protests gave confidence to millions of gays and forced a bigoted Bush administration to fund AIDS research and back down from the verbal belligerence toward gays that marked previous administrations.

Thousands of workplaces were pressured to provide domestic-partner benefits to lesbians and gays. Yet there has been almost no national mobilization for gay rights since the 1993 demonstration of hundreds of thousands in Washington, D.C., where the incoming Democratic administration was praised for its promise to improve the lives of lesbians and gays.

But the Democrats have reneged on those promises. According to the National Coalition of Anti-Violence Programs, more than fifty lesbian, gay, bisexual, and transgendered people have been reported killed in attacks since Matthew Shepard's murder, though the actual number of deaths is likely higher because many antigay attacks go unreported.

The strategy of electing Democrats to deliver civil rights for lesbians and gays has been a dismal failure.

Vote Kerry and Cobb: An Open Letter to Progressives

From Medea Benjamin, Peter Coyote, John Eder, Daniel Ellsberg, et al.
Published on www.commondreams.org, July 23, 2004

There is no greater political imperative this year than to retire the Bush regime, one of the most dangerous and extremist in U.S. history. As people dedicated to peace, economic justice, equality, sustainability, and constitutional freedoms, we are committed to defeating Bush.

The only candidate who can win instead of Bush in November is John Kerry. We want Kerry to replace Bush, because a Kerry administration would be less dangerous in many crucial areas, including militarism, civil liberties, civil rights, judicial appointments, reproductive rights, and environmental protection.

But while helping Kerry-Edwards defeat Bush-Cheney, we don't want to endorse Kerry positions that are an insult to various causes we support, including movements for global justice and peace that have burgeoned in recent years. Indeed, we want to communicate to Kerry and the world that we oppose many of his policies, including some that are barely distinguishable from Bush policies.

Accordingly, we encourage progressives to organize and vote strategically this year.

In "swing states," where few percentage points separate Bush and Kerry, we encourage activists to mobilize voters behind Kerry. (A frequently updated list of swing states is posted at www.swing04.com.)

In "safe states" (and Washington, D.C.), so overwhelmingly pro-Bush or pro-Kerry that we can be confident of who will win in November, we encourage activists to mobilize voters behind Green Party presidential candidate David Cobb.

In all states, we encourage activists to engage in election-year vigilance to ensure that all votes count, especially those of racial minorities—and to advocate for instant runoff voting and other reforms so that voters in future elections can support the candidate they most believe in without risk of electing the candidate they most oppose.

David Cobb has earned our endorsement in safe states by deftly steering the Green Party toward a nuanced strategy dedicated to ousting Bush, while seeking to grow a grassroots party that stands unapologetically for peace, racial and social justice, economic democracy, civil liberties, and genuine ecology. The Green Party gives political voice to movements that challenge Bush's Iraq policy and resist trade arrangements that trample on workers' rights, human rights, and the environment.

Despite a Democratic Party base that is increasingly progressive, anti-NAFTA/WTO and antiwar, John Kerry has lost the strong, brave voice he had as a young man who challenged the Vietnam War and now offers a faint echo of too many Bush policies—from Iraq and military spending to the global trade regime and corporate coddling (e.g., Kerry's plan to reduce corporate taxes).

We are disappointed that, four years after the Florida disaster, Kerry and leading Democrats (with exceptions such as Dennis Kucinich, Jesse Jackson Jr., and Howard Dean) do not promote common-sense electoral reforms like instant runoff voting that would once and for all eliminate the "spoiler" risk that deforms U.S. elections.

With our electoral system yet to be fixed, we are left this year with the improvised solution of endorsing one candidate in some states and another candidate in other states. This dual-endorsement solution is preferable to endorsing either a candidate with important positions we oppose or a solidly progressive candidate whose votes in swing states could help Bush get four more years.

In this crucial election year, we encourage progressives to work tirelessly to vote Bush out—as we build grassroots networks and coalitions to hold the Kerry administration accountable to the progressive values and policies shared by most Americans.

Signed:

Medea Benjamin, Peter Coyote, John Eder, Daniel Ellsberg, Angela Gilliam, Kevin Gray, Tom Hayden, Elizabeth Horton Sheff, Rabbi Michael Lerner, Robert McChesney, Norman Solomon.

Money vs. People: The Mystery of the 2004 Elections

By Peter Miguel Camejo
Published on www.greensfornader.net, July 29, 2004

There is a mystery to the 2004 presidential election; a silence has fallen on America regarding a glaring contradiction. As we enter the second half of 2004, there is massive popular opposition to the war in Iraq and to the USA PATRIOT Act—possibly a majority of Americans. Yet these same people are about to vote in overwhelming numbers for John Kerry for President.

But John Kerry and his running mate, John Edwards, gave President Bush eighteen standing ovations in January, voted for the war, say the war was right, insist on continuing the occupation of Iraq against its peoples' desires, want to increase the number of troops and nations occupying Iraq, voted for "unconditional support to Bush" for his conduct of the war, and backed Bush by voting against the U.S. Constitution for the Patriot Act.

The only explanation for tens of millions voting against their heartfelt opinions is the lack of free elections in America. There are no runoff elections. Without runoffs people are trapped. They fear expressing their true opinions. If they vote for what they are for they are told they will only elect Bush. They must learn to vote against themselves, to accept the con game of a two-party system. People are taught not to vote *for* what they believe but *against* an individual.

An unpopular policy once identified with an individual can be continued by replacing the individual, keeping the policy with modifications. In replacing Bush, Kerry pledges to more effectively forward the same policy of imperial domination.

If runoff elections existed tens of millions would vote against both Bush and Kerry and for peace. Once the myth of invulnerability of the two-party system is broken the dam against democracy and free elections will break. Already 25 percent of Americans are no longer registered Democratic or Republican; they seek alternatives.

The Democrats' fear of Ralph Nader is rooted in the programmatic conflict between their Party's stance and their supporters. This is the real story of the 2004 elections.

This mystery is never written about in the media—it is America's dark secret.

The 2000 presidential election was stolen when some sixty thousand people, primarily African Americans, had their right to vote illegally revoked in Florida. The film, *Fahrenheit 9/11*, opens showing one African-American congressperson after another asking for an investigation. But their cry for justice was squashed because not one Senator, not one Democrat, not Paul Wellstone, Barbara Boxer, Ted Kennedy, John Kerry, or John Edwards would defend democracy, and stand up for free elections.

Three and a half years later the Democratic Party has not lifted a finger to establish free elections in America. Not in a single state have they called for runoffs so Florida could never happen again. They could not make it clearer: the Democratic Party prefers that Republicans win elections, even without majority support, rather than allow free elections where a third party or an independent candidate could attract tens of millions from their base. Their answer is simple: Ralph Nader must not run, must not be an alternative.

If free elections were held with a runoff system like in most civilized nations, if proportional representation existed where if a point of view receives 20 percent of the vote its supporters would receive 20 percent representation, then every vote would count, and the Democratic Party as we know it today would no longer exist. The one hundred million people who never vote would have a reason to vote. New parties would appear and a representative democracy would begin to blossom in America.

Ralph Nader has created a small hole in the dam. The danger is real. The Democrats are on an all-out effort to attack the Nader/Camejo campaign because if voters begin to vote for what they want the entire electoral system would begin to unravel. If twenty million citizens voted for Nader it would be the beginning of the end of the two-party system. The Democrats would enter into a crisis, the ability of money to control people would begin to crack and the possibility of a democracy where citizens could vote for what they believe would be born. The Democrats are determined, not to beat Bush but to stop Nader, to protect the two-party, pro-corporate rule that America lives under.

That is what is behind all the talk of the miniscule funding by Republican citizens of Nader/Camejo. It is part of a relentless attack against free elections and the First Amendment of the Bill of Rights.

This is why the Democrats have organized a nationwide "hate Nader" campaign. They seek to obfuscate the issues. They seek to prevent the right of citizens to vote for Nader by preventing Nader even his right to be on the ballot. State by state thousands of citizens sign petitions to place Nader on the ballot; state by state the Democrats harass, seek technicalities to challenge the signatures, and try to prevent allowing the people a choice that is pro-peace.

The attack on Nader by the *San Francisco Chronicle* with a banner front-page article claiming Republicans are funding Nader is just one part of an ongoing campaign. In spite of the relentless attacks against Nader the polls continue to show ten million people behind Nader/Camejo.

Wealthy Democrats and Republicans both cross-finance their campaigns. It is standard practice for corporations to donate to both. Republicans donate millions to the Democrats. The very corporations that Democrats supposedly oppose, Enron, Halliburton, and Exxon, for example, all give funds to Kerry/Edwards. Kerry/Edwards have no plans to return a penny of their Republican or corporate backing.

These corporate/lobbyist funds are not really contributions. They are investments or bribes with an expected return of access and policy, precisely like the Kerry/Edwards call for lower taxes on corporations. This kind of contribution dominates the financing of Bush and Kerry as well as most major party candidates for Congress and Senate.

Corporations once paid 33 percent of the taxes received by the federal government. Now they pay under 8 percent, yet Kerry/Edwards are promising to lower their taxes further in spite of the half-trillion-dollar federal deficit per year and the increasingly regressive taxes on working people.

Against this domination of money over people stand Ralph Nader and the Nader/Camejo campaign.

The Nader/Camejo campaign is seeking votes from all citizens, Democrats, Independents, Republicans, Greens, and Libertarians.

Just as we seek their votes we ask all of them to help fund our campaign that opposes the war in Iraq, the US Patriot Act, and defends the health and well-being of our working people.

We especially ask for donations for the right to be on the ballot and for free elections in the United States, elections that respect the will of the voters, that favor runoffs (instant runoff voting) and proportional representation.

Most working people never give funds to any candidate. Those who do occasionally give to a candidate have no anticipation of personal financial gain. It is that kind of donor that represents the overwhelming majority of contributions to Nader/Camejo. The bulk of our contributions are in amounts below 100 dollars per person.

The Nader/Camejo campaign does not accept funds from Exxon, Enron, or Halliburton as Kerry/Edwards do. We do not accept funding from corporations!

We ask that Kerry/Edwards stop their hypocritical campaign about the miniscule funding we have received from citizens registered Republican. We ask that they stop their campaign against the American voters seeking to deny them a choice at the ballot box by allowing ballot access and an opportunity for voters who support Nader/Camejo to vote for them.

We, like all other candidates, do not, can not, and will not give donors lie detectors to ascertain their objectives in funding our campaign.

We have proposed a simple solution to the funding issue. Establish public funding of all campaigns to create fairness and end corruption. Kerry/Edwards and Bush/Cheney oppose public funding.

The choice is clear. Continue a corrupt electoral system that closes choices, forces citizens to vote against their conscience, and allows money to control people—or open up the electoral system, defend civil liberties, and establish free elections.

What You Won't Hear: Twelve Topics Democrats Will Duck at Convention
By Ralph Nader
Boston Globe, *July 25, 2004*

The Democratic National Convention that gathers in Boston this week to nominate John F. Kerry for president will be more like a coronation than a competition. Huzzahs, speeches, bands, balloons. These affairs have long lost any suspense or spontaneity, but somewhere amid the endless corporate schmoozing and lobbyist gladhanding, you'd expect an ounce of inspiration.

Instead, voters will watch (or, rather, *not* watch) as more than $13 million of their tax dollars (the amount allotted by the federal government for each convention) is spent on saying very little of substance.

Rather than ideas, this convention is about power and avoidance: the power of big business and special interests and the avoidance of any issues that might draw a clear distinction between our two leading political parties.

Here is a short list of what you won't hear this week, either on the convention floor or in the party's platform. Call them the twelve taboos.

1. You won't hear a call for a national crackdown on the corporate crime, fraud, and abuse that, in just the last four years, have robbed trillions of dollars from workers, investors, pension holders, taxpayers, and consumers. Among the reforms that won't be suggested are resources to prosecute executive crooks and laws to democratize corporate governance so shareholders have real power. Democrats will not shout for a payback of ill-gotten gains, to rein in executive pay, or to demand corporate sunshine laws. The convention will not demand that workers receive a living wage instead of a minimum wage. There will be no backing for a repeal of the anti-union Taft-Hartley Act of 1947, which has blocked more than 40 million workers from forming or joining trade unions to improve wages and benefits above Wal-Mart or McDonald's levels. One out of four U.S. workers is now being paid less than $8.75 per hour.

2. John Kerry claims that he will call for a review of all existing trade agreements, but he will not call for a withdrawal from the WTO and NAFTA. Trade agreements should stick to trade while labor, environmental, and consumer rights are advanced by separate treaties without being subordinated to the dictates of international commerce.

3. Kerry may suggest that President Bush's tax cuts for the wealthy be rolled back, but he will steer clear of any suggestion that our income-tax system be substantially revamped. Workers should keep more of their wages while we tax the things we like least at the source, such as polluters, stock speculation, addictive industries, and energy-guzzling technologies. Corporations should be required to pay their fair share; corporate tax contributions as a percentage of the overall federal revenue

stream have been declining for fifty years and now stand at 7.4 percent despite massive record profits.

4. There will be no call for a single-payer health system. Fifty-five years after President Truman first proposed it, we still need health insurance for everyone, a program with quality and cost controls and an emphasis on prevention. Full Medicare for everyone will save thousands of lives while maintaining patient choice of doctors and hospitals within a competitive private health-care delivery system.

5. There is no reason to believe that the Democrats will stand up to the commercial interests profiting from our current energy situation. We need a major environmental health agenda that challenges these entrenched interests with new initiatives in solar energy, efficiency in motor vehicles, and other sustainable and clean energy technologies. Nor will there be any recognition that current fossil fuels are producing global warming, cancer, respiratory diseases, and geopolitical entanglements. Finally, there will be no calls for ending environmental racism that leads to contaminated water and air in our cities, to toxic dumps in poorer neighborhoods, and to high toxicities in the workplace.

6. Democrats will not demand a reduction in the military budget that devours half the federal government's operating expenditures at a time when there is no Soviet Union or other major state enemy in the world. Studies by the General Accounting Office and internal Pentagon assessments support the judgment of many retired admirals and generals that a wasteful defense weakens our country and distorts priorities at home.

7. You won't hear a clarion call for electoral reform. Both parties have shamelessly engaged in gerrymandering, a process that guarantees re-election of their candidates at the expense of frustrated voters. Nor will there be any suggestion that law-abiding ex-felons be allowed to vote. Other electoral reforms should include reducing barriers to candidates, same-day registration, a voter-verified paper record for electronic voting, runoff voting to insure winners receive a majority vote, binding none-of-the-above choices, and most important, full public financing to

guarantee clean elections.

8. You will hear John Kerry speak about his "tough-on-crime" background as a federal prosecutor, but you will hear no calls for reform of the criminal justice system. Our nation now holds one out of four of the world's prisoners, half of them nonviolent. While they attempt to counter Republican charges that they favor criminals over victims, Democrats will say nothing about a failed war on drugs that costs nearly $50 billion annually. And they will not argue that addicts should be treated rather than imprisoned. Nor should observers hope for any call to repeal the "three strikes and you're out" laws that have filled our jails or to end mandatory sentencing that hamstrings our judges.

9. Democrats will ignore the Israeli peace movement whose members have developed accords for a two-state solution with their Palestinian and American counterparts. It is time to replace the Washington puppet show with a Washington peace show for the security of the American, Palestinian, and Israeli people.

10. The Democrats will not call for the United States to begin a military and corporate withdrawal from Iraq. Such a withdrawal would result in mainstream Iraqis no longer supporting or joining the insurgency. Troops from neutral, Arab, and other Muslim countries would temporarily replace U.S. forces as Iraqis get back their country through internationally supervised elections allowing for appropriate autonomy for the Kurdish, Sunni, and Shi'ite communities.

11. Seriously waging peace will be far cheaper than a permanent war economy which is generating huge deficits and distracting attention, talent, and resources from the American people.

12. Democrats will not stand up to business interests that have backed changes that close the courtroom to wrongfully injured and cheated individuals, but not to corporations. Where is the campaign against fraud and injury upon innocent patients, consumers, and workers? We should make it easier for consumers to band together and defend themselves against harmful practices in the marketplace.

To the voters I say: Don't hold your breath waiting for the Democrats to put people, not corporations, first. Watch as this convention abides by the twelve taboos.

David Cobb's Soft Charade: The Greens and the Politics of Mendacity

By Joshua Frank
Published on www.counterpunch.org, August 6, 2004

(The following is an expansion of a previous article. After receiving numerous e-mails from Campus Greens organizers, former Green co-chair Ben Manski, and many other irate Greens, I felt a need to clarify the misconceptions that are revolving around David Cobb's mundane campaign. And just to clarify, I've been registered Green since 1999, and worked on a number of ballot measures and campaigns.)

Green Party presidential candidate David Cobb has publicly said he is not running a "safe-state" campaign. In a rare interview with Steve Curwood of National Public Radio on July 2, when asked if he was running a "safe-state" strategy, Cobb replied, "No, it's not true. What I've said is I'm going to get on every ballot that I can possibly get on."

Sounds convincing. The guy is not only running in safe states, he wants to be on the ballot in as many states as possible. Fair enough. But is Cobb simply fabricating his own campaign's motives?

Indeed.

The fact is Cobb may not call what he plans to do a "safe-state" approach, but it is. As his Web site contends: "[Cobb] has said he will focus his campaign on states neglected by the corporate parties (i.e., 'safe-states'), he has also said that he will visit and campaign in any state that invites him."

Invites him? I wasn't aware presidential candidates had to be invited to a state in order to campaign.

His Web site declaration continues: "For example, he has pledged to visit the battleground states like Ohio and Pennsylvania to support their petition drives to put the Green Party candidate on the state ballots."

So Cobb has publicly announced that he will not actively campaign in swing states even if he is on the ballot, although he will work in those states for other Green hopefuls.

"[In swing] states, I'm acknowledging that there is a profound responsibility on the citizens," Cobb told Curwood in the NPR interview, "and they should weigh their options and decide how to spend their very precious vote."

Could you imagine John Kerry or George Bush muttering such feeble words: "Weigh their options?" I am no weathered campaign advisor, but I can imagine that it is a bad idea for any candidate to advise potential voters that they have a viable alternative to your own party's ticket. Shouldn't Cobb be trumping his campaign instead of asking voters to "decide how to spend their very precious vote"? Again, instead of fighting for the Green Party, he has oh-so-slyly admitted he sees quite a difference between Bush and Kerry. On what grounds he hasn't made clear.

As for Cobb's running mate Pat LaMarche, she is also a bit confused. Following Cobb's announcement that he wanted LaMarche to be his running mate, she said she would not commit to voting for herself and Cobb in November. "If Bush has got 11 percent of the vote in Maine come November 2, I can vote for whoever I want," she told the *Portland Press Herald/Maine Sunday Telegram.* "I love my country. Maybe we should ask them that, because if [Vice President] Dick Cheney loved his country, he wouldn't be voting for himself."

Later, perhaps realizing the stupidity of her remarks, LaMarche posted a press release on the Cobb campaign Web site. "I am honored to be the Green Party vice presidential candidate running with David Cobb," she lamented. "I want to reassure all members of the Green Party that, on November 2nd, I will be voting Cobb/LaMarche."

Glad we got that cleared up. It's too late, however. The cat is out of the bag. LaMarche, like Cobb, believes Kerry offers a stark alternative to George Bush's band of neocons. If some progressives feel that Kerry does, fine, but Greens shouldn't be the ones sparking that debate.

With all this it is clear that the Green Party may as well drop out of the presidential race. What's the point of running? If Cobb is attempting to build a party (as his defenders claim) grounded on the premise that Democrats offer a significant alternative to Republicans—there is little need for a Green Party to even exist. Just join progressive Democrats who are attempting to change the centrist tides from within the establishment. That seems to be working pretty well. Just ask Dennis Kucinich.

Parties to Injustice: Democrats Will Do Anything to Keep Me Off the Ballot
By Ralph Nader
Washington Post, September 5, 2004

This summer, swarms of Democratic Party lawyers, propagandists, harassers, and assorted operatives have been conducting an unsavory war against my campaign's effort to secure a spot on the presidential ballots in various states. It is not enough that both major parties, in state after state, have used the legislatures to erect huge barriers, unique among Western democracies, to third-party and independent candidacies. Now they are engaging in what can only be called dirty tricks and frivolous lawsuits to keep me and my running mate, Peter Miguel Camejo, off the ballot while draining precious dollars from our campaign chest.

This contemptuous drive is fueled with large amounts of unregulated money, much of it funneled through the National Progress Fund, an ostensibly independent group led by Toby Moffett, a former Democratic congressman who is currently a partner in a largely Republican lobbying firm called the Livingston Group. By contrast, to defend ourselves from the assault, we have to draw on funds that are limited and regulated by the Federal Election Commission.

News reports show that the National Progress Fund and other so-called independent 527 organizations (named for the section of the tax code under which they incorporate) were operating openly at the Democratic National Convention. They held meetings to discuss the best strategies and tactics to push the Nader/Camejo ticket off the ballot and they raised money from Democratic fat cats to accomplish their goals. It is evident that these "independent" groups are actually not independent but working closely with the Democratic Party.

In addition, chair of the Democratic Party of Maine, Dorothy Melanson, testified under oath in a public hearing before Maine's secretary of state last Monday that the national Democratic Party is funding efforts throughout the country to stop Nader/Camejo from appearing on ballots.

These ties with Democrats don't prevent the 527s from accepting help from entrenched corporate interests, or even Republican quarters, to finance challenges of the signatures we have collected to meet the requirements of ballot access. According to reports filed with the Internal Revenue Service, Robert Savoie, president of Louisiana-based Science & Engineering Associates, donated $25,000 to the National Progress Fund in June. A month before, Savoie gave $25,000 to the Republican National Committee.

In Pennsylvania, where a court last Monday barred us from appearing on the ballot, signature challenges have been mounted by Reed Smith, a law firm whose political action committee primarily gives to Republicans. A lawyer from the firm boasted to the *New York Times* that "8 to 10 lawyers in his firm were working pro bono on the case, 80 hours each a week for two weeks, and could end up working six more weeks." The firm is counsel to twenty-nine of the top thirty U.S. banks, twenty-six of the Fortune 50 companies, nine of the top ten pharmaceutical companies, and fifty of the world's leading drug and medical device manufacturers.

The melding of these interests demonstrates that it is the corporate-political duopoly that is working to limit voters' choices for this November. For all their talk about free markets, the major parties do not tolerate competition very well. They don't want voters to be able to consider a candidate who advocates health care for all; a crackdown on corporate crime, fraud, and abuse; a shrinking of the military-industrial complex and corporate welfare; a living wage for all full-time workers; and a responsible withdrawal from Iraq.

The zeal of these ballot access sentries comes from a refusal to respect the rights of millions of voters to have the opportunity to vote for candidates of their choice. With their organized obstruction of our campaign's efforts just to get a place on the ballots, these authoritarians want to deny Americans more voices, choices, and agendas. The voters are the losers.

Watching their bullying maneuvers and harassing lawsuits around the country, I marvel at the absence of condemnation by Senator John F. Kerry or Terry McAuliffe, the Democratic National Committee chairman.

Senator Kerry told us that he would look into this situation seven weeks ago but we have not heard back from him yet. Around the same time, McAuliffe told me in a phone conversation that he actively approved of these organized efforts, one of which is ironically called the Ballot Project. He urged me to run only in the thirty-one states considered to be locked up by one of the two candidates.

Challenging the signatures of your rivals is an old political tactic, and when you're collecting hundreds of thousands of signatures, there are bound to be some that don't withstand scrutiny. But the Democrats are not just seeking compliance with harsh election laws. They are using dirty tricks to intimidate citizens.

That's the way it seemed to a fifty-eight-year-old supporter of ours in Oregon. On August 12, 2004, she was at home with her two grandchildren when she answered a knock on her door and found a man and woman who she said began threatening her with jail if there was any false information on the petitions she was collecting for our ballot access. These people, who called themselves "investigators," were dispatched by a law firm that has worked extensively with Oregon trade unions that have supported Democratic candidates. In many states our signature gatherers have been subjected to similar treatment in what is clearly an orchestrated campaign.

And some people who merely signed Nader/Camejo petitions have also been pressured. One person in Nevada got a call from someone who urged him to admit that he was tricked into signing our petition. When the petition signer said he had signed voluntarily, the caller continued to try to persuade him to claim that he had not signed the petition. After numerous requests, the caller identified himself and admitted he was from the Democratic National Committee in Las Vegas. A call to the number on the caller ID was answered, "Hello, DNC." We have similar reports from around the country.

Ballot access laws are so arbitrary and complex that they leave small parties open to legal pestering. In Arizona, large Democratic donors hired three corporate law firms to file frivolous challenges to our clearly ample number of signatures. For example, 1,349 signatures of registered voters were invalidated because the person who collected them had given his or her correct full address but had neglected to include the correct name of the county. The purpose of these exercises are, in lobbyist Moffett's words, "to neutralize [Nader's] campaign by forcing him to spend money and resources defending these things."

A covey of Democratic operatives in Illinois convinced the election board to disqualify signatures because the registered voters had moved since registering to vote even though they still lived in Illinois. The Democratic Speaker of the state House of Representatives sent state employees, contractors, and interns to review and challenge our ballot access petitions. The speaker wouldn't say—when asked either by reporters or in a Freedom of Information Act request my campaign filed in July—whether these state employees took leave from their taxpayer-paid jobs.

In other states, Democratic operatives are using a grace period after the filing date and directly calling voters who signed, pressing them to withdraw their signatures or say that they were misled so that the Democrats could allege fraud later in court.

The Democratic Party's machine is operating in many other ways, too. Its apparatchiks were waiting at the Virginia secretary of state's office on August 20 to say that our signature gatherers did not arrive in time, when in fact they arrived with twenty-five minutes to spare. The head of the state Elections Division, who happens to be the former executive director of the Virginia Democratic Party, refused even to accept our petitions until she was ordered to do so by the state attorney general.

To excuse and distract from this accumulation of organized misdeeds, the Democrats are feeding the press the Big Lie that the Republicans are bankrolling and supporting us. If the Republicans were to spend one-quarter as much to support us as the Democrats are spending to obstruct our access to ballots and our supporters' civil liberties, we would be on all fifty state ballots by now.

We have not been accepting signatures obtained through organized Republican Party efforts in the three or four states where we have learned of such activity.

We are trying, of course, to win over some Republican and independent voters who voted for George Bush in 2000 but are furious with him over endless deficits, federal regulation of local education, corporate subsidies and handouts, the sovereignty-shredding World Trade Organization and North American Free Trade Agreement, the big-government-snooping Patriot Act and, lately, the Iraq quagmire.

In 2000 about 25 percent of our vote came from people who told exit pollsters they otherwise would have voted for Bush. Yet the most recent independent review of our current campaign found that only 4 percent of our donations came from people who have also given to the Republican Party. The Center for Responsive Politics found that this group of fifty-one people gave $406,000 to the Republicans and $53,000 to Nader/Camejo. Amusingly, however, the center found that our Republican backers gave even more, $63,000, to the Democrats.

When I talked to Kerry, I cautioned him that if he did not order a stop to the dirty tricks of his Democratic underlings and allies, he may face a mini-Watergate type of scandal. For Democrats and Republicans who care about civil liberties, free speech, and an equal right to run for elective office, this festering situation should invite their very focused demands to cease and desist.

Hand it to the Democrats to keep some costs down, though. A contractor they hired in Michigan to make phone calls to check the validity of our tens of thousands of signatures outsourced the work to India.

Only Progressive Unity Can Defeat Bush

By Zack Kaldveer, Media Coordinator, Greens for Kerry, and Sophie Mintier, Treasurer, Greens for Kerry
October 21, 2004

We consider this election to be the most important in a generation. The Bush/Cheney administration is the most extreme, incompetent, and dangerous in our nation's history. The prospects of a second term and the consequences it would have on our country and world led us to a simple question: "How do Greens and progressives participate in what was clearly becoming the most important challenge in a generation: ending the reign of George W. Bush?" The answer to that question is to vote for John Kerry in swing states.

We joined the Green Party because of its commitment to human rights, sustainability, economic and environmental justice, peace, and civil liberties. Indeed, if these are more than slogans, and truly represent our core principles, then uniting to defeat Bush was a moral imperative. For that reason, we formed Greens for Kerry (GFK), and our mission was simple: help beat Bush, mobilize to push Kerry to adopt a more progressive agenda if elected, and promote the growth of the Green Party on a grassroots level.

Like so many progressives, we are wholly unsatisfied with our current, money-driven, corporate-dominated political system and the limited options that a two-party democracy provides. But, given our current political reality, we believe it is our civic duty to help unseat George W. Bush, the mandatory first step if a larger progressive movement is to ever take shape. After November 2, if Kerry is elected, we must continue on with phase two of the long-term goal that most progressives share: building a political movement in America from the grassroots up. In less than four years this administration has weakened milestone environmental protection laws like the Clean Air Act (four hundred environmental rollback attempts); eliminated key labor rights fought for and won by those before us; dismantled what once were considered unassailable constitutional rights; appointed extremist judges to our country's federal courts; and established a new military doctrine of pre-emptive nuclear war.

As progressives we recognize that John Kerry is not an ideal choice. However, to deny the significant differences between the two candidates on issues ranging from environmental protection, nuclear proliferation, women's rights, the Supreme Court, and labor rights, is intellectually dishonest.

We ask that when you enter that voting booth you consider the worker making minimum wage who won't be receiving a $1.85 an hour raise ($3,848 more a year: Kerry proposes a $7.00 minimum wage) if Bush is re-elected; remember the single mother whose childcare services will be cut; remember the women whose reproductive rights will be jeopardized; remember the effect that Bush's policies will have on the air we breathe, the water we drink, and the food we eat. Then tell yourself it doesn't matter how you vote. This election is not an academic exercise—lives are at stake. But don't just take our word for it: Noam Chomsky recently remarked, "Anyone who says 'I don't care if Bush gets elected' is basically telling poor and working people in the country, 'I don't care if your lives are destroyed.'" He also quite rightly stated, "Then there is another choice: electing Bush or seeking to prevent his election."

Winona LaDuke, Nader's running mate in 2000, stated just this week, "I love this land, and I know that we need to make drastic changes in Washington if we are going to protect our land and our communities.... I'm voting my conscience on November 2; I'm voting for John Kerry."

In fact, seventy-five members of the Nader 2000 Citizens Committee recently signed a letter calling on swing-state voters to support Kerry, which included such progressive legends as Jim Hightower, Studs Terkel, Cornel West, and Howard Zinn. Are these individuals, who have dedicated their lives to strengthening our democracy and speaking truth to power all just sellouts? Or do they recognize something larger, something that we believe all of us feel on the deepest of levels—that our democracy, freedom, future, and past are under assault, and it is our job to put an end to it.

If you still aren't convinced, please consider using a key tool GFK and other progressive organizations are promoting this election year to both help defeat Bush and support third-party candidates like Ralph Nader and David Cobb called "vote pairing" (www.votepair.org). Vote pairing allows would-be Nader or Green Party voters in swing states to swap their votes with Kerry supporters in non-swing states. This allows you to vote your conscience, vote out Bush, and begin to turn our country around.

The world community, and the millions of Americans whose lives will be hurt by four more years of this administration are pleading that we help put an end to this imperial regime. We need to heed their call. Voting for John Kerry in swing states is our only realistic response.

An Open Letter to Former Naderites Running Scared in 2004*

By Ralph Nader
Published at www.votenader.org, October 27, 2004

I was saddened to read your open letter urging people to vote for John Kerry in 2004. Saddened, not because of the impact on my vote but because it signals more of the same surrender of some liberal thinkers.

Senator Kerry made it clear in the three debates with President Bush that he has no intention of getting out of the illegal occupation of Iraq. He is going to fight the war to win it and will send more troops if needed. He also showed that rather than challenging the military-industrial complex he intends to expand the military by forty thousand more troops. How can any peace activist support a candidate who holds those views? Even without the voice of the peace movement, about half the American public wants the U.S. out of Iraq. If the peace movement had stood for ending the Iraq occupation and demanding that their candidate do so then we would have had a very different debate in 2004. Now, no matter how the election turns out, we are likely to see a bloody offensive after the war and a quagmire that will become a civil war with the U.S. on the side of our puppet government against the Iraqi people.

Regrettably, the same is true for other popular progressive issues. Two-thirds of the public supports health care for all now, yet Senator Kerry has put forward a plan that leaves 20 million without health care. The American public believes that full-time workers should make a wage that they and their families can live on. Yet John Kerry only advocates raising the minimum wage to $7 an hour by 2007—this will keep wages at the equivalent of pre-1960 earnings—at a time when some CEOs are now earning $7,000 per hour. And, even on the environment, in

---

* A number of these people never worked for any group under my supervision. They are a tiny minority of the thousands of people who have worked in the groups I have founded.

the debates John Kerry made it clear he did not support the Kyoto Treaty—despite the clear evidence of global climate change and its ruinous impact on the environment. The women's movement has been told that Kerry will consider anti-choice judges and that he is proud of his vote for Justice Scalia. African Americans have been ignored, taken for granted, and their issues not even discussed.

If the liberal leadership had not surrendered to the Anybody-But-Bush mentality and demanded John Kerry support these issues they would have accomplished two important things. First, they would have made John Kerry a better candidate—rather than allowed him to become an echo of George Bush's policies. Second, they would have advanced the progressive agenda, rather than allowed this popular agenda to be ignored in a presidential election year.

Those of you who were asked to sign this petition by Robert Brandon, a Democratic Party operative, should know that he misled you with his false statement, claiming that Nader–Camejo are supported by "right-wing campaign donors." The Center for Responsive Politics found that only 4 percent of Nader–Camejo donations came from Republican donors, many from classmates who I have worked with on various social justice issues. Indeed, the Center found that the Democratic candidate, John Kerry, has taken more than $10 million from Republican donors—one hundred times more than Nader–Camejo has received. You should not confuse the conclusion of the letter with its deceptive predicates. You should have done your homework.

Finally, what have you said about the anti-democratic dirty tricks, political bigotry, harassment, and intimidation by the Democratic Party and the Kerry–Edwards campaign? We would welcome hearing from you if you want to join us in condemning these gross violations of civil liberties and Nader–Camejo and the millions of voters who are denied the candidate of their choice.

I plan to continue to fight for justice—there should be no holiday from that struggle no matter how this election turns out. We hope the scared liberal leaders who abandoned their principles in 2004 will find a way to find the courage of their convictions in the future and rejoin this effort.

Sincerely,

Ralph Nader

CHAPTER FIVE

Lessons from the 2004 Elections

Political Independence Is the Lesson of 2004 for Progressives

By Howie Hawkins
November 8, 2004

The 2004 election should jolt progressives into rejecting once and for all the self-defeating strategy of supporting the Democrats as the lesser evil. "Anybody But Bush" resulted in anything but the progressive agenda.

Progressives didn't lose on November 2. They lost long before November 2 when beating Bush became the central priority for most progressives. If Kerry had won, he would be sitting down right now with Bush during the transition period, two Skull and Bones brothers jointly planning escalation of the war in Iraq and the corresponding neglect of social and environmental crises. The only times prominent progressives got any widespread media coverage in this election was when they joined in the Democrats' $20 million attack on the independent antiwar, anti-corporate Nader/Camejo ticket.

Working people lost the election last April when the labor movement continued to support Kerry even after he pointedly prioritized deficit reduction and a military spending hike over social spending. By June, when Kerry reassured the Democratic Leadership Council, the organized corporate force in the Democratic Party of which he is a founding member, that "I am not a redistributionist Democrat," unions should have been in open rebellion against Kerry.

Environmentalists lost the election as soon as the leadership of the big environmental groups decided to attack rather than support the Nader/Camejo ticket. Nader/Camejo was the one ticket with both the will and potential capacity to put before the nation the urgent need for a demilitarization and solarization of the economy before the impending peak of oil and gas production and the food, heating, electrical, and other material supply lines of petro-industrial society start breaking down.

The peace movement lost the election when it collapsed into the pro-war Kerry campaign, thereby giving legitimacy to the post-election escalation of the war to colonize Iraq that we are now witnessing. Because Kerry was as pro-war as Bush, it was clear long before the vote on November 2 that the U.S. government, under Kerry or Bush, would escalate the war for oil in Iraq and cut domestic spending to pay for it.

The 99 percent Bush/Kerry vote should not be taken as a 99 percent mandate for sacrificing social needs at home to empire abroad. It's more like a 70 percent mandate. The November 5 AP/Ipsos poll showed seven in ten Americans think U.S. troops should stay until Iraq is "stabilized." But that is up 32 percent from earlier in the year, when polls showed that only a 38 percent minority, in both the May 11 CBS/New York Times poll and the September 13 Harris poll, said U.S. troops should stay until Iraq is "stabilized." That's what happens when two pro-war candidates debate who can best fight the war to "stabilize" Iraq and the peace movement supports one of them. Peace movement support for the pro-war lesser evil helped turn a pro-war minority into a pro-war majority.

Progressives who supported Anybody But Bush have to face the fact that their lesser-evil strategy suffered a crushing defeat in this election. Not only did unions and other nominally progressive political organizations blow a few hundred million dollars failing to elect Kerry; worse, progressives lost the battle of public opinion as the lesser-evil strategy took progressive demands completely out of the debate, thus enabling Kerry to join programmatically with Bush in a debate about which one of them could best promote a militaristic approach to Iraq, terrorism, the Patriot Act, and federal spending priorities.

Progressives made no demands on Kerry. They never threatened to take their votes to the progressive Nader/Camejo ticket. Progressives marginalized themselves by allowing Kerry to take their votes for granted.

The political lesson that progressives should draw from the 2004 election is that abandoning their demands to support the Democrats as the lesser evil is political suicide.

Progressives can best fight the right through their own party that can advance a real alternative to militarized corporate plunder without compromise because it is independent of the funding and influence of the corporate/military complex. So the next four years should be about:

- strengthening the Green Party as an alternative to the bipartisan consensus of the corporate-sponsored parties;

- recommitting the Greens to independent politics;

- building independent movements for peace, justice, and the environment that are oriented toward winning people over to their demands instead of merely delivering them to the Democratic Party; and

- giving those movements independent electoral expression, especially at the municipal level where the Greens can continue to win offices, begin transformation from below by exercising the considerable autonomous powers of municipalities, and demonstrate that there really is an alternative.

New Mexico: A Sobering Lesson for Practical Fusion
By Jack Uhrich
Green Horizon Quarterly, Fall 2004

The New Mexico Green Party made national headlines in 1994. Its candidates for governor and lieutenant governor, Roberto Mondragon and Steve Schmidt, received over 10 percent of the vote, and the favored Democrats in the race, Bruce King and Patsy Madrid, lost.

All of a sudden, seemingly coming from nowhere, the Greens were a power to be reckoned with in New Mexico politics. Over the next six years, they would become what David Cobb called a "flagship" state party of the national Green movement, looked to as a model by Green parties all over the country.

Actually, like all "overnight successes," there was a lot of unseen groundwork laid beforehand. The NM Green Party's first chairperson, Abe Gutmann, had gained 40 percent of the vote in a state legislative race in 1992, Andres Vargas received 42 percent the same year in a race for district attorney, and Steve Schmidt had helped lay the groundwork for all the Green electoral successes that were to come over the next several years with his proposed strategy of running "serious, credible, platform-based candidates and campaigns."

But today, after all that groundwork and success, the New Mexico Green Party is a shell of its former self. Its Web site doesn't appear to have been updated in almost two years. They've only elected two candidates in the last three years, and one of their elected officials, Santa Fe city council member Miguel Chavez, switched his registration from Green to Democrat in 2002. Further, the Greens' candidate for governor in 2002, who helped the party regain its ballot status, has also switched his registration to Democrat to help the Dennis Kucinich campaign, and many others in the Albuquerque area have done the same.

What Happened? What Lessons Can Be Learned?

What happened to the momentum of the New Mexico Greens? Is their fate indicative of larger issues within the Green Party nationally? Does their fate foretell problems to come in other states? What lessons can we learn from their successes and shortcomings?

Even though many independent and Democratic progressives (incorrectly) blamed the Greens for the Democrats' loss in 1994, there were also many progressives—both inside and outside of the Democratic Party—who were glad to see an alternative out there. In late 1995, this writer helped to pull together Green Party leaders and leaders of NM's Pro PAC (a political action committee for progressive Democrats). An informal compromise was worked out, whereby the Greens agreed not to run candidates against incumbent Democrats that we considered progressive and supportive of our platform. Essentially, New Mexico Greens were practicing what Abe Gutmann called "practical fusion," whereby, even though they didn't formally endorse some of the non-Green progressive candidates, Greens were tacitly supporting them by not running someone against them and splitting the progressive vote. And that type of principled, positive cooperation was reciprocated by progressive Democrats. Green Santa Fe city council member Cris Moore was endorsed by a key local union in his successful bid to become the first elected Green in New Mexico, Abe Gutmann was endorsed by Pro-PAC and the Sierra Club, this writer by the National Association of Social Workers, and other Greens were endorsed by key people-of-color, feminist, gay, and lesbian leaders who were active progressive Democrats. So Greens were seen as exercising their "Green clout" both ways, by helping progressive Democrats, as well as punishing conservative ones.

Change of Direction in 1996–97

Unfortunately, a number of events in late 1996 and early 1997 changed the direction of the Green Party and its strategy. First, the New Mexico Democratic leadership undercut the efforts of progressives in their own party, and blocked the Greens' attempts to run Democratic progressives like state legislator Max Coll and Carol Miller (who was still a Democratic candidate at that time) as fusion candidates on the Green Party ballot line. And in June 1997, the New Party lost its case for fusion before the U.S. Supreme Court, by a daunting 6–3 vote. Have a look at Micah Sifrey's *Spoiling for a Fight: Third Party Politics in America* (2002).

Just before the Supreme Court decision, in the spring of 1997, the New Mexico Green Party again made national headlines, when Carol Miller (now a Green), got 17 percent of the vote in a three-way special election for U.S. Congress. This time there was no denying the "spoiler" impact of a Green in the race. Conservative Republican Bill Redmond defeated Democrat Eric Serna by just 3 percent. Carol's 17 percent of the vote was a clear factor in Serna's defeat.

Following the exercising of the spoiler part of the party's "Green clout" in the 1997 race, even more progressive and moderate Democrats made overtures to move toward fusion, whether practical or legal. According to John Nichols, in the August 1997 issue of *The Progressive* magazine ("Spoiling for success: in New Mexico, the Green Party costs the Democrats a Congressional seat"), Bill Richardson, then the most prominent New Mexico Democrat, and a Latino, called for "early entreaties" to the Greens, and even talked about a Green-Democrat fusion ticket for Governor in 1998.

Also, in early 1998 Shirley Baca, a popular, progressive Chicana Democratic state legislator, approached the Greens about running as a fusion candidate for Congress in New Mexico's southern district, which had a reactionary Republican congressman. She was even willing to use her situation to put forth another test case on fusion to the New Mexico courts, which many Greens and legal experts believed they could have won.

At the same time, Greens continued to win on the local level. Fran Sena Gallegos was elected as a Santa Fe judge in March of 1996, Gary Claus was elected to the Silver City Council in May of 1997, and Cris Moore was re-elected to the Santa Fe City Council in March of 1998.

An Accumulation of High-Profile "Spoiler Races"

But the accumulation of high-profile "spoiler races" had begun to dampen the tenuous coalition the Greens had built with Roberto Mondragon and his progressive allies in the Chicano community. Roberto, a lifelong friend of Eric Serna's, who had worked together with him on the Rainbow Coalition, left the Greens and returned to Serna and the Democrats when the Greens endorsed Carol's run in 1997.

At this point the New Mexico Greens were at a crossroads. Legal fusion, at least as a national strategy, was dead. However, it was still legally possible in New Mexico, there was support for it among even some mainstream Democrats like Richardson, and, even without it, there were practical things that Greens and progressive Democrats had cooperated on up until then, and could continue to cooperate on. In other words, "practical fusion" was still possible, as both a state and a national strategy.

Carol Miller Chooses to Run for Congress Again: Party Is Split

However, at the Green Party's state convention in 1998, Carol Miller refused the urgings of a number of the elders in the party that she run for another, less volatile office, like secretary of state, where many felt she had a real chance of winning. Instead, she choose to run again for Congress, this time against popular New Mexico attorney general Tom Udall. As attorney general, Udall had protected the Greens' ballot status with a special ruling that he had issued, and he was supportive of many parts of the Green Party platform.

At that same convention, the Greens voted formally not to continue to seek fusion, but to instead push for IRV as its major electoral reform. They did stay out of the governor's race, but they refused to support Shirley Baca for Congress, or moderate Republican Lorenzo Garcia in his race for treasurer (even though he had gained the Greens their highest vote total ever in a statewide race, 33 percent, running as a Green in 1994).

Besides Miller's race, 1998 also brought two more spoiler races where the Democrats lost. Green Bob Anderson gained more than 15 percent of the vote in a special congressional election in Albuquerque in the spring of 1998, and then more than 10 percent in the general election in the fall. In both races, Anderson's percentages prevented the Democrat from winning and helped elect conservative Heather Wilson, who is now a national force in Republican politics.

In the meantime, Carol Miller received less than 4 percent in her race against Tom Udall, avoiding another Democratic loss. However, her decision to run caused a major split among Greens over the practical fusion versus the more purist spoiler/instant runoff voting (IRV) strategy. Many Greens in Carol's district and around the state had openly expressed concern about the spoiler effect of her run in the Udall race, and Abe Gutmann even went so far as to organize a "Greens for Udall" campaign. He was ultimately censured by the party for taking financial support from Udall for this effort, but his censure led to an ongoing internal struggle that ultimately split the party in two, and that continues to this day.

Movement Groups Angered by the Spoiler Campaigns

Along with that, Miller's insistence on running against Udall, coupled with the outcome of the 1998 Congressional races in Albuquerque, angered many in organized labor, the people-of-color communities, and other former allies of the Greens in the gay and lesbian, environmentalist, and women's movements. Most people agreed that the Democratic candidate in Albuquerque was particularly weak, but they also felt that the Republican, Heather Wilson, was infinitely worse. Consequently, in 1999, a coalition of progressive people-of-color groups attacked the New Mexico Greens with a public campaign that reached the national media, accusing them of being racist and not caring about working-class people.

The Greens eventually met with and worked out an uneasy truce with these groups, but the die was cast. From then on, for all intents and purposes, active alliances between the Greens and people-of-color organizations—as well as most of organized labor and other progressive groups—were essentially over.

In 2000, there was yet another high-level spoiler race in the Albuquerque congressional race, coupled with the impact of Ralph Nader's national race. So, in a period of six years, the Green Party of New Mexico found itself involved in six high-profile spoiler races, in addition to the Nader 2000 race. In each race, there were good reasons not to like the choices the Democrats offered. But in each case (except for the Udall race), the Republican who was elected in place of the Democratic candidate was measurably worse than the Democrat. And in the case of Udall's election, the state Green Party officially opposed him, and then punished the most prominent Green who supported him, alienating many of Udall's supporters, most of whom would have supported Greens in other races.

Democrats Shift Strategy: Wait Out the Greens, "No" To IRV

All of this set the stage for what has taken place since. Despite the Greens' continued arguments that IRV is ultimately in the Democrats' interest to support, the Democratic establishment appears to have chosen instead to wait out the Greens. They apparently believe that the Greens will eventually wear out their welcome with the people, who they think will ultimately decide that it's better to elect a bad Democrat—than vote for a Green and see an even worse Republican elected. And the Democrats' strategy seems to be working. At present there are only two elected Greens in office, down from a high of five in 2000.

New Mexico's experience with their own six spoiler races, combined with the impact of the 2000 presidential race, and the subsequent threat of a spoiling effect on other high-profile races, such as Paul Wellstone's U.S. Senate race in Minnesota in 2002, has left every state Green Party with a spoiler "albatross" that it must begin to address realistically. In order to implement practical reforms like instant runoff voting, Greens need to have at least a working relationship with Democrats, especially those closest to the beliefs and values of the Green Party platform. But the effects of continuous spoiler races, without an at least equal amount of counter-balancing cooperative efforts with the broader progressive community, have been to drive a wedge between the two camps.

A Different Green Strategy Is Needed

Obviously a different strategy is needed. I advocate that we return to the original New Mexico strategy of fusion, both legal fusion, where possible, and practical fusion where it isn't. That does not mean we should abandon the quest for IRV, or that we would never use the threat of spoiling a race. Practical fusion includes the threat of spoiler races, and the spoiler races in 1994 and 1997 obviously had some major positive outcomes toward building the party. Our initial judicious use of a combination of practical fusion and spoiling in the mid-1990s enabled us to come very close (one vote, in the last legislative committee) to getting IRV on the ballot as a constitutional amendment.

However, after 1997 the party became too rigid in its approach, too unwilling to accept certain political realities that they were not in a position to change at that time, and too lacking in collective knowledge about how to negotiate the Green clout they had built into practical accomplishments that they could continue to build on. Instead, the political purism of the New Mexico

Greens of the late-1990s (and this author embarrassingly includes himself as all too often a part of that purist camp), led to too few wins on the local level to counterbalance the effect of the high-profile spoiler races, and a growing unwillingness on the part of new candidates to step forward and run on the Green Party line. This left the public with the perception that the Greens may have admirable values and good ideas, but don't have the knowledge or the clout to make them reality.

What If!

Looking back, one cannot help but wonder, what if, after the 1997 race, Carol Miller had instead run for secretary of state and the Greens had instead supported Udall openly, as well as Shirley Baca in her southern New Mexico congressional race (a race she could also have run with our support)? Both Democrats were basically supportive of most of the Green Party platform. What if both of them had won, with open Green support? What if, instead of running in the second election in 1998, Bob Anderson had declared the first race as essentially the first outcome of an IRV-style selection process, with him being the candidate disqualified in the first round of voting, and thrown his support to the Democratic candidate in the second race? It's possible that New Mexico would now have possibly three Democratic congresspeople, instead of just one, and two of them more progressive than most Democrats in Congress.

Would not the Green Party in New Mexico also have looked different today? When progressives saw that the Green Party used their Green clout in more than just negative ways, the Green Party wouldn't have been yoked with the spoiler albatross. Green clout would be seen as a force that could help Democrats as well as hurt them. In turn, the New Mexico Green Party today would be enjoying increased support from labor, progressive organizations, people-of-color organizations, and progressive Democrats, all grateful for the critical support of the Greens—support that had been the key to victory in these elections. Perhaps then, Green Abe Gutmann's 45 percent vote for city council in 1997, and Melissa McDonald's 46 percent in her 2000 race for county commissioner, would have instead been stretched to a winning 51 percent, and Greens would have representation in the governments of two of the most influential counties in the state. Perhaps Tom Udall and other progressive Democrats would have been so grateful for our support that they would have continued their qualified support for the party, and we would be growing in numbers, candidates, and newly elected Greens, instead of scratching our heads as to what went wrong.

Unfortunately, members of the Green Party can't rewrite New Mexico's history. They can only learn from it, apply it to their own times, develop new strategies, and try to do better in their future work. But the history lesson of New Mexico is that it's time for a change in strategy, if the Green Party is to grow and thrive.

As we go to press, there is some indication that the climate in New Mexico is starting to change. Popular Green leader Rick Lass has decided to drop out of his race for the New Mexico state legislature, so as not to split the vote with a progressive Democrat, who has a better chance of winning, and who supports much of the Green Party platform. Perhaps once again, the New Mexico Green Party will provide a model for Green parties all over the country to look up to.

The Greens Are Enduring, Debating, and Learning

By Steve Welzer
Green Horizon Quarterly, Spring 2005

The Green Party has now run national electoral campaigns under conditions of Democratic Party incumbency (2000) and Republican Party incumbency (2004). There were specific circumstances and issues in each case, of course, but to the extent that general conclusions can be drawn and lessons learned from these experiences the party will benefit and go forward.

Perhaps the most significant observation is that the Green Party, running an appealing candidate, has a chance to be perceived by many progressives as a serious and welcome alternative when a Democrat has been occupying the White House, but when the incumbent administration is Republican many of those same progressives will view the candidate of the Democratic Party as enough of an alternative as to merit support; moreover, they will tend to adopt a rhetoric of "closing ranks" and harangue against "spoiling," putting pressure on the Green Party to avoid running a high-impact campaign.

Handling "Anybody But..."

The "ABB" (Anybody-But-Bush) syndrome made 2004 a difficult year for the Greens, but it was certainly instructive. What the Greens will need to do is learn to anticipate it (in its generalized form—"ABR"—Anybody But the Republican). If the Green Party could become the repository of memory for the electoral wing of the social change movement, it could be ready each cycle to graphically remind progressives about the extent to which they are invariably disappointed with Democrats in power—and about how the resurgence of alarmism when the Republicans are in serves no function other than to retard the development of a true alternative.

Another lesson of 2004 is that, internally, the Greens need to develop an organizational culture of steadfast independence. It was problematic that a significant number of Greens supported, worked for, contributed to, or voted for the candidate of the Democratic Party in 2004. Others reacted to the ABB pressure by opting for a low-impact, deferential presidential campaign. If they hope to overcome third-party marginalism, the Greens will need to project an image of gravitas while establishing in the minds of the voters a strong and clear-cut differentiation between themselves and both of the establishment parties.

Handling "Spoiler" Vilification

There is no way to know whether or not Al Gore would have won the 2000 election if the Ralph Nader/Green Party ticket had not attracted the highest percentage vote for a progressive third-party campaign since that of Robert LaFollette in 1924. It is conceivable that Nader did, in fact, "spoil" the election for Gore.

What's not in doubt is that the high-visibility impact of the 2000 campaign transformed and simultaneously provoked a crisis within the Green Party. On the one hand it was a step toward the party becoming viewed as a potentially serious new force in American politics and it catapulted the Greens to the front of the ranks among third-party initiatives. On the other hand, justified or not, it prominently associated the Green Party with spoiling. Nader's role in the election became fodder for the punditry; both he and the party found themselves confronted with a stinging campaign of vilification. (Seen on a Democratic Party discussion e-list: "GREEN=Get Republicans Elected Every November.")

The "spoiling" issue is a complex and difficult one that always has divided partisans of independent politics in this country, given our winner-take-all system—and it surely will continue to do so until thoroughgoing electoral-system reform is achieved. Groups and even individuals are torn about this issue. In recent years the Labor Party and the New Party foundered when they were not able to successfully come to terms with it. So it was not surprising to see the Green Party internally divided as the 2004 electoral cycle approached.

Some Greens were concerned that if the party was perceived to "again" be a factor in the defeat of the Democratic Party opponent to George W. Bush, an indelible "bull in a china shop" stigma would impede its organizing efforts for years to come. When Ralph Nader made it clear that he would not accede to any type of campaign strategy which involved less than an all-out effort, Greens concerned about spoiling resisted the idea of another Nader/Green campaign.

Others, to the contrary, felt it was specifically important for the Greens to show that the party would not back down in the face of the "spoiler" vilification. They asserted it would be a mistake to give any credence to the idea that the Green Party's 2.7 percent of the vote in 2000 constituted "too much of an impact," and they felt that a rejection of Nader could give the impression that the party was less than steadfast in its determination to become a serious electoral force.

Questions and Differing Perceptions about the Party's Role

Discussions leading up to 2004, while often focused on the "Nader question" showed the extent to which Greens have questions and differing perceptions about the appropriate role of their party vis-a-vis the establishment parties. Should there be any degree of contingency to our opposition? Is our growth dependent upon weaning progressives gradually out of the orbit of the Democratic Party? To what extent and under what circumstances should we take pains to be "good citizens of the progressive movement" by deferring to the fact that the Democrat is the immediate practical alternative in an important race?

These questions deeply divided the party in a year when many progressives were viewing the 2004 election as a national plebiscite on the legitimacy, policies, and war of George W. Bush. The Cobb/LaMarche campaign made a point of exhibiting understanding and tolerance for voters who felt they had to prioritize defeating Bush. This posture succeeded in getting attention and praise from those prone to advocating an "inside/outside" strategy (a July letter from progressives with that orientation toward the Democratic Party stated: "David Cobb has earned our endorsement in safe states by deftly steering the Green Party toward a nuanced strategy dedicated to ousting Bush, while seeking to grow a grassroots party. . ."). Pro-Nader Greens expressed concern that such a strategy compromised the party's independence to an unacceptable degree. The debate about this fundamental issue has by no means been resolved and is sure to continue. As it becomes recognized that the issue is, indeed, complex and that both positions have some merit, the discussion may very well become less rancorous and divisive.

Important to Keep Moving Forward

In order to learn from mistakes, regroup after divisions, benefit from internal debates, build consensus, and take advantage of organizational memory, a party must endure and keep moving forward. The Greens are well aware that prior attempts to build an alternative progressive political force in this country—Socialist, Progressive, Labor, Citizens, Rainbow—have failed to reach critical mass, disappearing or stagnating after a few electoral cycles or, at most, a few decades.

It is encouraging that the Green Party survived the difficult circumstances it encountered in 2004. Criticisms regarding the party's pace of growth, lack of cohesion, difficulty with fundraising, etc., need to be taken to heart, but, on the other hand, the critics should acknowledge the fact that among the group of third-party startup initiatives of the 1990s, only the Green Party has shown endurance. Working in the party's favor is the resonance of the Green politics movement worldwide. Ecological responsibility has emerged as a major theme of twenty-first century political discourse. And, to its credit, the U.S. Green Party has demonstrated a capability to take advantage of opportunity. The Nader/Green campaign of 2000 stepped into the spotlight when the Reform Party unexpectedly imploded and the Gore candidacy fizzled. In 2004 the Cobb campaign skillfully maneuvered into a position where it could spearhead the challenge to the election irregularities in Ohio. (William Rivers Pitt wrote: "The presidential candidates for the Green Party and Libertarian Party deserve the lion's share of praise and credit for the [challenge to the Ohio Electors in the U.S. Congress on Thursday, January 6th].... Cobb and Badnarik forced the Democrats to do the right thing, and that made Thursday a banner day for third parties in America." [www.truthout.org, 1/7/05])

Endurance in the Face of Crisis

So it turns out that there were some positive highlights to point to in a difficult year. It still remains to be seen whether or not the Green Party can accomplish what no other third party has been able to do in recent memory, i.e., break out of the marginal tier to gain widespread recognition as a viable oppositional force. The Greens must not allow "spoiler aversion" to hold them back. Not only is spoiling inevitable (there is no way to go from 1–4 percent of the vote to 30–40 percent of the vote without passing through levels that are sure to "spoil"), but, moreover, spoiling is an important tool in a third party's arsenal, a way to demonstrate why electoral-system reform is necessary.

Spoiling invariably elicits a degree of vilification—the Greens simply need to learn to take the heat. In the face of it, they must not back down from their provocative and consistent challenge to both of the establishment parties. They need to develop an organizational culture oriented toward displacing the Democrats rather than deferring to them. And they need to spark the interest of the broad ranks of the politically disaffected rather than being overly concerned about the reticence of the liberal intelligentsia or the vagaries of the Rep–Dem dance.

Perhaps the exposure to the ABB syndrome of 2004 will help inoculate the Greens against the virus of lesser-evilism going forward. In an article that appeared in *The Nation* after the election, Medea Benjamin wrote: "Many of us in the Green Party made a tremendous compromise by campaigning in swing states for such a miserable standard-bearer for the progressive movement as John Kerry. Well, I've had it.... For those of you willing to keep wading in the muddy waters of the Democratic Party, all power to you. I plan to work with the Greens to get more Green candidates elected to local office" ("Looking Back, Looking Forward," *The Nation* issue of December 20, 2004).

Approached with apprehension, 2004 may become viewed in retrospect as the year in which the Greens managed to endure in the face of crisis and even make some breakthroughs and learn some valuable lessons. If the Greens will continue to press forward with their challenge to the two-party system—boldly, consistently, and at all levels—it might not be too long before the electorate starts to recognize the Green Party as the viable new alternative the party is seeking to become.

Addendum:

In my *Green Horizon* article I discussed the significance of the 2004 campaign from the vantage point of the Green Party, but I did not address the ramifications of the Nader campaign. My own take on the latter can be summarized thus:

• The main positive, enduring result of the 2004 Nader campaign was the graphic demonstration of what lengths the establishment parties will go to when threatened. It was instructive for the third-party movement to see that.

• Nader will make a significant contribution to the movement if he continues to pursue remedies to the ballot-access barriers he encountered during the campaign.

• The 2004 Nader campaign did not yield many other positives. It would take quite a stretch of the imagination to call the campaign a success. A major problematic factor was the dissolution of the Ralph Nader/Green Party alliance. Both sides can be faulted to some extent for this casualty.

- The problem on the Green Party side, as analyzed above, was aversion to being perceived to "again" play the spoiler role. Many Greens got cold feet about the party's association with Nader. Misleadership allowed the anti-Nader forces within the party to jeopardize the relationship.

- There were two problems on Ralph Nader's side, attributable to him and his inner circle of decision makers:

  1. They failed to recognize the extent to which the interest in/sympathy for the 2000 candidacy was based on the idea that Nader was working to build a significant, permanent new alternative party. Going "independent" was a mistake. It resulted in loss of support, diversion of precious campaign resources to dealing with ballot-access problems, and a catch-as-catch-can series of unproductive alliances with forces more marginal than the Green Party.

  2. They are, as a group, deficient when it comes to working in or with organizations which aren't their own (i.e., organizations they didn't initiate or don't control). In the wake of the 2000 campaign they refused to or didn't know how to do the kind of internal organizational politicking that was needed to play a significant role helping to develop the Green Party into a serious new political force. It was not enough for Nader just to do some fundraisers for the party. He and his colleagues needed to get involved helping to guide or at least influence the Greens. Failure to do so resulted in a lost opportunity.

The Ralph Nader/Green Party alliance had great potential. Without such alliances (with figures of stature like Nader) the Green Party will grow much more slowly. Without organizational support, Nader now goes back to being perceived as a lone wolf—a heroic reformer who ultimately fell short of making a major impact in the arena of alternative politics.

Resurgence: The Green Party's Remarkable Transformation

By David Cobb
Green Horizon Quarterly, *Winter 2005*

A remarkable transformation has taken place in the public's perception of the Green Party. In one sense, you could say we've gone from being seen as spoilers to being hailed as saviors.

In the aftermath of the 2000 stolen presidential election, those who wanted to ignore the hard facts of voter suppression and fraud found the Green Party as an easy scapegoat. Never mind the massive disenfranchisement of African American voters in Florida or the blatantly political and unprecedented maneuvering of the U.S. Supreme Court, blame the outrageous results of the "election" on the Green Party. The die was cast, the spin spun and, to a great extent, the public bought it. The Green Party and our 2000 presidential candidate became persona non grata in many political circles.

Four years later, following another national election plagued by what could charitably be called irregularities, the Green Party has emerged as a champion of democracy.

This happened for two reasons. One, the Cobb/LaMarche Green Party presidential campaign did the right thing in Ohio by seeking a recount of that flawed and fraudulent election in order to protect the integrity of the democratic process. The second reason is because we ran a campaign in the first place. As Woody Allen has been credited with saying, 90 percent of life is just showing up. If we hadn't run a Green Party presidential campaign in 2004, as many people suggested, we would never have had the incredible opportunity of using the Ohio recount to shine a spotlight on the serious deficiencies of a dysfunctional electoral system.

The Ohio recount may be the best thing that has ever happened to the national Green Party. By demanding a recount (in conjunction with Libertarian Party presidential candidate Michael Badnarik), when we had no interest in the outcome of the election, we demonstrated a true nonpartisan commitment to ensuring the right to vote and the right to have all votes counted. By contrast, John Kerry, the Democratic Party's presidential candidate, refused to stand up either for himself or for the thousands of Ohioans who stood in line for hours in the rain to vote for him. Kerry never demanded a recount. After considerable hesitation and delay, he did file legal motions in support of our efforts, but that only amounted to saying "me too" to what our attorneys had already submitted. For many Democrats this dismal performance, following on the heels of Gore's botched recount effort in 2000, was simply too much.

The Cobb/LaMarche campaign was inundated with phone calls and e-mail messages from disgruntled Democrats. Thousands contributed financially to make the Ohio recount happen and many volunteered as observers for the recount itself. Many more sent messages saying that they were switching their party registration to Green; others hailed us as patriots.

The pinnacle of our post-election efforts came on January 6, 2005, when Representative Stephanie Tubbs Jones of Ohio and California Senator Barbara Boxer challenged the legitimacy of Ohio's electoral college votes, the first such challenge since 1877. This historic challenge was preceded by an inspiring rally held in Lafayette Park across from the White House which was organized by our campaign in conjunction with a number of other progressive organizations. I was honored to share a stage with such longtime civil rights activists as Reverend Jesse Jackson and Representative Maxine Waters before joining over four hundred people in a March on the Capitol which stretched for several blocks through the heart of Washington.

Party Continues to Grow

The Green Party continued to grow in 2004. We ran record numbers of candidates, elected more local officials, and registered more Green voters than ever before. Everywhere we went, we found enthusiastic and dedicated Greens hard at work in their local communities.

There is no question that this was an unusual and difficult year to run a Green Party presidential campaign. Although many Greens supported our campaign, others supported either Kerry or Nader/Camejo, dividing an already small constituency even further. That notwithstanding, the Cobb/LaMarche campaign was a spirited and principled effort embodying the best of Green values. We were unwavering in presenting a clear, alternative progressive agenda to the corporate parties. We told the truth. We consistently referred to John Kerry as a corporatist and militarist who supported the wars in Iraq and Afghanistan; the USA PATRIOT Act; the racist War on Drugs; the misnamed, one-size-fits-all No Child Left Behind Act; and as someone who failed to support single-payer, universal health care and a living wage for all American workers. Some Greens objected to the fact that we told another truth as well—that as bad as Kerry was, Bush was worse.

We ran a campaign that was significant not just for what it accomplished, but how we accomplished it. Our ticket was gender balanced; the only major ticket which could make that claim. Our campaign committee operated by consensus. As the presidential candidate, I was only one voice of many. We worked cooperatively in concert with state and local Green parties and we have, as promised, turned over our volunteer and donor lists to the national Green Party. And, despite negative attacks on us, we stayed positive the entire time.

As a result of all the campaigns the Green Party ran, from school boards to the presidency, we trained more activists, recruited more community leaders, and developed more skills and infrastructure. The Green Party is getting bigger, stronger, and better organized in each election cycle.

New Voting Rights Movement

The Green-inspired Ohio recount played a significant role both in the birth of the New Voting Rights Movement and in a fundamental transformation of the political landscape. The recount in Ohio (and in New Mexico) brought together Greens and Libertarians, longtime civil rights activists and new voting rights organizations. Our campaign also worked closely with Representative John Conyers and his staff, Reverend Jesse Jackson, Rainbow/PUSH, and a new group called the Progressive Democrats of America to document and publicize what went wrong in Ohio and what we can do to fix our broken election system.

Thanks to our part in the Ohio recount, the Green Party has gained new credibility and visibility as well as a leadership role in the New Voting Rights Movement. Election reform is now center-stage and has moved from being a peripheral issue pushed by "fringe" parties to a mainstream concern with the backing of leading civil rights organizations and members of Congress. It wasn't what we could have expected to be the result of our campaign as we set forth with the Cobb/LaMarche presidential campaign, but we did position ourselves to be ready for breakthroughs, and we couldn't be happier with the results.

Narcissism Runs Rampant: Diagnosing the Green Party

By Joshua Frank
Published on www.counterpunch.org, February 25, 2005

The ashes of the 2004 election battle have finally settled, and sadly the Green Party is buried in the rubble still gasping for air. Even so, if you have heard any of the sordid mutterings from staunch Green loyalists, they are spinning quite a different tale.

Take prominent Green apologist, Ted Glick, who has failed miserably at seeing the error of the Green Party's choice to run David Cobb this past year. "[Our vote total] was less than expected," he recently spewed in an online missive, "but the fact is that the cumulative vote for all fourteen 'third party' Presidential candidates on the ballot ... was a little less than 1.2 million." Apparently, to Mr. Glick, such a diagnosis somehow emancipates the Green Party's own tepid performance—for no third party did exceptionally well.

Not sure if the Greens' vote total was less than expected, however, as David Cobb told *CounterPunch* during the "height" of his quest for the presidency that he had "no goals for votes." Talk about a schmuck.

The Greens could, and should, have been vociferously opposing the war in Iraq and Afghanistan. But they opted for a "smart-growth" (read: safe-state) strategy instead, where they'd stay well below the electoral radar. They should have been on the front lines of the campaign scene, denouncing John Kerry and George Bush's neoliberalism and their handling of the downward economic spiral, civil liberties infringements, and environmental catastrophes. But instead the Green Party caved, and regardless of what Ted Glick and others claim, they paid a steep price, getting pounded at the polls as a result. A miserable sixth place.

David Cobb and his running mate Pat LaMarche earned a little over 118,000 votes on November 2, 2004. Even though only half a million people voted for Ralph Nader in 2004—a drastic decline compared to four years earlier when 2.8 million people voted Green—Nader still managed to garner five times as many votes as the Green Party on Election Day '04, despite being vilified by professional leftists, Greens, progressives, and bemused Democrats.

Many still cite the drastic reduction in votes for Nader in 2004 as evidence of failure. But it is wrong to compare his two runs in these terms. In the second case, Nader had no party to back him, and in the wake of the September 11 Anybody-But-Bush hysteria, many who were with Nader in spirit decided to cast their votes for John Kerry in hopes of unseating Bush. Political expediency didn't work however.

The Libertarian Party garnered some 200,000 more votes than Cobb. But who cares, right? Cobb got his wish. For he never wanted votes anyway.

An example of the ruin: In Minnesota, the Green Party has enjoyed majority status since 2000, but is now heading back to the political fringe. Cobb's poor vote total disqualified the Greens from $400,000 in public subsidies and automatic ballot access in the state. Looks like they will have to start over from scratch in the state, as well as Connecticut, Montana, Utah, Nevada, New Mexico, and Rhode Island, where the Green Party lost the presidential ballot access they had acquired during the 2000 election.

The Green Party didn't fare very well in local races either, where Cobb and others claimed they would stay strong. Failing to show up, the Greens were outgunned all across the board by Libertarians, Constitutionalists, Independents, and yes, even Socialists in some cases. But many Greens still claim that they "grew" in '04.

Green Party members Starlene Rankin and Mike Feinstein of California wrote in *Green Pages* following their November butchering that, "fourteen states ran the most Green candidates ever, and overall at least 431 Greens ran for office in forty-one states.... The Greens won 68 victories out of 431 races in 2004, including 12 city council seats and 18 victories overall in California. There are now a record 221 Greens holding elected office across the U.S."

Growing in numbers doesn't mean growing in strength. Currently the Green Party claims to have exactly 313,186 members in twenty-two states across the U.S. If this is indeed accurate, that means almost 200,000 of those members did not even cast a vote (let alone donate cash) for their party's presidential ticket in 2004.

How the hell can Ted Glick and others claim that this was a "success"? Not to mention their "smart-growth" strategy did not even elect the man they hoped would win: pro-war Democrat John Kerry.

Despite this "growth," sources at the Green Party headquarters reveal they are in dire straits financially. It isn't likely that the Green Party's D.C. office will have to close in the immediate future. Nevertheless if money doesn't start rolling in soon, sources admit, it may well happen down the road.

What is interesting is that Green Party "think tanks" have recently received big bucks from significant Democratic contributors, Richard and Marilyn Mazess of Wisconsin. According to the Federal Election Commission the Mazess clique have given well over $50,000 to the Democratic Party since 2003. They contributed some money to the Green Party following the election in 2004. And they also tossed Ralph Nader several thousand dollars this past election—perhaps to cover their own Democratic tracks.

Nonetheless, two spanking new Green Party nonprofits are now robust and thriving. The Green Institute, which is headed by ex-Green Party Operations Director Dean Myerson, and the Liberty Tree Foundation for Democratic Revolution, which is headed by ex-Green Party Chair Ben Manski (both Cobb backers), have collected a combined $500,000 from the Mazess duo.

Certainly this raises questions as to which direction the Green Party will proceed in the future. How much influence will these "think tanks" have, especially if the Green Party itself continues to struggle financially? Will it be replaced by these non-profit careerists? Will fruitless "smart-growth" campaigns continue to be the failing Green Party strategy?

To no surprise, David Cobb has parked his ass on the Board of

Directors at the Green Institute "think tank." And akin to Theodore Glick, Mr. Cobb still claims his losing campaign strategy was a winner. Narcissism runs rampant indeed.

This is not to say that there aren't spurts of dissension starting to pulsate within the party's grassroots. A quest to take back the Green Party is already underway. Many Greens are coming together under the banner of the "Green Alliance" to shift internal power away from Cobb and others, and back into the hands of the membership. Green Party veteran Peter Camejo, who was Ralph Nader's running mate this past election, is also contemplating the best way to mend the fractures currently leaking what little strength the Green Party has left.

Let's hope that Camejo, the Green Alliance and other like-minded Greens can join forces and topple the current party "leadership." If they aren't successful, 2004 won't be the worst election the Greens will ever endure.

Lessons from the 2004 Elections
By Peter Miguel Camejo
January 2005

The 2004 elections unmasked a great deal of the political realities of our nation. Most readers are aware the media is now under the control of a handful of large corporations all run by right-wing, generally Republican, worshippers of the market. Still it seems so peculiar how the most crucial issues of our time were simply never mentioned during the presidential campaign by either of the two pro-corporate parties.

Except for a pro-pollution quip by Kerry, little was said about the destruction of our planet and economy through global warming. In Missouri, Kerry stated that buying "a great big SUV is terrific, terrific. That's America." Both Kerry, and Bush joined in opposing the Kyoto Protocol during the debates to reassure corporate America of their commitment to profits over a future for our species.

The fact that 90 percent of the people have seen no rise in their inflation-adjusted income over the last thirty years in spite of the doubling of our GDP was of no concern to Bush or Kerry. The only real income gains went to the richest 1 percent. This income polarization and the growth of an underclass, with our minimum wage dropping (inflation adjusted in present dollars) from $8.50 to $5.15 since 1968 was never discussed.

The drop in corporate tax revenues that once provided 33 percent of federal government revenues but today provide only 7.8 percent likewise was particularly a taboo issue. The only comment in this regard was a call by John Kerry for further tax cuts for corporations. His proposal came at a moment when profit margins were the largest ever of GDP and the percentage of the budget from corporate taxes the lowest in decades.

The poorest 20 percent now pay the highest tax rate on their income for state and local taxes throughout the nation. In California the poorest 20 percent pay a rate 57 percent higher than the richest 1 percent of the population who pay the lowest rate of all. The general trend to an ever increasing regressive tax structure and the endless growth of corporate subsidies of course was never mentioned.

We could go on and on. Our antiquated electoral system, the growing violations of our Constitution and the rule of law internationally, and so on were never put before the people. The single most pressing world issue, the war in Iraq, became the centerpiece of the campaign as both Kerry and Bush fought over who was the most pro-war.

The Key to U.S. Elections

There was one peculiar event around the elections that received almost no analysis or discussion. The overwhelming majority of the supporters of John Kerry disagreed with their candidate on most major issues. Even in countries with completely distorted electoral systems, where money dominates and manipulates, it is quite unusual to see people voting massively for someone they consciously disagree with.

This simple fact tells how deep the corruption of the American political system has become. The *Boston Globe* reported 95 percent of the delegates at the Democratic Party convention opposed Kerry on the war. But these delegates are hopelessly corrupt people.

They are part of a system based on careerism and money. They accept the game and call it being realistic. That is to lie to the people, to lie to themselves; to act out a lie does not bother these people at all.

Dennis Kucinich, Howard Dean, and Al Sharpton—along with all the Democratic "left"—bought in to the fundamental lie of the presidential campaign. That lie is simple. They tell the people that the Democratic Party is not corrupt, is not an agent of corporate rule, and is not a defender of George Bush and his policies. They do not tell the people the elections are fixed from day one through the control of money and the media. Nor to they speak of the role of the so-called "two-party" system that prevents the real issues from being heard or debated, and that does not allow representative democracy (proportional representation), or even runoffs that would make it possible for people to vote for an opposition candidate. That lie is the essence of our electoral system. And in one sense it is the key issue of the elections.

This fact is a statement on the enormous success of the two-party, pro-money political system developed in the United States. It has achieved getting about half the people simply not to vote, and those who do vote even when they disagree with corporate domination vote in favor of what they oppose. Yet the people believe they somehow have chosen the government. Keeping this system in place is essential for the rule of a tiny minority over the majority in a complex modern economy. Open totalitarianism would have a very deep negative impact on the economy. Far better is the illusion of democracy. Crucial in this equation is the role "progressives," especially many of the liberal intellectuals, play.

Massive Capitulation of Liberals

The fact that the Democratic Party candidate was totally pro-corporate, pro-war, pro-Patriot Act, anti-poor, and against the environment did not stop the bulk of so-called "progressive leaders" from demanding not only a vote for Kerry but respect for corporate domination of our society—by not having any candidates appear that favored peace, or were anti-corporate. They openly sought to deny those progressives who disagreed with their capitulation to the Democratic Party the ability to express their opinion at the ballot box. In the end approximately half a million people did vote for peace and against corporate domination.

The Nader Factor

Never in our history have we seen such a massive effort to try and prevent an individual, Ralph Nader, from entering the race for the presidency. This massive anti-democracy campaign was led by so-called "progressive" organizations like *The Nation* and MoveOn.org. Throughout the campaign these groups became more openly direct agents of the Democratic Party.

The only other time in American history where the kind of viciousness expressed against Ralph Nader was ever seen was against the early abolitionists, the Liberty Party candidates (in the 1840s), who were labeled fanatics for daring to challenge the two pro-slavery parties of the time.

Why is this happening? Why the intensification of the broad capitulation of the progressive intelligentsia? For years they have backed the existing system through their subordination to the Democratic Party. But the new level of panic and intensity of their attack against anyone daring to challenge the Democrats is new.

U.S. Turns to Reverse Gains

The answer, I believe, is tied to the shift in the socio-economic reality since the 1970s. After the Second World War the United States made a worldwide effort to take markets from nations weakened by the war, primarily England and France. The move to gain world domination was combined with a campaign to offer concessions at home to win the backing of working people and draw in the power of the trade unions behind corporate international ambitions. Liberal support for the Democrats was associated with concessions. The Democrats, certainly deceivers then as now, acted more as brokers negotiating concessions in return for delivering support from minorities and working people.

This period ended with the Vietnam War, globalization, and the beginning of the micro-processor revolution during the 1970s. The shift can be traced to the rise of Japan's economy (actually economies throughout Asia in general), and the peak in oil inside the United States.

The U.S. corporate world found itself being challenged by international competitors in new ways. It now wanted to remove some of the concessions granted in the period from the thirties through the sixties. Once the Cold War ended, which left the U.S. as the only world military power, the shift accelerated. At each step the Democratic Party rose to the occasion, blocking any effective opposition to the take-back program of corporate America.

Unions were destroyed (from 37 percent of our workforce to 12 percent), the minimum wage was lowered, social safety nets were dismantled, the income gap widened, and some environmental regulations were lowered.

At each step scattered resistance appeared. As each union was attacked it would try to fight back alone, depending on its "friends" in the Democratic Party. As the corporate rulers saw so little resistance, and it became clear that they could depend on the Democrats' control over minorities and labor (later also the NGOs) they pressed forward with increasing take-back programs. The Patriot Act is now an open challenge to the Bill of Rights. The war in Iraq is an open break with any pretense to respect the rule of law internationally.

Thus the role of the Democrats as the broker-negotiator for labor, minorities, and women for concessions has shifted toward direct support of corporate policy since the 1970s. They now try to convince the people that the Republican pro-corporate platform is really in their own interests. That is, they have become open backers of the shift to the right.

During the 1990s interest in third parties reappeared. Polls showed a lowering in the support for the two parties. The Perot phenomenon showed how shallow the commitment to the two parties was at the beginning of the 1990s. Then in 2000 a nationally known figure, Ralph Nader, came forward with a pro-the-people platform and was backed cautiously by some progressive Democrats, such as Hightower, Moore, Dugger, and others. Ronnie Dugger had formed a "populist" party that would not run candidates lest it upset the Democrats. Other Democrats tried forming a third party that would endorse Democrats, called the New Party. Nothing came of these formations. Only the far more clearly independent progressive Green Party that was willing to run against

Democrats began to grow, at least a little, particularly in California.

Democrats were startled. They were doing their job supporting corporate America when suddenly an independent current was beginning to appear. Quickly they set out to stop the Green Party and the Nader phenomenon. Relying on their undemocratic spoiler electoral system, they placed the "blame" for the election of Bush on Nader precisely while they voted for everything Bush asked of them.

By 2004 the Democrats had proved they could contain the opposition and permitted corporate America to confirm Bush as an actually "elected" president. They had scared the Moores, Hightowers, and Duggers back into the fold from which I doubt they will dare stray again. These kinds of capitulations are not quickly reversed. However, if a mass break begins from below, these "progressives" will suddenly once again become interested in third-party politics and once again they will play the role of opposing those who actually are building an independent force.

So far the Democrats have shown they can contain the early attempts to develop a political movement representing the people. The key to the victory for Bush in 2004 was precisely the effectiveness of the Democrats. And the effectiveness of the Democrats was partially reflected in the inability of leading progressives to stand up against what will be recorded, in time, as the greatest fraud ever perpetrated on the American people, the Democratic Party.

The Rise of the Religious Right

These same liberals who cried out against Nader for running are all confused by the reappearance of an old traditional way to control the oppressed in our nation. The use of superstition combined with handouts. The rise of the religious right is the companion to the Democratic Party in controlling the oppressed majority. While a super-oppressed underclass is being created by globalization, including inside the United States, new religious formations are appearing, well funded, offering programs of token material assistance (as the governmental safety net is removed) while indoctrinating people to accept pro-corporate worship of the market with the usual promise of a reward in heaven. This organizing effort of the right is making gains precisely because of the failure of a progressive viable alternative to exist.

Could it get any better for the rich? If you can't brainwash them with superstition you have the Democratic Party "opposition" to corral and control them. It will be hard for corporate America to get the editors of *The Nation* reading the Bible, but voting Democratic is easy enough and either way it leads in the same direction. Watching the Democrats giving George Bush eighteen standing ovations at the State of the Union address in 2004 tells you all you need to know—including the moment when Bush called for ending the separation of church and state through his plan to give tax money to these rightist reactionaries who use the cover of being religious outfits.

The rise of Bush and his more open and explicit moves to not only take away socioeconomic concessions but begin to change the traditional framework—that is the constitutional rights of our political system—has made the more "progressive" types like *The Nation* editorial board panic. They have no confidence that the people could ever independently resist these attacks, so instead of helping build an opposition, calling on people to rebel from the Bush/Kerry platform of war and oppression, they call on everyone to forget about the economic take-backs or even the war issue and back the "lesser-evil" of the two pro-corporate, pro-war political organizations, the Democrats.

Their panic, as they begin to finally understand where corporate America is going, is quite open. They offer no solution. They can only shout words of hate against anyone who points out the dead end of their support for the Democrats. They have only one simple message: "vote Democrat." They offer no platform, no demands on the Democrats. They do not even dare to say to the Democrats: "If you continue to support Bush we won't support you." No, their support for the Democrats is unconditional. It is considered a "reality check" that cannot be altered, like gravity. The fact that 25 percent of our people are no longer registered Democratic or Republican and that polls find 38 percent do not consider themselves supporters of either party is of no concern to them. There is no hope. Surrender, unconditionally, to the rule of the corporate world and ask for mercy, vote Democrat.

Michael Moore is a perfect example. On national TV he called

Ralph Nader crazy for daring to run. Moore went on to speak about "we," meaning the future Kerry government, as though there was any connection between what Moore has advocated in his writings and movies and what Kerry would do. This delusional effort which swept an entire current of well-known progressive leaders from Chomsky to Moore has really revealed the failure of that layer to understand the nature of our society and the role of our two-party system. Deep down it shows a lack of belief that the American people could ever rise up and change America.

The Green Party

Within the Green Party this crisis resulted in the appearance of two opposing political currents. One current bent to the liberal capitulation and the other resisted the capitulation. What was new for those of us who have been around for the last fifty years fighting for social justice, peace, and democracy was not the capitulation but the existence of a rather broad resistance, at least in comparison to the sixties where the capitulation to the Democratic Party was quite generic.

Inside the Green Party two documents appeared expressing these two currents. One called for support for the concept of voting for a lesser evil, i.e., the Democratic Party, signed by eighteen leaders of the Green Party. The other, named the Avocado Declaration, called for opposing lesser-evil voting and supporting Green Party independence. The document of the lesser-evil current gave very little historical or socioeconomic explanation to back up the authors' views.

The Green Party nomination of David Cobb for president—the choice of the lesser-evil current—over Ralph Nader—the choice of the independent current—is now history. But what is not yet fully understood is that Cobb lost the primaries and the state conventions. Thus the Milwaukee convention of 2004 that nominated Cobb introduced another issue and a new crisis into the Green Party: internal democracy. The evidence is so overwhelming that the Milwaukee convention was packed that it is hard for Cobb supporters to deny it. It is sad that they show no remorse nor see the destructive result of rejecting majority rule. It is our hope that the next National Convention will return the Green Party to internal democracy and that Cobb and many of his supporters will help to do so.

The pro-lesser-evil current has every right to fight for their ideas and try to win a majority within the Green Party. If they were to become the majority, the pro-independence current should respect their right to promote their views in the name of the party. But the grave problem that arose in 2004 is that the lesser-evil current lost the votes of the membership but still succeeded not only in getting control of the convention but getting control of the national Coordinating Committee. The result has been a sharp decline of the Green Party nationally. Its funding has declined and the Green Party's strongest state organizations have begun to feel uneasy with the national leadership.

But in California and New York, the Green Party has continued to grow. In New York, registration in the Green Party grew by the thousands during 2004, now surpassing 40,000, and in California a new record of elected officials hit seventy-seven, while registration remained just under record levels of 160,000. These two states represent by themselves the majority of Greens in the United States and both states side strongly with the pro-independence current.

It is inevitable and normal that the Green Party will have internal differences and debates on these historic issues. As I traveled throughout the country campaigning, I met Green Party organizers who are stunned by what has happened and will leave the Green Party if its internal structure is not democratized.

In the present discussion on returning the Green Party to democracy Marilyn Ditmanson, the Treasurer of the Butte County Greens in California, expressed what many Greens feel when she wrote, "There are those of us who believe that the Green Party is important enough to spend our time to fix it. Right now the Green Party does not represent the will of its people. There are many of us who are on our last campaign for the Green Party—to bring democracy to the party. If we do not get democracy here we will find a political party or start one where we get democracy."

Across the nation, Green Steve Greenfield of New Paltz, New York, writes, "The will of the great majority as expressed in opinion surveys, primaries and ultimately in the ballot booths was overruled by 'electors' whose prime source of decision power was their ability to afford the transportation to Milwaukee."

It would be quite easy for the Cobb supporters to prove their claim that their victory was legitimate and that they did represent the majority. Take for example Maine, a state where the pro–Democratic Party wing of the Greens is well organized and in control of the Green Party apparatus. Maine is the state where a Green candidate was elected to the state legislature, but who openly announced his support for Kerry. Maine's delegation voted 95 percent for Cobb at the 2004 National Convention. Maine Cobb supporters have one little problem to explain. When the Green Party membership voted for who they supported and who they wanted as delegates they only voted 23.6 percent for Cobb while delivering 29.2 percent for Nader and giving Salzman and Camejo (who both supported Nader) another 12.9 percent, bringing the pro-Nader vote to 42.1 percent.

The Cobb supporters argue the delegates from Maine came around and changed their minds and voted for Cobb. If that were true, then all that the Cobb supporters need to do is present written statements from the nineteen delegates showing that only 23 percent (four delegates) had originally voted for Cobb and the other fifteen of their nineteen delegates had originally voted for other candidates, mostly pro-Nader, but had changed their minds. That is, that their delegation to the convention reflected their membership.

If they could do that they would have done so long ago. They know what we all know. The pro-Cobb Greens packed the Maine delegation in open disrespect for the will of the membership as was done in many other states. John Rensenbrink, one of Maine's lesser-evil leaders, wrote a piece claiming there was a shift in opinions at the last minute. Rensenbrink added something new in the debate, attempting to red-bait those who support independence. Rensenbrink wrote that the real danger to the Greens is socialists, specifically naming the Socialist Workers Party (SWP), and the International Socialist Organization (ISO) for joining the Green Party.

Rensenbrink is the editor of *Green Horizon Quarterly*, so you would think he would show some journalistic integrity and indicate some evidence for his assertions. But his statement is not backed by a single fact. Not a single member of the SWP is a member of the Green Party. Nor could Rensenbrink name a single delegate that "changed" his or her mind.

It is true that there are many socialists in the Green Party. Some, like members of Solidarity, have been members for years. Others, like the ISO, have recently joined in some areas. Both have played important and extremely positive roles in strengthening the influence of the Green Party. The ISO in particular has brought large numbers of young activists on campuses to help build Green Party campaigns and has done so in a totally principled manner. Both the ISO, Solidarity, and other socialist groups have helped expand Green Party influence within the labor movement and both have been welcomed by the majority of non-socialist Greens. Certainly that is what I have seen in California.

As Forrest Hill has shown, Cobb at best had about 25 percent support among Greens while those backing Nader had about 60 percent. The convention was stolen. It is not the first time nor will it be the last time a convention is stolen from its membership.

The Cobb supporters have another problem to explain in states where Cobb had lost the primaries or conventions but the convention delegates turned out to be over 90 percent for Cobb. The votes in the election show no such trend of a "shift" to Cobb away from Nader. In Maine, Cobb received 2,942 votes to Nader's 7,997—clearly Nader carried the majority of voters who had voted Green in 2004 and who did not vote for Kerry. Amazingly, Cobb support came in just around the percentage he got when the membership voted in Maine. In Wisconsin, we have a similar electoral result. Wisconsin is another Cobb last-minute miracle that gave him 94 percent of the delegates at the Milwaukee convention, but where he had received an even lower percentage of the membership vote than in Maine. But when the votes came in from Wisconsin, Cobb received 2,674 votes to Nader's 18,730, about 12 percent. Once again this reflected the actual vote strength Cobb had inside the Green Party.

Nader's campaign was an alliance between Greens and independents expressed in the Nader/Camejo ticket. The Greens who did not vote for Kerry voted in their overwhelming majority for Nader/Camejo, for a slate that favored independence and opposed lesser-evil politics.

The battle to build an independent electoral resistance to corporate domination clearly passed through the Green Party in the year 2000. It may not do so in the future unless the Green Party becomes once again a clearly independent political force.

The lesser-evil current in the Green Party has begun to shift more openly to a policy in support of the Democratic Party along the lines originally advocated by the now defunct New Party. Jack Uhrich, one of the more factional Cobb supporters, wrote an article for *Green Horizon Quarterly* making this view quite explicit. He argues the Green Party is not growing because it does not support Democrats and gives a detailed example in New Mexico. He names which Democrats the Greens should have supported and ends his article by pointing out there is hope since a Green has withdrawn in a race to help the Democrat win. He explains the decline of the Green Party in New Mexico as directly related to its policy of maintaining its independence from the two corporate parties, especially under the influence of Carol Miller, one of the leading pro-democracy and pro-independence Greens in New Mexico.

No Cobb supporter has made any comment disassociating themselves from Jack Uhrich's call for support to Democrats in partisan races. But the evidence continues to mount that the lesser-evil current is a minority in the Green Party. For instance, at the recent state plenary in California, the largest Green Party organization by far, it was clear that only a small minority believes the Green Party as an institution should endorse partisan Democrats.

In other states, like Utah, the lesser-evil wing has promoted splitting the Green Party. In Utah the pro-Cobb current simply declared itself the Green Party and began "expelling" Greens who supported Nader. The treasury of the Green Party was under the control of both a Nader and a Cobb supporter. The Cobb supporter went to the bank and emptied the account, taking all funds to the new "Cobb-only Green Party." The Cobb supporters then went to court seeking to have themselves declared the Green Party of Utah. They lost their requests after several attempts.

The national leadership has done nothing to stop the split in Utah. In fact, not one Cobb supporter has publicly opposed the pro-split action of their current in Utah. In the states where the largest active Green membership exists, the Cobb current is a minority and thus an open attempt to split the party is not likely at this time. The future of the Green Party lies in the balance. Some Greens who favor independence have quit, some on the right are joining the Democrats. There is some discussion of forming a new party, but most Greens believe the present crisis can be overcome. The fact is many of the Cobb supporters want there to be a Green Party and believe in democracy. I believe consensus can be reached on the issue of one person, one vote and a democratic process for nominating presidential candidates or endorsements can be created, in my opinion.

The party must accept and learn to live with conflicting political currents. This issue will dominate the history of the Green Party in the immediate future. As I proposed at the 2004 convention, the best way for Greens to proceed is to allow both currents to promote their strategy and for us to learn from each other, debate, discuss, and respect each other. My unity proposal at the Milwaukee convention, calling for both Nader and Cobb to be endorsed and allowing each state to respect its internal democracy for ballot status was unfortunately rejected by the Cobb current.

It is clear that such a compromise was not what the Democrats wanted to happen at the Green Party convention. They wanted Nader defeated. The last thing Democrats want is democracy and open discussion. They were overjoyed to hear of Cobb's "victory" at the convention. *The Nation* immediately ran a congratulatory article quoting only Greens who were Cobb supporters. Open Kerry supporters like Norman Solomon immediately announced he would join the Green Party now that it had come to its senses and was joining in the pro-Kerry effort.

While the Democrats fought tooth and nail to deny Nader ballot status, they tried to help Cobb. In New York, where 15,000 signatures are required, Cobb's small group of supporters were only able to collect 5,000. Even then the Democrats would not challenge their efforts and wanted Cobb on the ballot.

Progressive Democrats of America (PDA) are featuring David Cobb and Medea Benjamin on their Web site and at their national conference, while they rejected allowing Ralph Nader to speak. And of course they would not invite any Green who they did not consider a supporter directly or indirectly of John Kerry. Yet the PDA leadership agrees with the Green Party on many critical issues. Greens should work with them around specific issues. There is nothing wrong per se with Greens attending their conference and speaking at it. The issue is, do we promote their illusion that working in a pro-war, pro-corporate party is the course progressives should take? The lesser-evil current in the Green Party is rapidly moving to an inside/outside strategy because of their illusions in the nature of the Democratic Party. Ted Glick, Jack Uhrich, John Rensenbrink, and Medea Benjamin are among the most open advocates of this view.

The truth is, however, that the Democrats are now in disarray. They can't blame Nader for Bush's electoral victory and they haven't a clue of the role they played in helping Bush win. The polarization economically continues. The war and the attacks on our liberties continue.

Green Party relations with dissenting Democrats are quite important for the Green Party. The key is how this relationship is maintained. We should seek to work with Democrats around issues where we agree. But at the same time we must keep our independence and work to expose the reality of the Democratic Party. It is of great interest to us what happens in the Democratic Party.

While working with progressive Democrats is not the centerpiece to building the Green Party in my opinion, it is a factor both positive and negative. There will be an ideological struggle and collaboration around specific issues with many Democrats. The key is not to ever have the Green Party, as an institution, endorse candidates of the two parties representing the rule of money over people. In the end, a major split in the Democratic Party is inevitable due to the massive internal contradiction between what the Democrats support and who votes for them.

All these events point to our need to focus the growth of the Green Party outside of the "liberal intellectual" establishment and turn to the layers that, at least in California, have become the strongest base of voter support for the Greens. These include the poorest people, African Americans, Latinos, and youth. Our effort to build an independent alternative is still focused through the Green Party. Hundreds of thousands of people are members of the Green Party. We need to protect, build, unify, and win over the Green Party to a combative, independent stance.

In opposition to that perspective is the rising development from within the lesser-evil current for an inside/outside strategy, where the Green Party openly endorses Democrats, works with progressive Democratic Party organizations, and becomes a "fusion" pressure group from the outside. The problem with such a strategy is that it fails to understand the nature of the Democratic Party as a wholly owned subsidiary of the corporate world. We will never build a people's alternative force that does not see the Democrats as our opponents—rather than our allies.

Appendixes

Reexamining the Green Party Nominating Convention: A Statistical Analysis
By Forrest Hill
Published on www.greensfornader.net, September 28, 2004

In this analysis, I review in detail the methods used to allocate delegates to the presidential nominees at the Green Party National Convention and show how they led to the nomination of a candidate supported by a small minority of Green Party members. As you will see, the facts show that if the Green Party leadership had developed a system of voting based on the principle of "one person, one vote" (a system supported by the Green Party and all forces in the world that value democracy), Ralph Nader would have overwhelmingly carried the day and won the party's nomination.

The truth is that the Coordinating Committee (CC) of the United States Green Party, whether intentionally or not, created a voting system for the 2004 convention in Milwaukee that drastically undermined the political power of the majority of registered Greens in the country. This was especially true for Greens in California, where over half the registered Greens live.

In general, the CC extensively reduced the voting power of tens of thousands of Greens by relying heavily on the electoral college to determine the number of delegates for each state. This is perhaps not surprising, given that the number of representatives each state has on the CC is itself a function of the electoral college. For a party that proclaims to support the democratization of our election system (including abolishing the electoral college system) such non-representative democracy in the leadership is a concern.

The CC also developed several other ad hoc formulas, which have little relationship to the size of state party memberships, as a way to proportion delegates among states. The upshot of these formulations is that they allowed David Cobb, relatively unknown among Green Party members and a candidate who received only a small percent of the votes in statewide primaries, to win the Green Party nomination for president in 2004. This has resulted in a crisis within the party, not just because there is little support among the rank-and-file for Cobb, but also because the manner in which Cobb was nominated is perceived by many to have undermined key democratic values supported by the party's platform.

The CC has responded to criticism about the lack of democratic representation at the nominating convention by stating that the formula for delegate allocation in Milwaukee was approved in 2003 and according to Dean Myerson, political director of the USGP, "there were no complaints that it was an 'electoral college' then." While this statement may be true, it only reflects the fact that most Greens were totally unaware of the delegate allocation rules passed by the CC (and most still are), as well as the role the electoral college played in determining the outcome of the convention.

In this article I first critique the allocation rules developed by the national Coordinating Committee to determine the delegation size of each state. I then show how under the CC rules the voting power of an individual Green decreases dramatically across all states as the number of registered Greens in their state increases. Finally, I show what the outcome of the election at the National Convention would have been had the CC insisted on using a modified "one person, one vote" system, in which states where Greens cannot register are assumed to have some minimum number of active members based on empirical evidence.

1. Critique of the Delegate Allocation Rules

One of the arguments made for not using a one person, one vote system is that in many states voters are not allowed to register

Green. To try and solve this problem the national Coordinating Committee (CC) approved a system for calculating the number of delegates given to each state based on four criteria: 1. The number of electoral college votes, 2. The number of Greens elected to office, 3. The state's Green voting strength, and 4. The number of delegates each state has on the national Coordinating Committee.

These factors are weighted according to the formulas shown below.

Green Party 2004 Delegate Allocation Rules

Criterion 1: The state's electoral vote 0.5

Criterion 2: Greens elected 2000 through 2003. For each elected Green, award 1 point if the candidate garnered 500 or more votes, and 0.2 points if the candidate garnered less than 500 votes. Also award 0.2 points for each elected official who switched to the Green party *after* taking office.

Criterion 3: The state's Green Party Voting Strength 1.75. For most states, this criterion is based on the support presidential contender Ralph Nader received in the 2000 election. A state party may, however, substitute another 2000–2003 statewide race that had both Democratic and Republican opposition. To compute the electoral strength, multiply the number of votes cast for the candidate by the percentage of the statewide vote the candidate received, then divide by 100,000.

Criterion 4: The number of delegates that each state has on the Coordinating Committee 1.75.

Total the points from each of the four criteria and then round up *any* fractional part to the next largest whole number to determine the number of delegates the state will send to the Green Party Convention.

The fact that the CC decided to use a system that is not based on "one person, one vote" as one of the primary methods for determining the delegate count is a concern. However, what is even more troubling is that in their attempt to create a set of delegate allocation rules they somehow succeeded in creating a system that massively underrepresents the majority of Green Party members.

Below I have highlighted some of the major flaws in CC delegate allocation rules.

Criteria 1 and 4

First of all, Criteria 1 and 4 are essentially identical since the number of delegates that each state has on the Coordinating Committee is determined by the electoral college system (i.e., the number of delegates a state has on the CC equals the number of the state's electoral college vote). Thus, in terms of the proportion of delegates allotted each state, Criteria 1 and 4 yield the exact same result. Added together these criteria can be rewritten as a single rule that simply says the number of delegates a state has at the National Convention equals the number of the state's electoral college vote.

Given that the CC relied so heavily on the electoral college as a predictor of Green Party size in each state, one question we should ask is how well does the electoral college actually predict the number of registered Greens within states other than California (where 53.5 percent of registered Greens reside)?

Figure 1 shows the number of registered Green voters in the twenty-two states where Greens are allowed to register as a function of the number of electoral college votes. There is a small positive correlation only because of the large number of registered Greens in New York relative to other states. However, if we remove New York from this analysis (it is technically a statistical outlier[1]) the correlation between the electoral college vote and the number of registered Greens within states is totally uncorrelated. This means that for states with less than thirty electoral college votes (i.e., forty-seven states plus the District of Columbia), knowing the number of electors in a state tells you absolutely nothing about the number of registered Greens.

The dash line shows the general trend of the number of registered Greens as a function of the number of electors for states with less than thirty electoral college votes. While this trend is not significant, the fact that it is negative emphasizes how arbitrary and meaningless Criteria 1 and 4 are as rules for allocating delegates (i.e., for the majority of states, the size of their electoral college vote is totally unrelated to their success at building the party).

Criterion 2

The second criterion proposed by the CC to allocate delegates also has some serious flaws. This formula uses a point system based on the number of candidates elected to office between 2000 and 2003 and the number of votes cast for those candidates. The purpose of

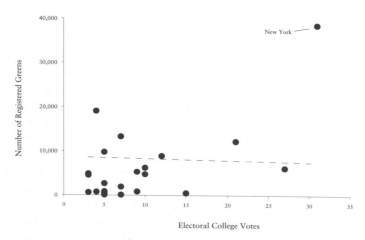

Figure 1. The number of registered Greens in each states (where Greens are allowed to register) as a function of the number of Electoral College Votes in each state. The dashed line shows the predicted trend between Electoral College Votes and Registered Greens for states with less than thirty Electoral College Votes.

this rule, we assume, is to allocate delegates to states according to how successful Greens have been at running for office. The major problems with this formula are: 1. it uses an arbitrary low-voting threshold to assign a value to each winning candidate, 2. it ignores the actual number of votes cast for "winning" candidates, 3. it does not distinguish between the relative difficulty of winning various races, and 4. it does not count races in which Green candidates received ten thousand votes, yet lost.

The problem with setting a low-voting threshold as a measure of success in local races is that changing the threshold by a relatively small amount drastically changes the proportion of delegates allotted to each state. For example, if the threshold is raised to one thousand votes (a relatively small number of votes to win an election), then Wisconsin and Pennsylvania would see the number of delegates allotted to them under this formula decline by about 40 percent.

If the point of Criterion 2 is to measure the relative number of active Greens in each state (assuming this can be determined by the number of elected Green officials), then a fairer method of assigning delegates would be to count the actual number of votes cast for winning candidates. Thus, the proportion of delegates allotted to a state is the number of votes cast for winning candidates in that state divided by the total number of votes cast for all winning Green candidates in the United States.

Figure 2 compares the proportion of delegates allotted states using the CC point system formula vs. the proportion of delegates that would have been allotted using the number of votes cast for winning candidates (data are for 2000 to 2003). Only the states with the ten highest delegate counts using these methods are shown. California does pretty much the same under both systems (receiving about 43 percent of the delegates), however, several states such as Pennsylvania and Wisconsin would receive a substantially lower percentage of delegates, while Oregon and Washington would increase the size of their delegation by at least a factor of two.

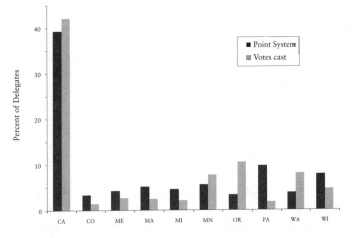

Figure 2. Percent of delegates that were allotted each state using the "winning" candidate point system described in Criterion 2 and the percent that would be allocated based on votes cast for "winning" candidates.

Of course if we want to allocate delegates based on the strength of local elections, why only use the number of votes cast for winning candidates? Since the conditions for winning a race vary greatly from state to state, why not measure local support for the Green Party by adding up the votes cast for all Green candidates in each state? This makes abundant sense when you consider that Laura Wells received 419,873 votes running for state controller yet lost (thus California receives no delegates for her efforts) while the combined vote total for all "winning" candidates in states other than California is 404,602. In fact, in 2002, six Greens ran for statewide offices in California and all of them received over 300,000 votes. On top of that, Matt Gonzalez received more than 100,000 votes running for mayor of San Francisco and was nearly elected to office. Yet, none of these races had any effect on the number of delegates allocated to California under the CC formulation.

In general, it makes no sense to use the number of officeholders as a way of distributing delegates among states. Delegates are supposed to represent a constituency, while the number of candidates holding office can depend on a number of factors that have nothing to do with the size of the Green membership. For example, Wisconsin has won several supervisor seats simply because they were uncontested, while in states like California (where developers are heavily involved in supervisor races), Green candidates usually need to get at least 20,000 votes to win, and are often heavily outspent by their opponents.

Figure 3 shows there is little relationship between the highly ad hoc method of distributing delegates using Criterion 2 and the number of registered Green voters within states. A correlation analysis between registered Greens and elected Greens is not significant (P > 0.15). Thus, given there is no relationship between the number of "winning" candidates and the size of statewide Green membership, this method of proportioning delegates should be dropped.

Criterion 3

The third criterion, the "voting strength of a state," is perhaps the most perplexing concept for allocating delegates, and one wonders what the CC was thinking when they came up with this rule.

The voting strength, as defined by the number and percent of the vote Ralph Nader received in the 2000 presidential election assumes that somehow there is a relationship between the support for Nader in a state and the influence of the Green Party. First,

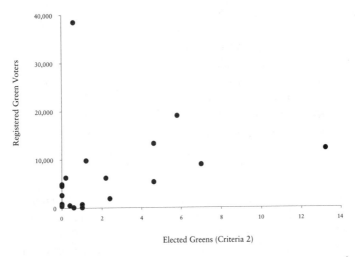

Figure 3. The number of registered Greens in twenty-two states where Greens are allowed to register as a function of the Greens elected to office between 2000 and 2003. The elected Greens score is calculated according to Criterion 2 in the delegate selection rules. Note that California was excluded from this analysis as it represents over half the registered Greens and is a statistical outlier.

Nader (and his political organization) in part must be given the credit for his support in 2000. Second, since the total number of registered Greens equals about one-tenth the number of votes received by Nader, and Greens tend to vote at the same rate as non-Greens (about 50 percent), the votes received by Nader were overwhelmingly cast by non-Greens. Finally, it is highly ironic that the CC decided to use Nader's showing in 2000 to disenfranchise Nader supporters in 2004.

It should be noted that even though we believe Criterion 3 is a highly arbitrary method of allocating delegates, in the case of California, the CC didn't even apply its own rule correctly. The rule states that the results of another statewide race that had both Democratic and Republican opposition can be substituted for Nader's presidential results. Using the results of Peter Camejo's 2002 gubernatorial race would have increased the delegate count by five in California, while the results from Laura Wells's race for Controller would have increased the delegate count by eight. Such oversight makes us wonder how accurately the CC applied its own set of ad hoc rules in other states.

Forgoing the will of the many for the few

While the intent of the delegate allocation rules was to allow all states to participate in the nomination of the Green Party presidential candidate, the fact of the matter is they do an incredibly poor job of representing the membership in states where Greens are allowed to register. This is disturbing given these states easily account for 90 percent of the active Greens in the United States. As we will show in the next section, states with large numbers of registered Greens were highly underrepresented at the convention, while states with small memberships were dramatically overrepresented. This heavily biased the voting results toward small states resulting in a victory for David Cobb.

2. Voting Power at the Convention

The defining principle that should have guided the national Coordinating Committee in developing their criteria for delegate allotment is "one person, one vote." It has been argued that since voters cannot legally register as Greens in twenty-seven states, Green Party members in these states would be disenfranchised if registration were the sole criterion used to allocate delegates, while states with high numbers of registered voters would be overrepresented.

Unfortunately, in their zeal to help fledgling states with small Green Party memberships (which is a noble cause), the national Coordinating Committee came up with a delegation formula that not only highly overrepresented small states but massively disenfranchised Green voters in populous states, especially California.

This is easily illustrated by calculating the voting power of Greens in states where they are allowed to register. The voting power is defined as the ratio of the number of national delegates to the number of registered Green voters. Greens from states with a high ratio have greater voting power (or representation) than Greens from states with a low ratio.

Figure 4a shows the voting power of each state relative to California, which has a delegate-per-voter ratio of 1/1,200. In general, Green Party members in eighteen states had at least twice the voting power of Californians, and in nine of these states Greens had at least ten times the voting power. More importantly, voting power among states decreases "exponentially" as the number of registered Greens in each state increases (Figure 4b). Thus the CC managed to come up with a system that almost completely disenfranchises the majority of registered Greens in states where they are allowed to register. Including the delegate count from states where Greens are not allowed to register (i.e., where membership is surely not more than a few hundred people) only makes

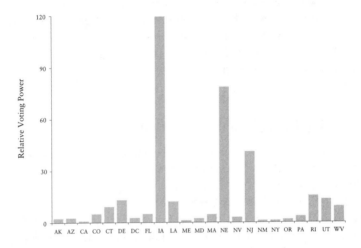

Figure 4a. Relative voting power of Green members at the National Convention in states where Greens can register to vote. Voting power is the number of delegates per registered Green, and the relative voting power is the ratio of the voting power of each state to the voting power of California (thus CA has a relative voting power of 1).

the situation worse.

Given the incredible inadequacies of the CC system to fairly allocate delegates among states, two questions arise: 1) how might we improve on this system to best approximate the principle of "one person, one vote" and 2) what would the outcome of the nominating convention have been if delegates were distributed according to this fundamental democratic principle?

A Democratic Method for Allocating Delegates

One way to implement a democratic one person, one vote sys-

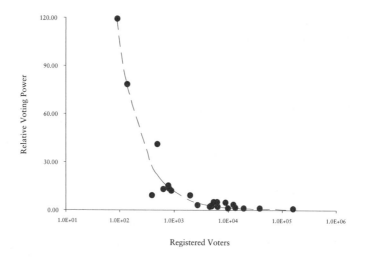

Figure 4b. The relative voting power of each state as a function of the number of registered Green voters. The X axis is on a logarithmic scale indicating that voting power decreases exponentially as the number of registered voters increases.

tem of representation given current limits on registration is to assume that states have some minimal number of Green Party members. There are numerous ways this minimum number could be determined. The most restrictive way would be to use the number of registered Greens in the state that has the lowest number of registered voters (in this case Iowa). The problem with this method, however, is that because of potential restrictions on registration in Iowa or other states with low numbers of registered Greens, these numbers would likely underrepresent active membership in several states (for example, Wisconsin).

For the sake of argument, we will assume the minimum number of active Greens in each state is equal to the geometric mean[2] number of Greens in the twelve states with the lowest number of registrants (52 percent of the states where Greens can register). The number of registered Greens in these states ranges from 90 (Iowa) to 4,832 (Arizona) and the geometric mean number of registered Greens is 825.

To estimate the proportion of delegates allocated to states using a one person, one vote system, we assume that all states, whether

Greens can register or not, have "at least" 825 active Green members. This would not only provide a generous estimate of the size of the active membership in states where Greens are not allowed to register, but also increase membership size in seven states where Greens are allowed to register (Delaware, Iowa, Nebraska, New Jersey, Rhode Island, West Virginia, and Utah).

The proportion of delegates allotted to each state is found by dividing the number of Greens in each state (using a minimum threshold of 825 Greens per state) by the total number of Greens in all states. Thus California would get 49 percent of the delegates (53 percent of registered Greens live in California), while states where Greens cannot register would each get approximately 0.25 percent of the delegates. So, for example, if there were, say, twelve hundred delegates at the convention, states like Iowa and Rhode Island would get three delegates.

By simply setting a minimum membership size, we ensure that all states are represented, yet create a delegation that fairly represents those states where Greens have been successful in building the party. There are other ways to set this threshold (some may argue for a round number like one thousand or two thousand). However, whatever method is chosen should be based on some sort of empirical evidence.

In essence using a system with a reasonable membership threshold does not punish states for being successful (which makes no sense if our purpose is to grow the Green movement), and provides an incentive for new state organizations to grow their membership.

3. Convention results using the democratic principle "one person, one vote"

The real delegate count

If the National Convention used a one person, one vote system to allocate delegates, what would have been the outcome of the presidential nomination?

To answer this question, we need to know the vote from all state primaries and caucuses.

Mysteriously, the national Green Party Web site, which provides a lot of information on the convention rules and the delegate count for each nominee, never posted the actual results of any state Green Party primary or caucus. Why was this information hidden from the membership? Neither did the Web site report on the turnout at the caucuses, which were often not well attended, nor how many people actually participated in the voting. Again the question is why? Therefore we are forced to work from e-mails.

Based on records from several e-mails, there is a strong indication that voter turnout in the caucus states was small (generally less than one hundred people) and that delegates may not have been proportioned according to the actual vote. For example, in Maine, Nader received 30 percent of the vote and was awarded six delegates while Cobb received 24 percent and was awarded seven delegates. Even more disconcerting is the fact that almost all the Maine delegates representing Nader voted for Cobb at the convention. Green Party officials must guarantee that delegates who represent a candidate are individuals who support that candidate (i.e., they are not simply appointed). The fear that the delegation was packed with Cobb supporters is one of the reasons a large number of Greens do not accept the results of the 2004 convention.

While we have managed to ascertain the vote in fifteen state caucuses via e-mail communications (see appendix), the vote of the majority of states cannot be found anywhere on the GPUS Web site (this information appears to have been suppressed by the Green Party). Thus, to determine the outcome of the presidential nomination using a one person, one vote election system, we calculated the percent of votes received by each candidate using the delegate count posted on the Green Party's Web site.[3] This undoubtedly favors Cobb; however, it is the best information available on how Greens actually voted.

Table 1 shows the percent of delegates that would have been allotted to each candidate under a one person, one vote (OPOV) system versus the CC's delegate allocation rules. There are a couple of points to note. First, the percentage of delegates for Cobb under OPOV is about half of what it was at the national convention. This is due to the fact that most of Cobb's victories were in small states where, as shown above, the voting power of Greens was dramatically elevated under the CC rules. Second, the percentage of delegates allotted to Peter Camejo is more than twice as high under

OPOV vs. the CC rules, due to the fact that he overwhelmingly won the California primary, receiving 63 percent of the total vote (or as reported in the press, 75.3 percent of the Greens who actually cast votes). Under OPOV, Camejo has 50 percent more delegates than Cobb, while under the CC rules Cobb is allotted almost three times as many delegates as Camejo. Finally, there is a substantial change in the percentage of uncommitted votes due to a high number of write-in ballots in California.

In general, these patterns indicate that the biggest flaw in the CC voting system was that it massively underrepresented the will of the Green membership in California. This seems particular egregious, given that almost fifty thousand Greens voted in the California primary, while the turnout at any other primaries or caucus meetings (as far as we know) never exceeded one thousand participants.

Table 2 shows the percentage of Greens who supported Nader or candidates running as a stand-in for Nader (Camejo, Miller, and Salzman) versus Cobb. Under a democratic one person, one vote system, the delegates representing Nader supporters outnumber Cobb by more than 2–1, while under the CC rules Cobb received more delegates than all Nader supporters combined. The fact that the CC rules for allocating delegates so drastically alters the outcome of the election is the prime reason that so many Green Party members do not believe the National Convention was legitimate.

Candidate	Delegates OPOV	Delegates CC rules
Peter Camejo	33.4%	15.5%
David Cobb	24.1%	40.1%
Kent Mesplay	1.8%	3.1%
Carol Miller	2.2%	1.2%
Ralph Nader	14.0%	15.3%
Lorna Salzman	8.0%	5.2%
Other	0.9%	4.4%
No Nominee	4.8%	9.6%
Uncommitted	10.8%	5.6%

Table 1: The percentage of delegates allocated to each candidate using a one person, one vote (OPOV) system in which all states are assumed to have at least 825 Green members, and the percentage of delegates allotted under the CC delegate rules.

Candidate	Delegates OPOV	Delegates CC rules
Nader Supporters	57.6%	37.2%
David Cobb	24.1%	40.1%

Table 2: The percentage of the delegates allocated to Nader supporters versus Cobb supporters under one person, one vote (OPOV) versus the CC rules.

Outcome of a democratic convention

As many know, Ralph Nader did not seek the Green Party "nomination." The reason he chose this course was because in November of 2003 when he was deciding whether to run for president, the Greens were divided about their national strategy. Many Greens in leadership positions did not want to run a candidate at all, while others only wanted to run in states where the race was not competitive between Republicans and Democrats.

After Nader announced in December that he did not plan to seek the Green Party nomination a lot of Greens began to urge him to reconsider. He finally relented and said that if the Greens decided not to run a candidate that he would accept their endorsement. To help ensure that Nader received the endorsement of the party, several candidates, including Peter Camejo, Carol Miller, and Lorna Salzman, put their names on various ballots around the country to run as stand-ins for Nader. Nader's name was also added belatedly to the ballots of several states.

The voting procedure developed by the CC for the convention stipulated that the only way the party could endorse Nader (or any other candidate for that matter) was if over 50 percent of the delegation first voted for "no nominee," and over 50 percent of the delegation voted to endorse a candidate using Instant Runoff Voting.[4]

During the first round of voting, the number of votes cast for each candidate was proportional to the number of votes they received (i.e., the results in Table 3). Since no one received a majority of votes during the first round of voting, the nomination process proceeded to a second round of voting, at which point candidates who ran for Nader would have instructed their delegates to vote for "No Nominee."

Table 3 shows the results of the second round of voting under a one person, one vote system. We have not changed the uncommitted category as there is no way to know how they would have voted; however, if these delegates voted in a manner that was consistent with the Green rank and file then most of them would have voted for "No Nominee." Thus under any kind of fair system, it is unlikely that Cobb would have gotten more than 30 percent of the vote and so his nomination should have been resoundingly defeated.

Candidate	Percent of Delegates
No Nominee	62.4%
David Cobb	24.1%
Uncommitted	10.8%
Other	2.9%

Table 3: Outcome of the second round of voting under a system of one person, one vote representation. The No Nominee category represents the sum of the delegates for Camejo, Miller, Nader, Salzman, and the No Nominee category.

Given that the votes for candidates representing Nader/Camejo accounted for 57.6 percent of the delegates, the endorsement of Nader would have been assured following the defeat of Cobb.

Conclusions

The real tragedy of the 2004 Green Party National Convention is that the party leadership got away with creating a highly undemocratic set of rules, which allowed a candidate with minority support among the rank and file to win the party's nomination for president. It is this point, and not the nomination of David Cobb himself, that has thrown into doubt the legitimacy of the national governing body and its supporters.

To make matters worse, there are several other problems that are not dealt with in this analysis. The first is that the CC implemented a system of voting that denied delegates the right to vote for endorsement without first voting against nominating a candidate. This problem was exacerbated by making candidates who were running as stand-ins for Nader drop out of the polling after the first round if they themselves were not willing to accept the nomination.

Second, many of the state delegations were packed with Cobb supporters who voted for Cobb after the first round, once they were no longer mandated to vote for one of the pro-Nader candidates. For example, in Maine where Nader and Salzman supporters won the caucus vote and Cobb only received 24 percent of the vote, eighteen out of nineteen delegates voted for Cobb in the second round of voting. The California vote was also not respected by the delegation as many switched to Cobb in the second round of voting. These and other examples have led many Greens to fear that the delegation was intentionally packed with Cobb supporters.

Finally, the behavior of much of the leadership toward Ralph Nader prior to the 2004 National Convention is inexcusable. Between 2001 and 2004 Nader appeared at forty-four Green Party fundraisers in thirty-one states (out of his own costs) and continued to promote the Green Party. In fact, there is no doubt that he has done more to build the Green Party than any other single individual. Yet over the past couple of years he has suffered the slings and arrows of many on the Steering Committee, as well as constant attacks from David Cobb and others for not being registered Green, for not sharing the names of all his donors with the GPUS or the Cobb campaign, and for not doing enough to build the party. It is this attitude that makes many Greens feel the CC intentionally devised their delegate allocation rules to weaken Nader's chance of receiving the party's endorsement.

This paper is not meant to provide a definitive solution of how voting should be carried out at future conventions. It does, however, show the importance of creating a system that fairly represents the Green Party membership. Given that the distribution of party members is heavily consolidated in a few states, using the electoral college (a system which itself does not fairly represent voters in America) to determine the voting power of each state must be stopped. All future elections for the presidential nomination of the Green Party must be based on the "principle" of one person, one vote. To do otherwise will only serve to alienate the membership and continue to divide the party.

Appendix

Below is a record of the vote in fifteen state caucuses obtained from e-mails sent by members of various state parties. We have no way of knowing whether these are accurate, but we believe they represent the turnout in many of the caucus states.

CONNECTICUT
John Battista
How many attended the state caucus?
  Attendance was 49 to pick 15 delegates
Delegates assigned to each candidate
  7 Nader, 4 Cobb, 3 No Candidate, 1 Camejo
Second round of voting at the convention
  8 Cobb, 7 No Nominee

DELAWARE
How many attended the state caucus?
  25 Greens picked 7 delegates
Delegates assigned to each candidate
  6 Cobb, 1 Camejo
Second round of voting at the convention
  7 Cobb

OHIO
Paul Dumouchelle
Secretary, Green Party of Ohio
How many attended the state caucus?
  43 attended the caucus and 46 voted by e-mail to pick 25 delegates
Delegates assigned to each candidate
  12 Cobb, 5 Mesplay, 4 No Nominee, 1 Abstention

ILLINOIS
How many attended the state caucus?
  Thanks for inquiring. We had about 50 people at the state convention. About 40 of them were qualified members of the Illinois Green Party. I believe about 35 (of the 40) participated in the nominating portion of the convention.
How many registered Greens are there in IL? If not a registration state, what is the membership of the GPIL?

We don't have any registered Greens, as Illinois does not allow you to register as a party member. The only current indication of party in Illinois is a record of which ballot you choose at a primary, which (with a few local exceptions) the Illinois Green Party has not yet qualified for. We do however have approximately 500 members of the IGP.

Delegates assigned to each candidate

11 Cobb, 4 Mesplay, 7 No Nominee

MARYLAND

From Kevin Zeese

How many attended the state caucus?

60 people picked 12 delegates

Delegates assigned to each candidate

5 Cobb, 3 Camejo, 2 No Nominee, 1 Nader, 1 Miller

MAINE

Ben Meiklejohn

How many attended the state caucus?

A total 171 votes cast statewide, Ralph Nader has earned the most votes with 51 total or 30 percent of all votes cast (excluding abstentions). David Cobb received 41 votes, or 24 percent. The rest of the votes were divided among 13 candidates.

Delegates assigned to each candidate

7 Cobb, 6 Nader, 2 None of the Above (NOTA), 2 uncommitted

Second round of voting at the Convention

18 Cobb, 1 No Nominee

MICHIGAN

From Marc

How many attended the state caucus?

Total vote count over the two-day period was 85

How many registered Greens are there in MI? If not a registration state, what is the membership of the GPMI?

We can't register. Our membership was last stated at 483 dues-paying members.

Delegates assigned to each candidate

13 Bier-Beemon (favorite daughter), 10 Nader, 8 Cobb, 1

Mesplay

NEBRASKA
Conversation with Dante:
How many attended the state caucus?
> Don't make me cry. We only had 40 at the most. We weren't that big to begin with and with the state of things we're even smaller.

How many registered Greens are there in NE? If not a registration state, what is the membership of the GPNE?
> We are partly a registration state meaning that only 1 of the 3 districts have ballot access. That district has just over 100 registered members.

Delegates assigned to each candidate
> 9 delegates for Cobb

NEW JERSEY
How many attended the state caucus?
> 75 people attended (total GPNJ dues-paying membership is approximately 280).

Delegates assigned to each candidate
> 9 Nader, 4 Cobb, 3 Uncommitted, 1 No Candidate

NORTH CAROLINA
From Gray Newman
How many attended the state caucus?
> We had 14 Greens from our locals pick 10 delegates for the convention. We have plus or minus 250 Greens in our locals but I know of quite a few more who do not live near locals.

Delegates assigned to each candidate
> 8 Cobb, 1 Camejo, 1 Salzman

GEORGIA
Joell
How many attended the state caucus?
> In Georgia the State Green Convention location was changed three times. Eventually it was held in Savannah and was attended by 17 Greens. While Georgia GP has never attained State Party status (11,000 write-in votes were cast for Nader in 2000), they were allotted 11 delegates to the convention.

Delegates assigned to each candidate
11 for Cobb

PENNSYLVANIA
How many attended the state caucus?
250
Vote
99 Cobb, 74 Nader, 62 No Candidate/Abstain, 3 Other, 1 Camejo
Delegates assigned to each candidate
16 Cobb, 12 Nader, 9 NOTA

TENNESSEE
From Katey Culver
How many attended the state caucus?
The Green Party of Tennessee Annual Meeting and 2004 Convention was held Fri–Sun May 21–23. Twenty-five Greens were at the meeting; also attending were two teenagers, six toddlers, and two cooks.
Vote
The actual tally was 19 voting members; 17 Cobb, 1 NOTA, 1 Camejo
Delegates assigned to each candidate
9 Cobb, 1 NOTA

TEXAS
Source: David Pollard
How many attended the state caucus?
There were 55 certified state delegates and about a dozen alternates that picked the 35 delegates for the convention
How many delegates will actually attend the National Convention?
Currently we have 19 people expecting to go to the expense of traveling and lodging up in Milwaukee. If less than 18 actually are able to make it to the convention, Texas will not be able to vote its full allotment of delegates at the convention. So there is to a small degree a self-limiting factor for states that are disinterested in the presidential campaign.
Delegates assigned to each candidate

25 Cobb, 9 No Nominee, 1 Camejo/Mesplay
Second round of voting at the convention
34 Cobb, 1 No Nominee

WISCONSIN

How many attended the state caucus?
596 people attended with 102 of 134 districts reporting. Some of the organized caucuses had no participants.

Vote

NO CANDIDATE	130 votes	22.41%
NONE OF THE ABOVE	105 votes	18.10%
UNDECIDED	104 votes	17.93%
WRITE-IN	93 votes	16.03%
DAVID COBB	70 votes	12.07%
LORNA SALZMAN	28 votes	4.83%
PETER CAMEJO	24 votes	4.14%
KENT MESPLAY	8 votes	1.38%
CAROL MILLER	7 votes	1.21%
PAUL GLOVER	6 votes	1.03%
NO ENDORSEMENT	3 votes	0.52%
SHEILA BILYEAU	2 votes	0.34%

Second round of voting at the Convention
31 Cobb, 1 Mesplay, 1 No Nominee

ARKANSAS

From Anita, no response on number attending.

Arkansas' seven delegates to the National Convention will be committed to David Cobb as a result of voting at our state convention today. The decision was unanimous.

Proposals to the GPUS from Greens for Democracy and Independence

Presented at GPUS National Committee meeting, July 21–24, 2005

Proposal ID 153
Proposal: Strengthening Internal Democracy in the GPUS
Presenters: Green Party of New York State, Green Party of

Vermont
Discussion: July 4–24, 2005
Voting: July 25–31, 2005

Background

To maintain our party's unity we must institute internal democratic reforms that ensure that all viewpoints are respected, all members can participate fully in the institutions of the party, and all decisions truly reflect the will of the Green Party membership.

In order to strengthen internal democracy in the Green Party of the United States, we ask the State Committee of the Green Party of New York State to approve the following proposals.

Proposal

The Green Party of New York and the Green Party of Vermont call upon the GPUS to strengthen internal democracy by adopting a national policy based on the principle of one person, one vote.

To facilitate the adoption of one person, one vote, we call upon the GPUS to require all accredited state parties to estimate the size of their state membership relative to other states, and that a neutral commission be set up to evaluate the claims made by each state.

One Person, One Vote

It is imperative that all members in the Green Party recognize that our national decisions reflect the true will of our members and that their opinions and votes are fully counted and respected.

The Green Party internal structures must correspond with the principle of one person, one vote. No member of the Green Party may have more or less representation than any other Green Party member when selecting the party's presidential ticket and its national leadership bodies.

State representatives to national leadership bodies and selection of delegates for National Conventions must correspond to the principle of one person, one vote. Any existing regulations that conflict with this principle are invalid and must be adjusted to correspond to it.

The principle of one person, one vote must be respected along with our principles of gender parity and diversity on the issues the party has declared relevant for our nation and our time.

Determining State Membership Size

Before the Green Party can implement one person, one vote representation, we must develop methods to fairly determine the membership size of each state. Given that more than half of the states in the United States do not allow citizens to register for any third political party, each state party will have to use different methods for estimating membership sizes.

States can estimate their membership size using registration numbers, number of elected Greens, votes cast for local, statewide, or presidential Green candidates, or whatever method they deem appropriate. All estimates by any one state must be contrasted with estimates from all other states to determine the overall percentage of delegates allotted that state.

Neutral Commission to Certify Membership Size

Based on the principle above, a special commission should be established that, as clearly as possible, represents the Green Party members and its differing political currents, geographic spread, and other factors such as gender and race. The commission will be selected by the National Committee and will meet every two years in odd numbered years.

Each state will be asked to provide an estimate of their membership size based on any combination of direct and/or indirect methods they deem as appropriate. The commission will review each state's claims and their premises. They will either agree or make their own estimate. In cases where there is disagreement between the committee and a state, every attempt will be made by both parties to resolve the dispute.

Once the membership size for each state has been certified by the commission, these values will be used to determine the proportion of representation each state gets in our national governing bodies and at the National Convention.

Representation for delegates and for election of the National Committee members will follow the certification of membership state by state in a formula that will be based on a one person, one vote criterion.

This proposal does not provide a rule or bylaw change; it is a call for rulemaking. It is a general resolution that provides guidance and recommendations for a working group established to craft and introduce proposals for actual rules or bylaw amendments. Such a working group would be convening under a charge to formulate proposals that are in accordance with the general principles outlined in each proposal and would be presented to the National Committee in the form of proposed bylaws and/or rules and procedures. The working group should be called into existence immediately upon adoption of this resolution, include members from all GPUS member states and caucuses, and submit formal proposals to the National Committee within ninety days of this resolution's adoption. The resulting proposals, wherever they consist of rules or bylaws or changes to rules or bylaws will require a two-thirds vote of the National Committee in order to pass.

Timeline

This proposal is to be presented for vote to the 2005 National Committee meeting, to be held July 21–24, 2005.

Proposal ID 154
Proposal: Delegate Selection to the National Convention
Presenter: Green Party of New York State, Green Party of Vermont
Discussion: July 4–24, 2005
Voting: July 25–31, 2005

Proposal

The Green Party of New York and the Green Party of Vermont call upon the GPUS to strengthen internal democracy in the selection of delegates to our leadership bodies and to the presidential nominating convention, based on the principle of one person, one vote.

To facilitate this process we call upon the GPUS to require that the selection of delegates to our National Convention respect the vote of the membership by ensuring that:

1) The number of delegates pledged to each candidate is proportioned according to the vote, whether a state uses primary, regional caucus, or a state nominating convention to choose a presidential nominee.

2) A delegate may not go to the National Convention repre-

senting a candidate (or proposal) that they did not vote for in their state's primary or caucus, unless specifically bound to support that candidate (or proposal).

3) During the first round of voting at the National Convention, delegates must vote for their designated candidate (or proposal position) to ensure that the will of the membership is respected. Should a second round be necessary, the delegates from any state may cast votes in accordance with instructions from their own state party organizations should such instructions be issued, or be free to vote their conscience if no such instructions are given. In all subsequent rounds, delegates are free to vote their conscience based on what they believe is the best for the Green Party.

4) Where possible, state Green parties should hold official primaries to facilitate the greatest possible participation by their members. Where no primaries exist, every effort should be made to ensure that all state party members receive ballots. The GPUS should help facilitate these efforts in cases where the states have limited resources to poll their membership. In all cases, the GPUS should report the number of voters participating in a state election and the number of votes received by each candidate on their Web site.

This proposal does not provide a rule or bylaw change; it is a call for rulemaking. It is a general resolution that provides guidance and recommendations for a working group established to craft and introduce proposals for actual rules or bylaw amendments. Such a working group would be convening under a charge to formulate proposals that are in accordance with the general principles outlined in each proposal and would be presented to the National Committee in the form of proposed bylaws and/or rules and procedures. The working group should be called into existence immediately upon adoption of this resolution, include members from all GPUS member states and caucuses, and submit formal proposals to the National Committee within ninety days of this resolution's adoption. The resulting proposals, wherever they consist of rules or bylaws or changes to rules or bylaws will require a two-thirds vote of the National Committee in order to pass.

Timeline

This proposal is to be presented for vote to the 2005 national Green Party meeting, to be held July 21–24, 2005.

Proposal ID 155
Proposal: Green Party Affirmation of Independence
Presenter: Green Party of New York State, Green Party of
  Vermont

Background

If the Green Party does not affirm its independence from the corporate parties, its existence will be compromised and its unity endangered. Furthermore, the Green Party will face internal strife and conflict as Greens debate which Democrat or Republican qualifies or does not qualify for support.

A policy of political independence is fundamental to our future growth and survival as a political party and should be as universal as our Ten Key Values.

In order to make political independence a policy in the Green Party of the United States, the Green Party of New York and the Green Party of Vermont ask GPUS to approve the following proposal.

Proposal

The Green Party of New York and the Green Party of Vermont call upon the GPUS to affirm its complete political independence from the Democratic and Republican Parties by adopting a national policy that states and acknowledges the following:

1) That the institution of the Green Party of the United States, as defined by its national organizations and by its presidential and vice presidential candidates, will not endorse, place on its ballot lines, urge a vote for, raise funds for, urge a vote against, or otherwise oppose just one of the two corporate party candidates (which amounts to backhanded support for the other corporate party candidate), or in any way run its campaign or make any GPUS resources available to assist either or both major corporate-supported parties or their partisan candidates. The GPUS urges its member state parties to observe these principles in their conduct of state campaigns and general operations, and recommends that all state parties adopt this as policy.

2) That an endorsement by the Green Party of corporate-controlled parties and their partisan candidates represents a movement away from the core of our founding principles of the Ten Key Val-

ues and toward the dissipation of our political identity, and therefore, while state Green parties have the unfettered right to name
and/or endorse candidates in any manner of their own choosing
with no interference or intrusion by GPUS, it is GPUS policy to not
grant support of any kind to partisan candidates of any corporate-
supported party through the Coordinated Campaign Committee
(CCC), official GPUS media, or activities of GPUS standing committees and caucuses.

3) That, as an independent political party, it is not only our
right, but our duty to politically challenge the corporate parties in
elections and to make demands of them to foster greater electoral
democracy in America. This affirmation does not apply to other
third parties or independent candidates whose platform reflects our
Ten Key Values. We recognize that we do not live in a representative democracy and that to build such a democracy we must work
with other political organizations. Thus, the Green Party may endorse and work with other political parties or candidates that are
independent of corporate domination and where there is agreement
on issues in harmony with our Ten Key Values.

This affirmation does not in any way restrict the Green Party,
or its members, from working with individuals from the corporate
parties on issues we support such as non-violence, social justice,
electoral reform, or environmental sustainability. The Green Party
is not a centralized party. It welcomes political diversity and encourages its members to express their views openly and publicly on
any matter they wish, including the right to support, work for, or
vote for a candidate from any party. Members may do so as individuals, as organized committees, as members of state organizations, county organizations, county committees, or as members of
a local Green Party chapter. Such action does not contradict the
Green Party's institutional independence, since these individuals or
organizations are autonomous and do not represent the official
policy of the Green Party of the United States itself.

This proposal does not provide a rule or bylaw change; it is a
call for rulemaking. It is a general resolution that provides guidance and recommendations for a working group established to
craft and introduce proposals for actual rules or bylaw amendments. Such a working group would be convening under a charge
to formulate proposals that are in accordance with the general

principles outlined in each proposal and would be presented to the National Committee in the form of proposed bylaws and/or rules and procedures. The working group should be called into existence immediately upon adoption of this resolution, include members from all GPUS member states and caucuses, and submit formal proposals to the National Committee within ninety days of this resolution's adoption. The resulting proposals, wherever they consist of rules or bylaws or changes to rules or bylaws will require a two-thirds vote of the National Committee in order to pass.

References

This proposal is to be presented for vote at the 2005 National Committee meeting, to be held July 21–24, 2005.

Which Way Forward for the Green Party?
By Ashley Smith and Forrest Hill
August 26, 2005

At the July 21–24, 2005, National Committee meeting in Tulsa, Oklahoma, the Green Party arrived at a fork in the road. The delegates voted down resolutions offered by Greens for Democracy and Independence designed to ensure proportional representation inside the party, national delegates accountable to the expressed will of the membership, and political independence from the two corporate parties.

This vote seems to fly in the face of everything that the Green Party stands for.

As Maryland senatorial candidate and Green Party member Kevin Zeese rightly points out, "the overwhelming majority of Greens support real democracy—based on the principle of one person, one vote—and want the Green Party to stand for something different than the Democrats or Republicans."

"The Tulsa decisions exacerbate the already growing rift in the party. The ramifications of these decisions must be reversed if the Greens are to truly challenge the corporate parties. This can only happen if Greens across the country are willing to fight to take back their party. Only an uprising by the membership will reinvigorate the Green Party," added Zeese.

At Tulsa, two currents came into conflict over the future of the party, a radical wing embodied by the Greens for Democracy and Independence (GDI) and a liberal wing that supports internal policy-making over political organizing.

GDI argues that the Green Party must become the political expression of the living social movements to challenge the corporate duopoly at the ballot box. It came into being to resolve the political and organizational crisis that wreaked havoc in the Green Party during the 2004 election.

The crisis started in the period leading up to the nomination of Green presidential candidate David Cobb, who argued for a "safe states strategy" in battleground states during the 2004 election campaign. This tactic was viewed by many Greens as a backhanded way of adopting a political strategy of capitulation to the Democratic Party in order to defeat Bush.

The safe-state strategy was supported primarily by small state parties, who were disproportionately represented at the 2004 National Convention. Based on this undemocratic apportionment, Cobb won the nomination, and for the first time ever, the Green Party embraced a lesser-evil political strategy.

The Cobb campaign for president garnered only about 120,000 votes, or about one-third of the registered Greens in the country. More importantly, there was virtually no support for Cobb from activists outside the party. As a result of this disastrous showing, Green parties in several states lost their ballot lines.

Since the election, the division between GDI supporters and the liberal wing of the national Green Party has become more apparent.

Many in the liberal wing have aligned themselves with organizations like the Progressive Democrats of America (PDA), whose stated aim is to transform the Democratic Party from within. In fact, David Cobb has appeared on many PDA panels and is prominently featured on their Web site.

The PDA is organizing to bring progressive activists into the Democratic Party, with the hope that it can be transformed from within. If the AFL-CIO—which is heavily involved in the Democratic Party and backed by millions of members—has failed in this effort, the PDA with its meager forces stands no chance of succeeding. The PDA has a greater chance of derailing the Green Party's efforts to challenge the corporate parties, than moving the Democrats to the left.

Greens for Independence and Democracy seek to reassert the central mission of the Green Party as the political arm of the social movements. GDI has been the driving force in developing proposals to institute democratic reforms and assert the independence of the Green Party from the corporate parties. GDI has presented these proposals publicly on its Web site and at state party meetings, where they have won majority support from state parties in New York, California, Florida, Vermont, and Utah—parties that represent the majority of Greens in the country.

Divisions Intensify in Tulsa

The Tulsa meeting was essentially a contest between the two wings of the party played out through the same undemocratic apportionment scheme that distorted the outcome of the 2004 Milwaukee convention. Under this scheme California and New York have only about 16 percent of the votes on the National Committee (NC), even though more than two-thirds of all registered Greens live in these two states.

Since liberal delegates to the NC overwhelmingly represent the smaller state parties—many with less than one hundred members—they control almost two-thirds of the vote. Delegates from states supporting GDI represent most of the Greens in the country, yet are a minority voting bloc on the NC.

Conflict between the two wings erupted early in the convention over which delegates to seat from Utah, a state where two groups claim to be the official Green Party. The original Utah Greens split into two factions in 2004 over which candidate—Cobb or Nader—to put on their state's ballot line. The leadership body only recognizes the "Cobb Party," while the "Nader Party" is recognized as the official Green Party in Utah by the secretary of state's office.

During roll call, the "Cobb Party" delegates were automatically seated by the leadership body. GDI delegates later protested this decision and proposed seating one Utah delegate from each party. This proposal was voted down by the liberal wing fifty-seven to thirty-four (with four abstentions).

Following this skirmish, Peter Camejo and David Cobb spoke to the body, each describing a different strategy for the future of the party.

Camejo stressed building the Green Party as the political expression of the mass social movements. He supported allowing many political tendencies to exist in the party. He even went so far as to apologize to David Cobb for any misstatements he may have made against him during the campaign. Finally, he called upon the Green Party to stand up to the Democrats and argued its independent challenge to the two-party system is "the spirit of the future."

Cobb repeated many of Camejo's points, but then emphasized an exclusionary message. Condemning what he called sectarianism—his label for anyone who opposed his safe-states strategy, or believed in building a left wing of the party. In an answer to a question after his speech, Cobb denounced *CounterPunch*'s Alexander Cockburn, saying that he "represents why the sectarian left has failed." The not-so-subtle message was that the Green Party should exclude those who oppose supporting liberal Democrats in their election campaigns.

The GDI Proposals

The real conflict in Tulsa broke out when GDI presented their proposals on internal democracy and independence to the NC. Since these proposals had already been passed by several state parties and discussed on the NC's listserv, GDI encouraged all delegates to provide comments, concerns, and amendments.

The liberal wing did not argue against the content of the proposals. Instead they raised objections concerning bylaws, implementation, and procedure.

After a long period of debate—during which the governing Steering Committee (SC) left the room to caucus (without explanation) and anti-GDI forces lead delegates in doing "the Wave" and singing "Oklahoma" and "Take Me Out to the Ball Game"—the NC voted down all three proposals by an average vote of fifty-eight to thirty-four (with three abstentions).

The vote on the GDI proposals completely mirrored the vote to seat both Utah delegations, and drew a clear delineation between the two factions of the party. There is no question that the undemocratic apportionment scheme has allowed a liberal bloc of delegates to gain the upper hand in the national leadership body of the Green Party. As one GDI member put it, "If the liberal wing is able to maintain its dominance of the party and orient the Greens into subordinating themselves to the Democratic Party, the Green Party will likely whither away like the Working Families Party and the New Party before them."

The Future of GDI

The opportunity and responsibility for GDI members is immense. The Democrats continue to ratify the Bush administration's program and thereby keep stoking frustration with the two-party system. The Democrats continue to support the occupation of Iraq, voted for the renewal of the Patriot Act, gave the margin of victory for the passage of CAFTA in the Senate, and stand prepared to confirm the nomination of antiabortion Reaganite John Roberts to the Supreme Court.

Today, millions of workers, women, gays, Latinos, Blacks, Arabs, Muslims, and other oppressed populations find no electoral expression within the two corporate parties for their demands and aspirations. Many have grown frustrated with the failure of the lesser-evil strategy of voting for the Democrats and are looking for an alternative. Unfortunately, the present leadership of the Green Party is set to direct them right back into the arms of the Democratic Party.

In 2004, leaders of all the various social movements suspended their efforts in order to mobilize the vote for Kerry—even though Kerry opposed almost all of their demands. Nine months after the election those social movements are still demobilized. Hopefully, the demonstration against the war scheduled for September 24 will mark the return of mass social movements after a long hiatus for the elections.

The disenfranchised in America form a large latent electoral force, which GDI and supporting state Green parties must connect with to renew the Green Party. Such a coalition offers the hope of galvanizing the Greens and the broader social movements to build a genuine third party rooted in this country's excluded majority and its mass movements that will fight and not join the corporate parties.

The contest between the two visions of the Green Party as expressed by the two wings of the NC is not just a fight for the soul of the Green Party, it is a fight to win the hearts and minds of people to break with lesser-evilism and build a no-holds-barred challenge to corporate politics. It is also a fight for maintaining and growing the social movements during election periods.

While the current undemocratic NC of the Green Party is taking the road back to the Democratic Party, the GDI current is considering how to galvanize individuals and state parties to take the road of democracy and independence.

Notes

Introduction

1. Martin Luther King Jr. speaking on why he came out against the war in Vietnam despite the condemnations he expected from liberals and civil rights leaders, in "To Chart Our Course for the Future" (address at SCLC Ministers Leadership Training Program, Miami, February 23, 1968) in *The Autobiography of Martin Luther King, Jr.,* ed. Clayborne Carson (New York: Warner Books, 1998).
2. Peter Miguel Camejo, "Green Party Unity," June 14, 2004, published on http://www.avocadoeducationproject.org. Reprinted in this collection.
3. An analysis of the National Election Study exit poll data by Harvard political scientist Barry Burden shows that only 9 percent of the people who thought Nader was the best candidate actually voted for him. If people had not voted strategically for the lesser evil, Nader would have had over 30 million votes instead of 2.9 million and might have won the election, especially if he had been allowed into the debates. Burden also shows that Nader would have won the 2000 election using the Condorcet system of preference voting in which voters rank each candidate against every other candidate, the system that most voting-system experts consider the fairest and most accurate way to reflect voters' preferences. 2000 was the only presidential election for which there is exit polling data to conduct a Condorcet election retrospectively in which the Condorcet winner was not the actual winner. See Barry C. Burden, "Minor Parties and Strategic Voting in Recent U.S. Presidential Elections," *Electoral Studies*, in press, available online at http://www.people.fas.harvard.edu/~burden/esfinal.pdf.
4. Mitofsky International, "California Recall Election Exit Poll—October 7, 2003," available at http://www.mitofskyinternational.com/california/CAGV0230H.HTM.
5. J. R. Ross, "Greens Reject Endorsement of Ralph Nader," Associated Press, June 26, 2004; Rick Lyman, "Greens Pick a Candidate Not Named Nader," *New York Times*, June 27, 2004; "Greens Reject

Nader Endorsment, Back Cobb," *MSNBC.com*, June 27, 2004; Rupert Cornwall, "Greens Reject Nader Bid for White House," *The Independent* (UK), June 29, 2004.

6. P. J. Huffstutter, "Green Party's Choice Could Be Kerry Boost," *Los Angeles Times*, June 28, 2004.

7. Available online at http://www.pollingreport.com/wh04gen.htm. Another reason for the decline in Nader's support in opinion polls was that polling organizations did not include Nader as an option in polls in states where he was denied a ballot line, which came to fifteen states in total after Labor Day.

8. The representation formula read:

"States will be allocated delegates slots based on the following formula:

1) Number of Electoral College members multiplied by 0.5

2) Number of Coordinating Committee members multiplied by 1.75

3) Number of Elected Greens that are listed by and accepted by the Coordinated Campaign Committee* on or before 12/31/03 multiplied by 1.00

*Electeds who received 500 or more votes will be given a value of 1, Electeds who received less than 500 votes or no vote totals known by the CCC will receive a value of 0.2.

4) Election Strength* derived from the 2000 Presidential Election multiplied by 1.75. States wishing to use a statewide race may do so as long as the Green candidate had Democratic and Republican opposition.

*number of votes for Nader multiplied by percentage of Nader's vote in the state divided by 100,000.

Add the four factors together and round up. This number will equal the number of delegates."

(Gray Newman, "[usgp-coo] corrected additional language to AC proposal," Coordinating Committee e-mail list, November 11, 2003)

This formula was never actually voted on by the Coordinating Committee (now called the National Committee), but only posted to the National Committee e-mail list during the week of voting on the accreditation rules proposal, which had listed the number of delegates for each state without describing the method by which the numbers were determined. (See Proposal 55: Accreditation of Delegates to the 2004 Nominating Convention at http://green.gpus.org/cgi-bin/vote/propdetail?pid=55.)

Expressed mathematically, the total delegates for a state were (.5 x electoral college vote) + (1.75 x Coordinating Committee delegates) + (1 x Elected Greens) + (1.75 x Statewide Green vote, Nader 2000 or other).

At the abstract level, the formula weighted the factors as follows:

10% to the electoral college vote

35% to National Committee delegates

20% to Elected Greens

35% to Statewide Green vote (Nader 2000 or other)

Because most states did not have elected Greens and some states did not have Nader 2000 or other statewide votes to win bonus delegates, in practice the formula gave much higher weighting to the electoral college vote. If we look at the total number of delegates from all states at the Milwaukee Convention owing to each factor to get the percentage that came from each factor, the result is:

33.9% come from electoral college vote factor
25.6% come from National Committee delegates factor
14.3% come from Elected Greens factor
22.5% come from Statewide Green vote factor

Thanks to New York State's 2004 delegate coordinator, Roger Snyder, for deciphering how the formula worked in theory and practice.

9. The primary, caucus, and convention results are posted on the Green Party Web site at http://www.gp.org. Candidates Sheila Bilyeau, Peter Miguel Camejo, Paul Glover, Carol Miller, and Lorna Salzman supported the endorsement of Nader. The Green presidential primary votes were as follows:

	CA	DC	MA	NM	R I	Total
Sheila Bilyeau		71				71
Peter Camejo	33,753					33,753
David Cobb	5,086	142		156	71	5,455
Paul Glover			78	55		133
Kent Mesplay	913		60	16	16	1,005
Carol Miller				345		345
Lorna Salzman	4,759		217		56	5,032
No Candidate		50			29	79
No Preference			236			236
Write-Ins		123	208		15	346
Blank			73			73
Total	44,589	386	1,069	628	131	46,803

10. David Cobb, "Green Party 2004 Presidential Strategy," distributed at the Green Party National Committee meeting in Washington, D.C., July 17–20, 2003. Emphasis in original. Reprinted in this collection.

11. John Rensenbrink and Tom Sevigny, "The Green Party and the 2004 Elections: A Three-Dimensional Strategy," May 1, 2003. Reprinted in this collection.

12. Ted Glick, "A Green Party 'Safe-States' Strategy," July 1, 2003. Reprinted in this collection.

13. Michael Tomasky, "Gang Green," *American Prospect Online*, July 23, 2003, http://www.prospect.org/web/page.ww?section=root&name=ViewWeb&arti cleId=1256.

14. Michael Albert, "Election Plan?" *ZNet*, August 12, 2003, http://www.zmag.org/content/showarticle.cfm?ItemID=4037; Tom Hayden, "The Democrats in Iowa: Field of Dreams?" *AlterNet*, August 12, 2003, http://www.AlterNet.org/story.html?StoryID=16584.

15. Peter Miguel Camejo et al., "Open Letter to Ralph Nader (Green Gubernatorial Candidates' Statement)," December 1, 2002. Reprinted in this collection.

16. Jeff Proctor, "Kucinich Visits UNM Campus," *Daily Lobo*, October 15,

2003, http://www.dailylobo.com/news/2003/10/15/News/Kucinich.Visits.Unm. Campus-528668.shtml. Kucinich stated in his campaign video that he will bring Greens into the Democratic Party. Greens in California and New York as well as New Mexico reported phone banking from the Kucinich campaign trying to get Greens to re-register as Democrats to support Kucinich in the primaries. See the discussion of Kucinich's Green reregistration efforts in Peter Miguel Camejo, "The Crisis in the Green Party: The Magic Number 39 and My Meetings with Cobb, Kucinich, and the Steering Committee," *CounterPunch*, April 6, 2005, http://www.counterpunch.org/camejo 04062005.html.

17. Micah Sifry, "Ralph Redux?" *The Nation*, November 24, 2003, http://www. thenation.com/doc.mhtml?i=20031124&c=1&s=sifry. Sifry's article was posted on *The Nation*'s Web site on November 6. *Mother Jones*' online "Daily Mojo" gave this story more play by using Sifry's quotes from anti-Nader Greens in "Never Say Nader," November 11, 2003, http://www. mother jones.com/news/dailymojo/2003/11/we_603_02a.html.

18. "Statement on Green Strategy 2004 and Call for Dialogue and Action," posted on the Portside listserv, November 17, 2003. Reprinted in this collection.

19. For a balanced account of the arguments and actions of both sides of this split up through 1996, see Greta Gaard, *Ecological Politics: Ecofeminists and the Greens* (Philadelphia: Temple University Press, 1998).

20. Nancy Allen cited by Steve Herrick, "Re: ASGP-COO here's something you may not have seen...," August 31, 2000, on the ASGP CC e-mail list.

21. John Rensenbrink, *Against All Odds: The Green Transformation of American Politics* (Raymond, Maine: Leopold Press, 1999), 205.

22. American Greens have also lost their programmatic focus on the changes in political institutions needed to make society a grassroots democracy. In the 1980s and early 1990s, many Greens focused on using local elections and municipal charter reforms to create grassroots-democratic structures of governance based on citizen assemblies and their wider coordination through councils of assembly-mandated delegates as a fundamental alternative to the centralized and hierarchic structures of the nation-state. See "Libertarian Municipalism," in Murray Bookchin wrote extensively on this approach. See Janet Biehl, ed., *The Murray Bookchin Reader*, ed. Janet Biehl (London: Cassell, 1997), and Biehl with Murray Bookchin, *The Politics of Social Ecology: Libertarian Municipalism* (Montreal: Black Rose Books, 1997).

23. Charlene Spretnak and Fritjof Capra, *Green Politics: The Global Promise* (New York: E. P. Dutton, 1984), 203.

24. Charlene Spretnak, "A Green Party—It *Can* Happen Here," *The Nation*, April 21, 1984, 472–478.

25. Rensenbrink, *Against All Odds*, 129.

26. Nader spoke on independent politics to a January 11, 2004, forum in New Hampshire, sponsored by the Committee for a Unified Independent Party, a Newmanite front. The next day Doug Ireland blasted Nader on *The*

Nation's Web site ("Nader and the Newmanites," January 12) for getting "in bed with the ultrasectarian cult-racket formerly known as the New Alliance Party." Democrats Wesley Clark, Howard Dean, John Edwards, Dennis Kucinich, and Al Sharpton also participated by sending representatives or answering questionnaires to the New Hampshire forum, but they escaped the ire of Ireland, who condemned Nader's run under any circumstances. Cobb and his supporters made much of Nader's attendance at this forum. In March, Ted Glick's "2004 and the Left" highlighted this as one of Nader's "questionable alliances." In late April, Cobb reportedly said in a public forum that Nader was "taking contributions from people Cobb called 'thinly veiled racists.'" (Doug Matson, "Green Party Hopeful Speaks His Mind," *Santa Fe New Mexican*, April 26, 2004.) In the ensuing controversy in the Greens that Cobb's remark engendered, Dean Myerson, now a Cobb campaign spokesperson, made it clear to Carol Miller of New Mexico, who had complained about this negative campaigning by Cobb, that Cobb was referring to the New Alliance connection: "New Alliance people were working on or coordinating petitioning efforts [for Nader], who also have supported Buchanan. It is the connection to Buchanan that led to David's characterization." (Carol Miller quoting Dean Myerson, "Spin is not an answer," May 19, 2004.) The "New Alliance people" are concentrated in New York City. As one of Nader's two field coordinators in New York State, I know that they did offer to coordinate the New York petition drive, but were rejected by the Nader campaign. Their members collected about fifteen hundred of the twenty-eight thousand petition signatures for the Nader/Camejo ballot line that were submitted in New York State.

27. Greg Palast, "The Screwing of Cynthia McKinney," *AlterNet*, June 18, 2003, http://www.gregpalast.com/detail.cfm?artid=229&row=1; Mark Donham, "Cynthia McKinney vs. Condi Rice: Why Do the Democrats Want to Deny Her Seniority?" *CounterPunch*, December 9, 2004, http://www.counterpunch.org/donham12092004.html; Cynthia McKinney's letter of April 2005, reprinted on the ActionGreens listserv, April 22, 2005, in message 32438, "Same Ol' Dirty Tricks—Representative Cynthia McKinney (D-GA)," http://groups.yahoo.com/group/ActionGreens/.

28. It should be noted that the liberal and radical tendencies in the Greens and the positions they took on the 2004 campaign are general trends. Some individuals associated with each tendency joined with the other tendency on the 2004 campaign strategy debate. For example, Mike Feinstein, Annie Goeke, Carol Miller, and Lorna Salzman had been prominent in the ASGP but supported Nader in 2004. On the other side, Joel Kovel had been active in left Green tendencies but supported Cobb in 2004 (Joel Kovel, "Green Follies," *CommonDreams.org*, June 23, 2005, http://www.commondreams.org/views04/0623-01.htm).

29. Jan Jarboe Russell, "Growing the Party is Green Presidential Hopeful's Top Priority," *San Antonio News-Express*, December 7, 2003, http://www.mysanantonio.com/opinion/columnists/jrussell/stories/1094333.html.

30. The quote is from the Supreme Court's unsigned majority opinion in *Bush v. Gore*, 531 U.S. at 104. On the Republicans' vote suppression and the Democrats' capitulation, see Jeffrey Toobin, *Too Close to Call* (New York: Random House, 2001), Greg Palast, *The Best Democracy Money Can Buy* (New York: Penguin, 2003), and Alison Mitchell, "Black Lawmakers Protest as Congress Certifies Bush Victory; Gore Gavels Down Lingering Bitterness Over Bush Victory," *New York Times*, January 7, 2001.

31. A media consortium, including the *New York Times*, the *Washington Post*, the Tribune Co. (*Los Angeles Times, Chicago Tribune, Newsday*, and others), the *Palm Beach Post*, the *St. Petersburg Times*, the *Wall Street Journal*, Associated Press, and CNN, spent nearly a year and $900,000 having the respected National Opinion Research Council (NORC) at the University of Chicago reexamine every disputed ballot in the 2000 Florida presidential election. NORC found that Gore won the popular vote in Florida when all disputed ballots were examined. See Dan Keating and Dan Balz, "Florida Recounts Would Have Favored Bush, But Study Finds Gore Might Have Won Statewide Tally of All Uncounted Ballots," *Washington Post*, November 12, 2001; Jim Naureckas, "Not That It Was Reported, But Gore Won," *Newsday*, November 15, 2001, http://www.commondreams.org/views01/1115-02.htm; and Toobin, *Too Close to Call*, 278–281.

32. Much of the commentary blaming Nader, such as the Epilogue to Michael Moore's *Stupid White Men* (New York: Regan Books, 2001), claims that Nader concentrated his efforts in the swing states in 2000 as if he were trying to help Bush beat Gore. In fact, an analysis of candidate appearances and campaign advertising shows that Nader spent far more campaign resources in the safe states than in the swing states in 2000 and proportionately far fewer resources in the swing states than Bush and Gore. See Barry C. Burden, "Ralph Nader's Campaign Strategy in the 2000 U.S. Presidential Election," *American Politics Research*, forthcoming, available at http://www.people.fas.harvard.edu/~burden/ apr1.pdf.

33. Jeff Horwitz, "Nader vs. the Green Party?" *Salon.com*, June 24, 2004, http://www.salon.com/news/feature/2004/06/24/cobb_campaign/index_np.html; Ted Glick, "The Green Party in 2004: More Than Party Survival," *ZNet*, February 7, 2005, http://www.zmag.org/content/showarticle.cfm?SectionID=90&ItemID=7186.

34. Jack Uhrich, "Re: [usgp-dx] I've Had Enough of Nader's Attacks on the GPUS," February 25, 2004, message on the Green Party discussion list.

35. Annie Goeke interview, June 1, 2005.

36. Ralph Nader, *Crashing the Party: How to Tell the Truth and Still Run for President* (New York: St. Martin's Press, 2001).

37. Cobb and his supporters would claim that Nader refused to share the volunteer and donor lists from the 2000 campaign. As a field coordinator for upstate New York for the 2000 Nader campaign, I know there was no problem using the volunteer lists for party organizing. Having talked with people on both sides of the controversy about the donor-list sharing, I

believe some staff miscommunications on both sides made coordination more difficult than it needed to be. But in the end, Nader's campaign did share those lists with the national Green Party and a fund-raising letter from the Greens to those lists went out.

38. The Cardwell and Sprague commentaries on the Bastrop convention of the Green Party of Texas, along with the text of the bylaw amendment, can be found on the ActionGreens listserv archive at http://groups.yahoo.com/group/ActionGreens/. Cardwell's statement is in message 30720, February 10, 2005, and Sprague's statement and the bylaw amendment are in message 30734, February 11, 2005, in the thread "Anti-Democratic actions of Cobb in Texas."

39. Jack Uhrich, GP-US National Committee discussion e-list, March 14, 2004.

40. Nader's December 22, 2003, letter is reprinted in this collection, as are his March 24, 2004, and June 25, 2004, letters to the Greens requesting their endorsement for his independent campaign.

41. Greg Gerritt, *Green Party Tempest: Weathering the Storm of 2004* (Providence, RI: Moshassuck River Press, 2005), 7, 11, 13, 17–18, 28.

42. Available online at http://greens4democracy.net.

43. Medea Benjamin et al., "An Open Letter to Progressives: Vote Kerry and Cobb," July 23, 2004. Reprinted in this collection.

44. Cobb press release cited in Glick, "The Green Party in 2004."

45. David Cobb, interview by Michael Albert, "Why Run?" *Z Magazine*, September 2004, http://zmagsite.zmag.org/Images/albert20904. html; CounterPunch Wire, "The Quotations of David Cobb: He Doesn't Care How Many Votes He Gets," *CounterPunch*, September 13, 2004, http://www.counterpunch.org/cobb09132004.html.

46. Joshua L. Weinstein, "LaMarche says she'll vote for whoever can beat Bush," *Portland Press Herald*, June 30, 2004; Susan M. Cover, "LaMarche Launches Campaign," *Kennebec Journal/Central Maine Morning Sentinel*, June 30, 2004.

47. Hannah Plotkin, "Green Party VP Wants Bush Out—At Any Cost," *The Dartmouth*, October 25, 2004. For similar LaMarche statements during and after the campaign, see "Pat LaMarche Stumps in Nebraska," Associated Press, August 3, 2004; Martha Stoddard, "Green V.P. Candidate Says: Vote Your Heart," *Omaha World-Herald*, August 3, 2004; Christopher Arnott, "Not Easy Being Green," *New Haven Advocate*, August 5, 2004; Michael Reagan, "Green Party's LaMarche Runs a Strategic Campaign," *Brunswick ME Times Record*, September 20, 2004; Clarke Canfield, "Pat LaMarche Urges Residents to 'Vote Their Conscience,'" Associated Press, October 7, 2004; Pat LaMarche, "Greetings from Green Vice Presidential Candidate Pat LaMarche to the Greens," October 30, 2004; Michael Reagan, "Green Party Aims to Grow," *Brunswick Times Record*, November 12, 2004.

48. David Cobb, "Resurgence: The Green Party's Remarkable Transformation," *Green Horizon Quarterly* 6, (Winter 2005). Reprinted in this collection. For similar claims from Cobb's campaign leadership, see

Blair Bobier and John Rensenbrink, "Groundbreaking Presidential Campaign Goes Overtime," *Green Pages* 8 (Winter 2004), http://www.gp. org/greenpages/content/volume8/issue4/oped2.php and Ted Glick, "The Green Party in 2004," reprinted in this collection.

49. Mike Feinstein, "Green Party Election History–By Year," http://www. feinstein.org/greenparty/electionhistory.html.

50. Mike Feinstein, "Draft Green Party Voter Registration Update: Trends in U.S. Green registration, a month-by-month comparison, April 2000– present," May 9, 2005, http://web.greens.org/stats.

51. *Ballot Access News*, February 2004 and December 2004.

52. Alexander Cockburn, "Don't Say We Didn't Warn You—Lessons They Won't Learn from November 2: A Word from Nader; A Last Look at Kerry and Michael Moore," *CounterPunch Weekend Edition*, November 6–7, 2004, http://www.counterpunch.org/cockburn11062004.html.

53. David Cobb, "Resurgence: The Green Party's Remarkable Transformation," reprinted in this collection. The other post-election analyses from the Cobb leadership that make no comments on its impact on the campaign issues and debate are Bobier and Rensenbrink, "Groundbreaking Presidential Campaign Goes Overtime"; Glick, "The Green Party in 2004"; and Gerritt, *Green Party Tempest*.

54. Tom Hayden, "When Bonesmen Fight," May 8, 2004, *thepolitic.org*, posted on ZNet, May 22, 2004, http://www.zmag.org/content/ showarticle.cfm?SectionID=37&ItemID=5577.

55. The few organizations and institutions on the left that did not surrender to Anybody But Bush should be noted. Among political organizations, two independent socialist groups, the International Socialist Organization and Solidarity, put significant energy into the Nader/Camejo campaign. Among media institutions and pundits, Alexander Cockburn and Jeffrey St. Clair of *CounterPunch*; the radical youth e-journal, *Left Hook* (www.lefthook.org); and Greg Bates (*Ralph's Revolt: The Case for Joining Nader's Rebellion*, 2004) and Joshua Frank (*Left Out!: How Liberals Helped Reelect George W. Bush*, 2005) of Common Courage Press stood almost alone among the left intelligentsia against the lesser-evil politics of the Anybody-But-Bush tide.

56. For a discussion of some of the contemporary ties between big corporate foundations and progressive media and NGOs, see Charles Shaw, "Regulated Resistance: Pt. 2—The Gatekeepers of the So-Called Left," *Newtopia Magazine*, May 3, 2005, http://www.newtopiamagazine. net/modules.php?op=modload&name=News&file=article&sid=40. For a case study of how liberal corporate funding worked to co-opt and pacify the Black power movement of the 1960s, see Robert L. Allen, *Black Awakening in Capitalist America* (New York: Anchor Books, 1969; Reprint: New Jersey: Africa World Press, 1990).

57. The visibility of a few antiwar Democrats like Dennis Kucinich, Barbara Lee, and Cynthia McKinney can obscure how overwhelmingly the Democrats have supported Bush's war and repression agenda. Key votes in Congress include:

War Powers, September 14, 2001: Only one (Barbara Lee) of 212 House Democrats and none of the fifty Senate Democrats voted against the resolution authorizing President Bush to use military force against anyone associated with September 11 attacks without a Declaration of War by Congress. This resolution was the legal basis for the invasion and occupation of Afghanistan.

Patriot Act, October 24–25, 2001: Only one (Russell Feingold) of fifty Senate Democrats and fifty-three of 212 House Democrats voted against.

Iraq War Resolution, October 10, 2002: Only twenty-one of fifty Senate Democrats and 126 of 212 House Democrats voted against. These relatively high votes against the Iraq war resolution were the result of intensive lobbying by the peace movement. A month before the vote, only a few Senate Democrats and about twenty-five House Democrats were committed to opposing the Iraq war. Once the invasion was launched, even this core opposition shrank, as the following votes show.

"Unequivocal Support" for Iraq War, March 22, 2003: As the invasion of Iraq began, none of the forty-eight Senate Democrats and only eleven of 204 House Democrats voted against this resolution expressing "unequivocal support ... for [President Bush's] firm leadership and decisive action in the conduct of military operations in Iraq as part of the on-going Global War on Terrorism."

1ˢᵗ Supplemental Appropriation for Iraq and Afghanistan Wars, $79 billion, April 3, 2003: None of the forty-eight Senate Democrats and only nine of 204 House Democrats voted against.

2ⁿᵈ Supplemental Appropriation for Iraq and Afghanistan Wars, $87 billion, October 17, 2003: Only eleven of forty-eight Senate Democrats and 119 of 204 House Democrats voted against.

3ʳᵈ Supplemental Appropriation for Iraq and Afghanistan Wars, $25 billion, June 22–24, 2004: None of the forty-eight Senate Democrats and only fifteen of 204 House Democrats voted against including this supplemental funding in the Defense Department appropriation.

4ᵗʰ Supplemental Appropriation for Iraq and Afghanistan Wars, $82 billion, May 6, 2005: None of the forty Senate Democrats voted against the Senate or conference committee versions. Only 34 of 202 House Democrats voted against the House version of the bill on March 15. On May 5, only fifty-four House Democrats voted against the final version reported out of the House-Senate conference committee, with the increase in no votes due to objection to anti-immigrant provisions added in conference, not to funding the Iraq and Afghanistan occupations.

58. See, for example, Benjamin et al., "An Open Letter to Progressives." In September, another statement by prominent Nader 2000 supporters called for a Kerry vote in swing states without even calling for a Nader or Cobb vote in safe states. It referred readers to the same www.swing04.com Web site used by the July 23 statement to identify swing states. See "Nader 2000 Leaders Organize to Defeat Bush," September 14, 2004, http://www.vote2stopbush.com.

59. The comparison between Nader's 2000 and 2004 vote totals must also take into account the fact that the Nader/Camejo ticket was denied ballot access in many populous states where Nader was on the ballot in 2000, including Arizona, California, Illinois, Massachusetts, Ohio, Oregon, Pennsylvania, and Texas. The totals cited are the Federal Election Commission's official totals. We will never know how many more write-in votes Nader/Camejo received. Hawaii, Oklahoma, and Oregon do not even count write-ins as a matter of election law. Many other states do a poor job of counting them.

60. E. J. Kessler, "Billionaire Liberals Seek To Fund Idea Mills," *Forward*, January 21, 2005, http://www.forward.com/main/article.php?id=2575.

61. David Rosenbaum, "Kerry Team Settles Dispute with Kucinich Delegates Over Iraq," *New York Times*, July 11, 2004; "Did Kucinich Sell Out Anti-War Democrats?" *Democracy Now!* July 14, 2004, http://www.democracynow.org/article.pl?sid=04/07/14/1410234; Charley Underwood, "A Kucinich Delegate in Boston and the Totalitarian Democratic Party," August 1, 2004, http://bellaciao.org/en/ article. php3?id_article=2305.

62. Seymour Hersh, *The Price of Power: Kissinger in the Nixon White House* (New York: Summit Books, 1983), 128–133; Michio Kaku and Daniel Axelrod, *To Win a Nuclear War: The Pentagon's Secret War Plans* (London: Zed Books, 1987), 164–168.

63. Carl Davidson and Marilyn Katz, "Moving from Protest to Politics: Dumping Bush's Regime in 2004," April 28, 2003, http://www. cc-ds.org/Peace%20 and%20Justice/moving_from_protest_to_politics.htm.

The phrase "From Protest to Politics" in the title of the Davidson/Katz paper seems to reflect a conscious retreat from the radicalism of 1968 that developed in response to the liberalism of 1964. As a national officer of Students for a Democratic Society (SDS) between 1966 and 1968, it could not have been lost on Davidson that this phrase resurrected the liberal slogan that civil rights leader Bayard Rustin coined after the Johnson landslide of 1964. Rustin was the principal organizer of the 1963 March on Washington and a harsh liberal critic of Black, student, and antiwar radicals. In calling for a continuation of the moratorium on demonstrations called by the civil rights leadership in the summer of 1964 in deference to Johnson's campaign, Rustin argued that the liberal/labor/Black electoral coalition behind Johnson demonstrated an electoral realignment that was creating a permanent Democratic majority for progressive reform. (Bayard Rustin, "From Protest to Politics: The Future of the Civil Rights Movement," *Commentary*, February 1965). Radicals reached the opposite conclusion, arguing that demonstrations and, indeed, disruptive resistance were needed to pressure the power structure for reforms. They pointed to the fact that Johnson delayed action on the Voting Rights Act until after the 1964 election, and then moved on it only after the widely televised Alabama state trooper brutality against civil rights marchers in Selma in March 1965 created a national public climate that forced his hand. The other major pending civil rights legislation, the Fair Housing Act, languished until the aftermath of the King assassination in 1968.

Among those radicals was Carl Davidson, whose proposal adopted by SDS to support draft resistance at the very end of 1966 gave SDS its counter-slogan to Rustin's in 1967, "From Protest to Resistance." The National Mobilization Committee adopted that slogan for the famous October 21, 1967, antiwar demonstration at the Pentagon later that year. The McCarthy liberals, in turn, threw Rustin's slogan back at the mobilization for the Pentagon demonstration to convince antiwar youth to support their candidate as a more "realistic" strategy. McCarthy played the role in 1968 that Kucinich did in 2004 in seeking to head off a third-party insurgency. In announcing his candidacy on November 20, 1967, McCarthy said he wanted "to provide an alternative for those who become cynical and make threats of support for third parties or fourth parties or other irregular political movements." McCarthy was trying to head off the movement for an independent Peace and Freedom ticket. A ticket headed by Martin Luther King Jr. and Dr. Benjamin Spock had been promoted in the lead-up to the National Conference for a New Politics in September 1967. That conference failed to support an independent ticket in 1968, but the independent Peace and Freedom movement continued in California and other states and ran independent antiwar slates in several states under various names. See Kirkpatrick Sale, *SDS* (New York: Vintage, 1974), 313–316; Dave Dellinger, *More Power Than We Know: The People's Movement Towards Democracy* (New York: Anchor, 1975), 89–91; Michael Friedman, ed., *The New Left of the Sixties* (Berkeley: Independent Socialist Press 1972), 35–93.

64. Pushing Roosevelt toward his Second New Deal in 1935 was left to economically progressive but socially reactionary demagogues such as Huey Long, Father Coughlin, Gerald L. K. Smith, and Dr. Frances Townsend, who coalesced in the 1936 Union Party presidential campaign of Representative William Lemke that received 2 percent of the vote. "In 1935, ... when a poll by the Democratic National Committee revealed that Huey Long was likely to receive three to four million votes if Long ran for president as an independent in 1936, FDR launched what became known as 'the second hundred days,' during which time the Social Security Act, the Wagner Act, and the 'soak the rich' Wealth Tax Act were passed." Douglas O'Hara, "The Merchants of Fear: Smearing Nader," *CounterPunch*, February 24, 2004, http://www.counterpunch.org/ ohara 02242004.html.

65. Kevin Spidel, inteview by William Rivers Pitt, "Ordinary Heroes and the Rising Power of the Roots," *Truthout*, January 27, 2005, http://www. truthout.org/docs_05/012805U.shtml.

66. Media Benjamin, "A Special Message from Media Benjamin," posted on the Progressive Democrats of America Web site, March 14, 2005, http:// www.pdamerica.org/ postcards/medea-letter_3-14-05.php.

67. Mitofsky International, "California Recall Election Exit Poll—October 7, 2003," http://www. mitofskyinternational.com/california/ CAGV0230

H.HTM.
68. Katherine Q. Seelye, "Nader Emerging as Threat Democrats Feared," *New York Times*, October 16, 2004:

> Though he hurts Kerry more than Bush, there's a potential that he hurts Bush, too," said Anna Greenberg, a Democratic pollster who has examined Nader voters, although she said that potential Nader voters were difficult to find and hard to track. She said the profile of likely Nader supporters was changing and beginning to resemble that of voters who supported Ross Perot, the third-party candidate in 1996, rather than those who supported Nader in 2000. His backers then tended to be split equally between men and women and were white, liberal and college-educated, according to pollsters. But Greenberg said voters who support him now tend to be white men, blue-collar, fiscally conservative, populist, against open trade, angry about the high cost of health care and prescription drugs and fiercely opposed to the war in Iraq.

69. A June 2004 Gallup poll found that "With Nader thrown in, Kerry's percentage among Black voters declined from 81 percent to 73 percent. Nader drew 10 percent of Black voters, dropping Bush to only 9 percent. Among Latino voters in a three-way race, Kerry's support fell from 57 percent to 52 percent, while Bush's fell from 38 percent to 35 percent. Nader was the choice of 8 percent of Latino voters." "Poll: Kerry Leads Among Minority Voters," *CNN.com* July 7, 2004, http://edition.cnn.com/ 2004/ALLPOLITICS/07/06/gallup.poll/. After Nader did not receive the Green Party's support at the end of June, his numbers among all groups fell considerably. But election day exit polls showed that the proportion of Nader's voters that were non-white was 48 percent (5 percent Black, 36 percent Latino, and 7 percent other non-white), far higher than for Kerry (34 percent) and Bush (12 percent). Exit polls also showed more union households in Nader's base (33 percent) compared to Kerry's (30 percent) and Bush's (18 percent). Considering all the liberal hand-wringing over what the "moral issues" vote meant in 2004, it is worth noting that more voters who identified moral issues as why they voted for their candidate were in Nader's voter base (57 percent) than Kerry's (8 percent) or Bush's (35 percent). See the exit poll conducted by Edison/Mitofsky for the National Election Pool (ABC, AP, CBS, CNN, FOX, NBC), http://election. cbsnews. com/election2004/poll/poll_p____u_s__all_us0.shtml.

70. Todd Chretien, "The Dem Plot Against Nader: Florida Comes to California," *CounterPunch*, August 5, 2004, http://www. counter punch.org/chretien08052004.html.

71. Noam Chomsky, "The Non Election of 2004," *Z Magazine*, January 2005, http://zmagsite.zmag.org/Jan2005/chomsky0105.html. On the moral values question, Chomsky reports:

> In some polls, "when the voters were asked to choose the most urgent moral crisis facing the country, 33 percent cited 'greed and materialism,' 31 percent selected 'poverty and economic justice,' 16 percent named abortion, and 12 percent selected gay marriage" (Pax Christi). In others,

"when surveyed voters were asked to list the moral issue that most affected their vote, the Iraq war placed first at 42 percent, while 13 percent named abortion and 9 percent named gay marriage" (Zogby). Whatever voters meant, it could hardly have been the operative moral values of the Administration, celebrated by the business press.

Introduction Part II

1. Ronnie Dugger, "Ralph, Don't Run," *The Nation*, December 2, 2002, http://www.thenation.com/doc.mhtml?I=20021202&s=dugger.
2. Eric Alterman, "Bush's Useful Idiot," *The Nation*, September 16, 2004, http://www.thenation.com/doc.mhtml?i=20041004&s=alterman.

Chapter 1

A Green Party "Safe-States" Strategy

1. This does not mean all individual Democrats are "bad guys." There are a not-insignificant number of people like Kucinich and Sharpton, progressives with solid histories of often-courageous activism. Over time it is essential that the third-party movement help to bring these people out of the Democrat Party and into a genuinely progressive independent political formation.
2. "Focusing" on the safe states should not be understood to mean that the Green Party would only put their candidates on the ballot in those states. In the "unsafe" states where there is significant Green organization—which is most of them—it is to be expected that state organizations will nominate or petition to put presidential/vice-presidential candidates on the ballot. I support this.
3. I've researched presidential voting results for 2000, 1996, and 1992. This research yielded twenty-three states with over 103 million people in them with voting results from those three years which make it extremely likely the winner will be from the same party as was the case in all three of those presidential election years. There are another five states with over 35 million people in them which are very likely to go the same way as in 2000. There's a good chance, based upon what happened in 2000, that, in the last month or two of the campaign, the key time period, there will be another 5–10 states that will fall into this category of a near-sure thing for Bush or the Democrat. To see the basis for these projections and the specific twenty-eight states, write to me.

Chapter 3

How the Greens Chose Kerry Over Nader

1. Garance Franke-Ruta, "No Tie—Cobb! The True Story of How a Man You've Barely Heard of Beat Ralph Nader for the Green Party Nomination." *American Prospect*, Web exclusive: June 28, 2004.
2. John Rensenbrink and Patrick Mazza, "Report on the ASGP Middleburg Meeting 1996," http://www.mainegreens.org/directaction/voices/jrensen/middle.htmz.
3. From *The Nation*, November 3, 2003. Ralph Nader's Skeleton Closet, http://www.realchange.org/nader.htm.
4. "NoKerryNoBush, Dems Promote Fake Greens for Kerry Org," SF Indymedia, Friday April 09, 2004, http://sf.indymedia.org/news/2004/04/1689628.php
5. "Why John Kerry?" Greens for Impact, http://www.greensforimpact.com/doc/wjk.cfm
6. Walt Contreras Sheasby, "George Soros and the Rise of the Neo-centrics," *Citizine*, http://www.citizinemag.com/politics/politics-401_soros_neocentrics.htm.
7. Sheasby, "Democrats Launch Anti-Nader Campaign," *Citizine*, May 28, 2004, http://www.citizinemag.com/commentary/commentary-0405_walt sheasby.htm
8. Belinda Coppernoll, "Truth at the GP Nominating Conv. in Milwaukee," COMMENTS@truthout.org, June 28, 2004.
9. Rick Lyman, "The Greens Gather, Sharply Split Over Nader's Run," *NY Times*, June 26, 2004, www.nytimes.com/2004/06/26/politics/campaign/26greens.html.
10. 2004 Delegate Allocation Details, http://gp.org/convention/delegate_1.html.
11. Carlos Petroni, "Green Party Delegates at a Crossroads. Battle between the Left and Demogreens in Milwaukee," *SF-Frontlines*, Saturday, July 3, 2004, http://www.sf-frontlines.com/modules.php?op=modload&name=News&file=article&sid=745&mode=thread&order=0&thold=0.
12. Kevin McKeown, "Milwaukee report," Greens CA listserv: grns-cal-forum@greens.org, June 28, 2004.

Appendix

Reexamining the Green Party Nominating Convention: A Statistical Analysis

1. Outliers are measurements that are extremely large or small compared with the rest of the sample data and are suspected of misrepresenting the population from which they were collected. Using the Grubb's outlier test, the probability that the number of registered Greens in California fits with

the distribution of the remainder of the data is less than 5 percent.

2. The geometric mean is a measure of the central tendency of a data set (like the average) that minimizes the effects of extreme values (like Iowa in this case).

3. Green Party roll call vote at the National Convention, http://www.thegreenpapers.com/T04/Gr-Nom.phtml.

4. National Convention Voting Procedures, http://green.gpus.org/vote/displayproposal.php?proposalId=82.

Contributors

Peter Camejo is a financier, businessman, political activist, environmentalist, author, and one of the founders of the socially responsible investment movement. Camejo has fought for social and environmental justice since his teens. He marched in Selma, Alabama, with Dr. Martin Luther King Jr., rallied for migrant farm workers, and was active against the war in Vietnam. His most recent run for office was as Ralph Nader's running mate in the 2004 election. Camejo ran as the Green Party candidate in the 2003 gubernatorial recall election in California and in the 2002 governor's race.

Todd Chretien was the California student coordinator for the Nader/LaDuke 2000 and the Medea Benjamin for Senate 2000 campaigns, and the Nader/Camejo 2004 northern California field coordinator. He is a member of the Green Party in Oakland, California, and a frequent contributor to the *International Socialist Review* (www.isreview.org).

David Cobb was the Green Party nominee for president in 2004. He served as the general counsel for the Green Party of the United States, and was the Green Party of Texas candidate for attorney general in 2002. In 2000, he managed Ralph Nader's presidential campaign in Texas.

Walt Contreras Sheasby was an ardent advocate, organizer, and social theorist. He ran four times for public office and served as editor for *Capitalism Nature Socialism*. He was a veteran of the civil rights movement and antiwar movement of the 1960s. He was an active member of the Green Party in California until his life was tragically cut short by West Nile virus in August 2004.

Mark Dunlea is former chair of the Green Party of New York State and is the author of *Madame President: The Unauthorized Biography of the First Green Party President* (Big Toad Books, 2004), which imagines what would have happened if a Green had been president on September 11, 2001.

Joshua Frank is a writer living in New York. He has appeared as a political commentator on MSNBC. His investigative reports and columns have appeared in many publications, among them: *CounterPunch*, *Z Magazine*, *Common Dreams*, *Clamor*, *Green Left Weekly*, and *Left Turn* magazine. He is the author of the newly released, *Left Out! How Liberals Helped Reelect George W. Bush* (Common Courage Press, 2005).

Ted Glick is the national coordinator of the Independent Progressive Politics Network (www.ippn.org), and is the author of a twice-monthly "Future Hope" column distributed nationally. He was an active member of the David Cobb Green Party presidential campaign leadership team throughout 2004.

Matt Gonzalez is the first member of the Green Party to win elective office in San Francisco, winning over 65 percent of the vote in a runoff election to become a member of the Board of Supervisors in 2000. In 2003, he was elected as the president of the Board of Supervisors and ran for mayor of San Francisco and was narrowly defeated in the runoff election. He currently is a lawyer in San Francisco and is active in the Green Party.

Howie Hawkins is a teamster and Green activist in Syracuse, New York. He has been active in movements for peace, justice, the environment, and independent politics since the late 1960s, and in the Green Party in the U.S. since it began organizing in 1984.

Forrest Hill has served on the Coordinating Committee for the Green Party of California, is a member of the Green Party National Delegation and California State Finance committees, and has helped coordinate campaigns for Ralph Nader, Peter Camejo, and Aimee Allison. He has a Ph.D. in oceanography from Massachusetts Institute of Technology and has worked as an environmental consultant to ensure compliance with the Endangered Species Act. He is currently a financial advisor in the field of socially responsible investing.

Alan Maass is the editor of *Socialist Worker* newspaper (www.socialistworker.org), and author of *The Case for Socialism* (Haymarket Books, 2004).

Carol Miller is a public health administrator who first rose to prominence in the New Mexico Green Party by running for Congress in 1997. She was active in the Nader for President Campaign 2000 and sought the Green Party nomination for president in 2004. She has actively worked for health care reform as a member of the White House Health Care Task Force, serving two terms as president of the New Mexico Public Health Association and six terms on the Governing Council of the American Public Health Association.

Dean Myerson serves as executive director of the Green Institute (www.greeninstitute.net). He was national secretary of the Association of State Green Parties from 1997 to 1999, coordinated the Green Party's 2000 National Nominating Convention in Denver where Ralph Nader was nominated, and also served on the Nader 2000 national staff. From late 2001 through October 2003, Myerson was national political coordinator of the Green Party of the United States and ran the Green Party's office in Washington, D.C.

Ralph Nader has founded or organized more than on hundred civic organizations, authored numerous books and articles, and was the Green Party candidate for president in 1996 and 2000. He ran for president as an independent in the 2004 election. His most recent book is *The Good Fight* (HarperCollins, 2004).

Rachel Odes is a Green Party member and activist in Oakland, California, and was a national organizer for the 2004 Nader/ Camejo campaign.

John Rensenbrink is a cofounder of the Green Party and former U.S. Senate candidate for the Green Party of Maine. He was also a cochair of the Green Party of Maine and is currently coeditor of *Green Horizon Quarterly* (www.green-horizon.org).

Tom Sevigny is a founding member of the Green Party of Connecticut and has served as the state's co-chair and one of Connecticut's National Committee Representatives.

Ashley Smith is a Green Party member in Vermont and is on the editorial board of the *International Socialist Review*. His writing ap-

His writing appears regularly in *Socialist Worker* and on CounterPunch. He was the Vermont coordinator for the Nader/Camejo 2004 campaign.

Sharon Smith writes the "Which Side Are You On?" column in *Socialist Worker* (www.socialistworker.org) and is a frequent contributor to the *International Socialist Review* and *CounterPunch*. She recently authored the book *Women and Socialism* (Haymarket Books, 2005) and *Subterranean Fire* (Haymarket Books, 2006).

Norman Solomon's most recent book is *War Made Easy: How Presidents and Pundits Keep Spinning Us to Death* (Wiley, 2005). His writings are archived on the Web at www.normansolomon.com and www.WarMadeEasy.com.

Jeffrey St. Clair is the cofounder and coeditor of the newsletter *CounterPunch* (www.counterpunch.org). An award-winning investigative journalist, his recent books include *Been Brown So Long It Looked Like Green to Me* and *A Dime's Worth of Difference: Beyond the Lesser of Two Evils* (CounterPunch, 2004).

Jack Uhrich is a member of the South Carolina Green Party Steering Committee and was Fund-raising Director for the Green Party of the United States.

Donna J. Warren is a former Green Party candidate for lieutenant governor of California and ran for Senate as a Green in 2001. She is a founder of the South Central Green Party, and helped found a Green Party chapter in East L.A. She sued the CIA and the Department of Justice in 1998 for their complicity in the destruction of South Central by crack cocaine and is an activist with Families to Amend California's Three Strikes (FACTS).

Steve Welzer was the state coordinator for the Green Party of New Jersey (GPNJ) and was a founding member of the GPNJ in 1997. He has been active in the Green movement for fifteen years. He is currently coeditor of *Green Horizon Quarterly* (www.green-horizon.org).

Sherry Wolf is on the editorial board of the *International Socialist Review* (www.isreview.org) and has written articles on "The Origins of Gay Oppression" and "The Democrats and War: No Lesser Evil."

Sources

Chapter One: Green Independence? The Debate Begins

Howie Hawkins, unpublished letter to *The Nation*, November 14, 2002. Reprinted with permission.

Appeal to Nader from Green gubernatorial candidates, sent December 2002.

The Avocado Declaration, published online at http://www. avocadoeducationproject.org, January 1, 2004. Reprinted with permission.

John Rensenbrink and Tom Sevigny, "The Green Party and the 2004 Elections: A Three-Dimensional Plan," *Green Horizon Quarterly*, Spring 2003. Reprinted with permission.

Howie Hawkins, "For a Green Presidential Campaign in 2004," presentation at regional Greens meeting, Freeville, NY, June 28, 2003. Reprinted with permission.

Ted Glick, "A Green Party 'Safe States' Strategy," published online at http://www.znet.com, July 1, 2003. Reprinted with permission.

David Cobb, "Green Party 2004 Presidential Strategy," presentation at Green Party National Committee meeting, July 17–20, 2003. Reprinted with permission.

Chapter Two: Green Tactics and Strategy

Howie Hawkins, "'Strategic Voting' Is Strategic Suicide," *Synthesis/Regeneration* 32, Fall 2003. Reprinted with permission.

Sharon Smith, "Debating the Election: The Democrats Don't Deserve Our Support," *Socialist Worker*, September 19, 2003. Reprinted with permission.

Norman Solomon, "Debating the Election: We Have a Responsibility to Work to Defeat Bush," *Socialist Worker*, September 19, 2003. Reprinted with permission.

Statement on Green Strategy 2004 and Call for Dialogue and Action, eighteen Green Party activists, circulated online, December 14, 2003, archived at http://www.sfgreenparty.org/news/news. gem.

Greens for Nader, "Run Ralph Run, But as A Green,"an open letter to Ralph Nader, December 10, 2003. Reprinted with permission.

Ralph Nader, "Letter to the Steering Committee and the Presidential Exploratory Committee of the Green Party," December 22, 2003. Reprinted with permission.

Green Party Steering Committee, "Letter to Ralph Nader Urging Reconsideration of Withdrawal," December 24, 2003.

Ralph Nader, "Endorsement, Not Nomination," letter to the Steering Committee of the Green Party of the United States, March 24, 2004. Reprinted with permission.

Greens for Nader, "Greens Should Endorse Nader," circulated online, April 15, 2004.

The Nation Editors, "An Open Letter to Ralph Nader," February 16, 2004. Reprinted with permission.

Ralph Nader, "Whither *The Nation*? An Open Letter" February 19, 2004. Reprinted with permission.

Ted Glick, "2004 and the Left," published online at http://www.dissidentvoice.org, March 30, 2004. Reprinted with permission.

Howie Hawkins, "Endorse Nader," *Green Horizon Quarterly*, Summer 2004. Reprinted with permission.

Peter Miguel Camejo, "Letter to *The Nation*," June 17, 2004. Reprinted with permission.

The Nation Editors, "It's Not Easy Being Green," June 17, 2004. Reprinted with permission.

Chapter Three: The Milwaukee Convention

Peter Miguel Camejo, "Green Party Unity," circulated online, June 14, 2004. Reprinted with permission.

Ralph Nader, "A Few Thoughts for the Green Party," presentation at Green Party National Committee meeting, June 25, 2004. Reprinted with permission.

Alan Maass, "The Green Party's Step Backward," *Socialist Worker*, July 2, 2004. Reprinted with permission.

Ted Glick, "Green and Growing: An Activist Report Back from the Green Party Convention," published online at http://www.dissidentvoice.org, June 29, 2004. Reprinted with permission.

Walt Contreras Sheasby, "How the Greens Chose Kerry over Nader,"published online at http://www.unrepentantnadervoter.com, July 19, 2004.

Jeffrey St. Clair, "Suicide Right on the Stage: The Demise of the Green Party," published online at http://www.counterpunch.org, July 2, 2004.

Norman Solomon, "Why I Changed My Voter Registration Today," published online at http://www.commondreams.org, June 28, 2004. Reprinted with permission.

Todd Chretien, "A Reply to Norman Solomon and Medea Benjamin: Believing in a Green Resistance," published online at http://www.counterpunch.org, July 26, 2004. Reprinted with permission.

David Cobb, "Growing the Green Party," *In These Times*, July 16, 2004. Reprinted with permission.

Carol Miller and Forrest Hill, "Rigged Convention, Divided Party: How David Cobb Became the Green Nominee Even Though He Only Got 12 Percent of the Votes," published online at http://www.counterpunch.org, August 7, 2004. Reprinted with permission.

Dean Myerson, "A Response to Miller and Hill," August 11, 2004. Reprinted with permission.

Peter Miguel Camejo, "Cut and Run: The Green Party 2004 Convention," circulated online, August 17, 2004. Reprinted with permission.

Chapter Four: Independence versus Anybody But Bush

Matt Gonzalez, "Why Vote for Ralph Nader?" *San Francisco Examiner*, July 14, 2004. Reprinted with permission.

Donna J. Warren, "A Letter to the Black Caucus from a Black Woman Living in South Central," *San Francisco Bay View*, July 14, 2004. Reprinted with permission.

Sherry Wolf, "From 'Maverick' to Attack Dog: Howard Dean's Gay Bashing of Ralph Nader," published online at http://www. counterpunch.org, July 10, 2004. Reprinted with permission.

Medea Benjamin, Peter Coyote, John Eder, Daniel Ellsberg, et al., "Vote Kerry and Cobb: An Open Letter to Progressives," published online at http://www.commondreams.org, July 23, 2004.

Peter Miguel Camejo, "Money vs. People: The Mystery of the 2004 Elections," published online at http://www.greensfornader.net, July 29, 2004. Reprinted with permission.

Ralph Nader, "What You Won't Hear: Twelve Topics Democrats Will Duck at Convention," *Boston Globe*, July 25, 2004. Reprinted with permission.

Joshua Frank, "David Cobb's Soft Charade: The Greens and the Politics of Mendacity," published online at http://www.counterpunch.org, August 6, 2004. Reprinted with permission.

Ralph Nader, "Parties to Injustice: Democrats Will Do Anything to Keep Me Off the Ballot," *Washington Post*, September 5, 2004. Reprinted with permission.

Zach Kaldveer and Sophie Mintier, "Only Progressive Unity Can Defeat Bush," published online at http://www.changein04. com, October 21, 2004.

Ralph Nader, "An Open Letter to Former Naderites Running Scared in 2004," published online at http://www.votenader.org, October 27, 2004. Reprinted with permission.

Chapter Five: Lessons from the 2004 Elections

Howie Hawkins, "Political Independence Is the Lesson of 2004 for Progressives," November 8, 2004, written for this volume.

Jack Uhrich, "New Mexico: A Sobering Lesson for Practical Fusion," *Green Horizon Quarterly*, Fall 2004. Reprinted with permission.

Steve Welzer, "The Greens Are Enduring, Debating, and Learning," *Green Horizon Quarterly*, Spring 2005. Reprinted with permission.

David Cobb, "Resurgence: The Green Party's Remarkable Transformation," *Green Horizon Quarterly*, Winter 2005. Reprinted with permission.

Joshua Frank, "Narcissism Runs Rampant: Diagnosing the Green Party," published online at http://www.counter punch.org, February 25, 2005. Reprinted with permission.

Peter Miguel Camejo, "Lessons from the 2004 Elections," January 2005, written for this volume.

Appendixes

Forrest Hill, "Reexamining the Green Party Nominating Convention: A Statistical Analysis," published online at http://www. greensfornader.net, September 28, 2004. Reprinted with permission.

Green Party of New York State, Green Party of Vermont, Proposals to the Green Party of the United States from the Greens for Democracy and Independence. Presented at GPUS National Committee meeting, July 21–24, 2005.

Ashley Smith and Forrest Hill, "Which Way Forward for the Green Party?" August 26, 2005, written for this volume.